IMAGES
of America

ANCHORAGE

On the Cover: At once a homeland of the Dena'ina people, a site of industrial development and military power, and the center of Alaska's population, Anchorage emerged in the 20th century as the 49th state's largest city and one of the world's great urban regions of the Far North. (Courtesy of the Anchorage Museum.)

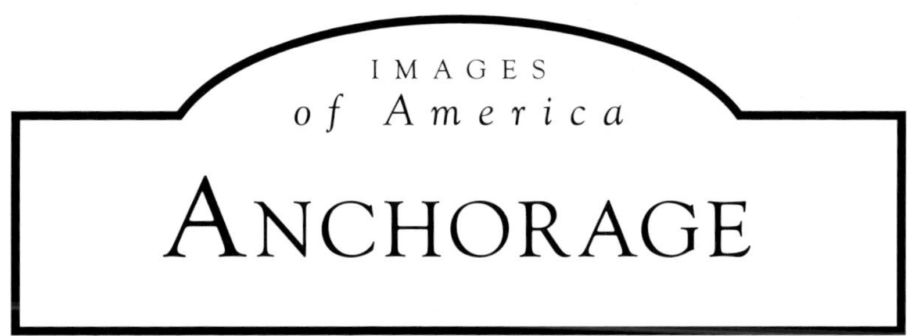

Ian C. Hartman and the
Cook Inlet Historical Society

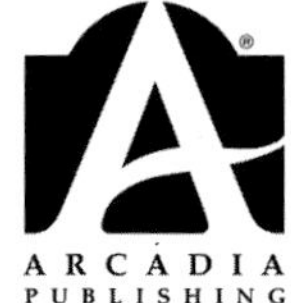

ISBN 978-1-4671-6231-9

Published by Arcadia Publishing
Charleston, South Carolina

Printed in the United States of America

Library of Congress Control Number: 2024952273

For all general information, please contact Arcadia Publishing:
Telephone 843-853-2070
Fax 843-853-0044
E-mail sales@arcadiapublishing.com

Visit us on the Internet at www.arcadiapublishing.com

This book is dedicated to my love and inspiration, Jenell Hartman, and to the memory of Poe and Cole Hartman.

Contents

Acknowledgments 6

Introduction 7

1. A Native Place 9

2. The Alaska Railroad Creates a Town 17

3. Life at the Edge of the Forest 31

4. A Military Community 59

5. Anchorage Comes Apart 77

6. A Municipality Comes Together 91

Bibliography 126

About the Cook Inlet Historical Society 127

ACKNOWLEDGMENTS

The images in this book are courtesy of the Anchorage Museum's archives and its extensive collection of historic Anchorage photographs (unless otherwise noted). The author and the Cook Inlet Historical Society thank the Anchorage Museum for its partnership on this project and support of Anchorage's history. This book would not have been possible without support from the Atwood Foundation and the Cook Inlet Historical Society. I've worked most closely with Heather McClain and Monica Shah at the museum's archives, and I'm grateful for their assistance. The Cook Inlet Historical Society appreciates the museum's leadership under the direction of Julie Decker and looks forward to a bright future of collaboration and cooperation. Eli Williamson served as an intern at the University of Alaska Anchorage and helped choose the photographs. I also thank fellow Cook Inlet Historical Society board members Judy Bittner, Jim Blasingame, Ayse Gilbert, Laura Koenig, Susan LaGrande, Aaron Leggett, Dick Mylius, Bruce Parham, Jennifer Romer, and David Tarcy for their service to Anchorage's historical community.

Introduction

By one definition, Anchorage is a young community. Its history as an organized town dates to 1915, and its modern boundaries as a municipality were set only in 1975. By another definition, however, Anchorage is quite old. The Native peoples of the region, the Dena'ina, have lived, harvested, subsisted, and stewarded the abundant resources of the land for generations.

The book presents a snapshot of life in Anchorage and a brief portrait of how it has changed over the course of the 20th century. The points of emphasis in this book include the built environment, activities and entertainment, and the people who have contributed to the community in one way or another. Some are well known and have taken on leadership roles in business and politics. Others are not as well known, but they have made a mark on Anchorage nonetheless. Anchorage is an exceedingly diverse community, and the book aims to capture at least some of that diversity. Aside from the vibrant Alaska Native community, Anchorage has become a site of international migration over the last 100 years.

From its days as a railroad construction camp, European families arrived in great numbers. Asian Americans and Pacific Islanders have become a sizable presence in the city, and their roots in Alaska are deep and consequential. Likewise, Black men and women have played an outsized role in Anchorage's history, and so too have Hispanic members of the community. International migration has shaped Anchorage's more recent history. Many are surprised to learn that some of the most diverse zip codes and schools in the United States are found in Anchorage, Alaska. At last count, 112 languages are spoken among the students enrolled in the Anchorage School District. And Bettye Davis East Anchorage High School, by some measures, is the most diverse high school in the nation.

This modest and brief book cannot effectively capture the nuance, depth, and complexity of Anchorage's history, growth, and development, but it can at least whet the appetite for one to learn more while providing a broad photographic overview of our community. To do so, I have divided the book into six topical chapters that roughly proceed chronologically through the 20th century.

The first chapter recognizes the Alaska Native presence in the area that would become Anchorage. The Dena'ina people are present not just in the first chapter but throughout. But it is paramount to ground one's knowledge of Anchorage's history in the recognition and acknowledgment of the Native peoples who have lived on these lands for over a thousand years and continue to positively shape the community and contribute to its vitality.

The second chapter depicts the centrality of the Alaska Railroad as the rationale for the creation of the modern townsite we know today as Anchorage. Curiously, the flag of the Municipality of Anchorage features a prominently placed anchor in the center, backed by a tall, full-rigged ship and a jet airplane just to the right. Missing from the municipality's flag is a train. Yet Anchorage as we know it today would not exist if it were not for the Alaska Railroad. The railroad's construction set into motion an economic boom that forever transformed Alaska and ensured that the Southcentral region would soon become the commercial and population center of the territory and, eventually, the state.

The third chapter builds off the second to explore the growth of the community between the construction of the Alaska Railroad and the middle of the 20th century. These were optimistic years in the young town, and the photographs depict enthusiasm and ambition among the population. Anchorage grew during these decades and developed into a modern community with many of the modern conveniences one would find in almost any midsize town around the country. Still, the conditions and remote location challenged Anchorage residents and led to a robust spirit of civic engagement. During these decades, a construction site had quite literally transformed into a town abutting a great forest, the Chugach National Forest to be precise.

The fourth chapter shifts focus to highlight the role and impact of the military in Anchorage. Beyond the Alaska Railroad, perhaps no single institution has had as large of a social and economic impact on the town as the nation's armed forces. Hosting two military bases, Fort Richardson and Elmendorf Air Force Base (now Joint Base Elmendorf-Richardson, or JBER), Anchorage and its surroundings has among the highest populations of active duty and retired service members of any metropolitan region in the country. Moreover, due to Alaska's strategic location in the North Pacific and Arctic, its military installations have played an important role in the nation's defense and its geopolitical posture.

The book's fifth chapter showcases the impact of what was arguably Anchorage's most catastrophic day: Good Friday, March 27, 1964. On that fateful day, a magnitude 9.2 earthquake struck Anchorage and its surroundings. The US Geologic Survey estimated that its epicenter was about six miles from College Fjord in Prince William Sound and about 75 miles due east of Anchorage. While the death toll in Anchorage proper was miraculously low, the damage was extensive. The photographs, many of which are iconic at this point, depict streets that collapsed, buildings and homes that sank into the ground, steel railroad ties that were bent and twisted as if they were tinfoil, and entire landscapes that shifted and heaved over the course of nearly five long, excruciating minutes. However, Alaskans rebuilt, and Anchorage emerged stronger and more resilient.

The final chapter depicts a community coming together in the aftermath of the earthquake. In a strictly legal sense, the modern municipality of Anchorage also came together. The City of Anchorage and the outlying borough merged into a single governing municipality in 1975, thus the name of the chapter. Additionally, these years correspond to a period when Anchorage had grown considerably wealthier due to an influx of oil revenue. Anchorage leaders embarked on an ambitious program to upgrade the city's civic and cultural institutions, lean into the possibilities of tourism, and elevate the growing city into a national and even international destination. While there were certainly bumps along the way, there is little doubt that Anchorage at the end of the century had come a long way from its early days as a construction site for the Alaska Railroad.

One

A Native Place

The area known today as Anchorage is by far Alaska's largest city. It has also been home for over a thousand years to the Dena'ina, the Indigenous people of Southcentral Alaska. The Dena'ina refer to the river around which Anchorage's modern townsite would later develop as Dgheyaytnu, or Stickleback Creek. There, Dena'ina families established seasonal fish camps before heading upland to bountiful hunting grounds.

However, many Alaskans remain unfamiliar with the area's history as Dena'ina Ełnena (Dena'ina Land). In fact, references to European explorers who claimed Alaska for one colonial power or another dot the landscape. Perhaps none of these figures is as well known as Capt. James Cook. It was Captain Cook, after all, who in 1778 planted the British flag and claimed the land and waters of Tikahtnu (what became known as Cook Inlet) for the British Empire. But while the British never established a permanent presence in Alaska, the Russian Empire claimed much of the North Pacific Coast and Bering Sea for over 130 years (1732–1867). Still, the land and waters around Anchorage remained firmly under the stewardship of the Dena'ina until the 20th century.

In the decades following the 1867 Treaty of Cession between the United States and the Russian Empire, American prospectors established modest settlements on the Kenai Peninsula, not too far from what would become Anchorage. One prospector, James Girdwood, settled along Crow Creek in 1896. His settlement, now known as Girdwood, is situated within the present boundaries of the municipality of Anchorage.

Indeed, waves of settlers, migrants, and fortune seekers have traveled to the community they have only known as "Anchorage" for well over 100 years. These men and women have come great distances to claim a piece of their American dream. Yet Anchorage remains synonymous with the ancestral homelands of the Dena'ina people. Acknowledging and learning from their enduring presence is fundamental to understanding the history of the community. While Anchorage has experienced tremendous growth and demographic transformation, it remains a home to the Dena'ina and a place that reflects its Native heritage.

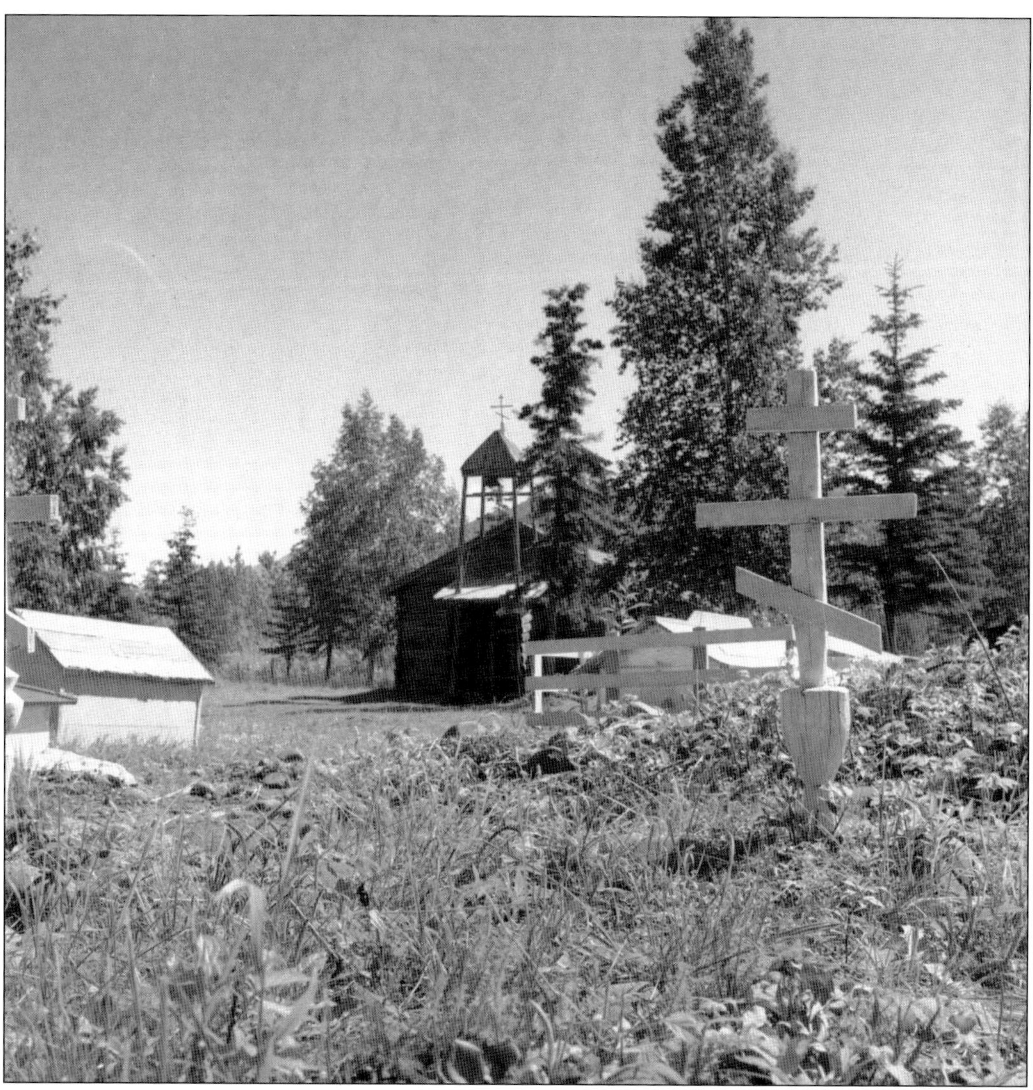

The oldest built structure in the Anchorage municipality is the St. Nicholas Russian Orthodox Church. The church was originally built in the nearby settlement of Knik in 1875 and was relocated to the Native village of Eklutna in 1895. Grave sites are seen in the foreground, a reminder of the toll that colonization had taken on the Dena'ina people. Between 1836 and 1839, roughly half of the Dena'ina died during a smallpox epidemic that spread across Southcentral Alaska. The Russian relationship with the Dena'ina was complicated and defined by tension and tragedy. While the European colonizers introduced various illnesses and diseases, they at times provided inoculations, as was the case with the Russian Orthodox church. The Russian influence in Alaska is most clearly seen in the proliferation of Russian Orthodoxy, a faith that roughly 25,000 or about five percent of Alaskans, many of whom are Alaska Native, practice today.

This broadside view of the St. Nicholas Russian Orthodox Church was likely taken in the 1910s, likely between 15 and 20 years after it was first constructed. Its location in the Native village of Eklutna is about one mile inland from the Knik Arm. Built of hand-hewn spruce logs, the church is just over 16 feet wide and 26 feet in length. Its interior was constructed of plank puncheon flooring. In addition, the interior of the church retains icons and artifacts associated with Russian Orthodoxy. The structure was added to the National Register of Historic Places in 1972.

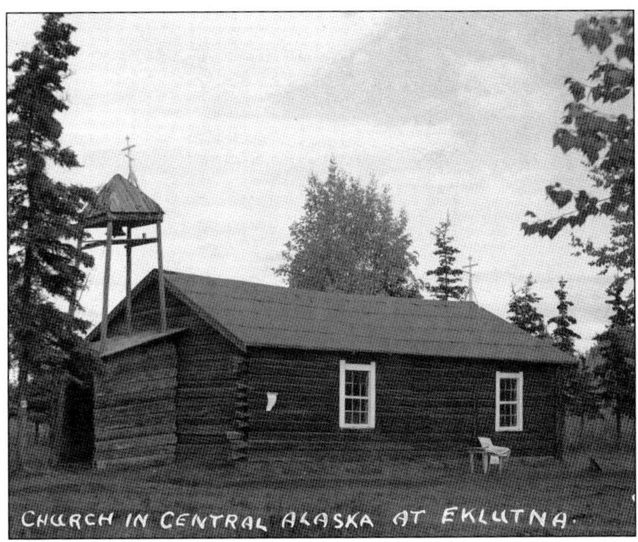

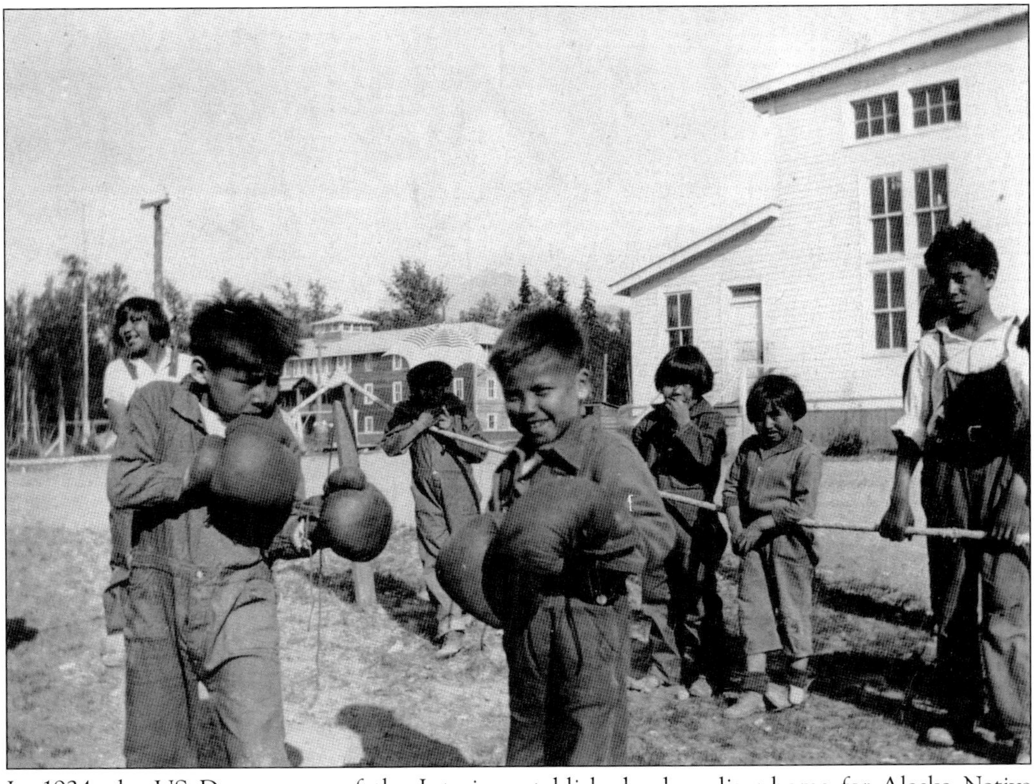

In 1924, the US Department of the Interior established a boarding home for Alaska Native children whose parents died during the 1918 influenza epidemic. The facility was located near the Eklutna village, about 30 miles from downtown Anchorage. It was named the Eklutna Industrial School and provided vocational training to Alaska Native students. The school enrolled over 100 students by the 1930s. But without a consistent source of funding, it deteriorated. When members of Congress visited the school in 1945, they found the conditions so deplorable that they ordered it closed immediately. The students were transferred first to Fort Raymond, near Seward, and then to Mount Edgecumbe, a boarding school in Sitka, in 1947.

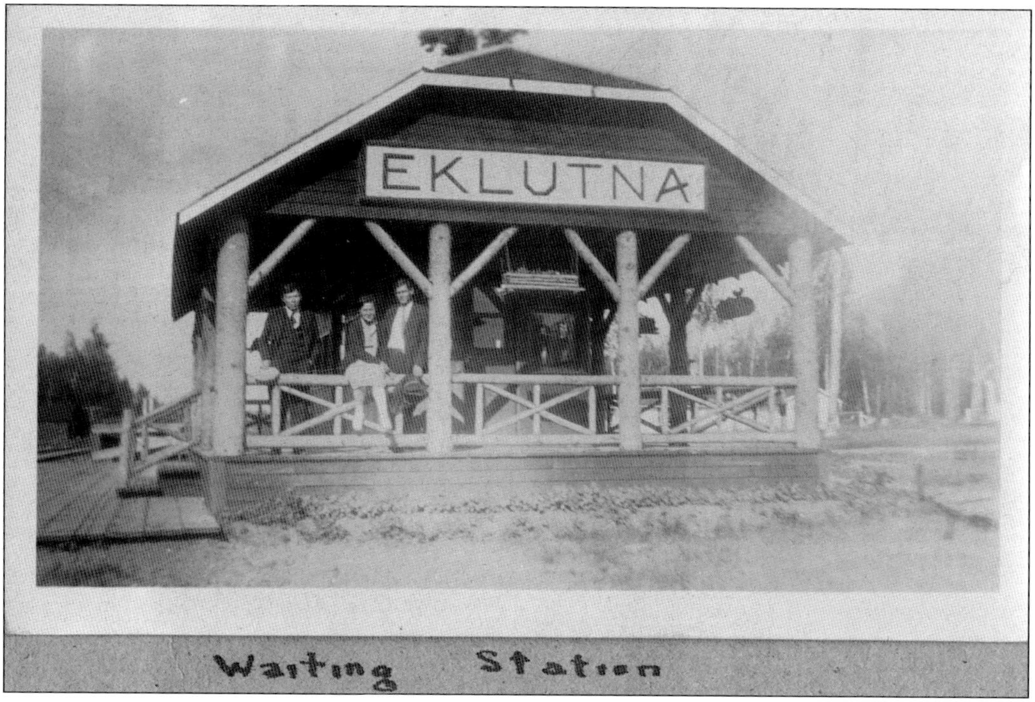

The Eklutna railroad station is pictured in the 1920s north of the Anchorage townsite. The Alaska Railroad traversed traditional Dena'ina lands. And while the railroad provided economic opportunities for many, it also disrupted the lives and culture of the Dena'ina in the area.

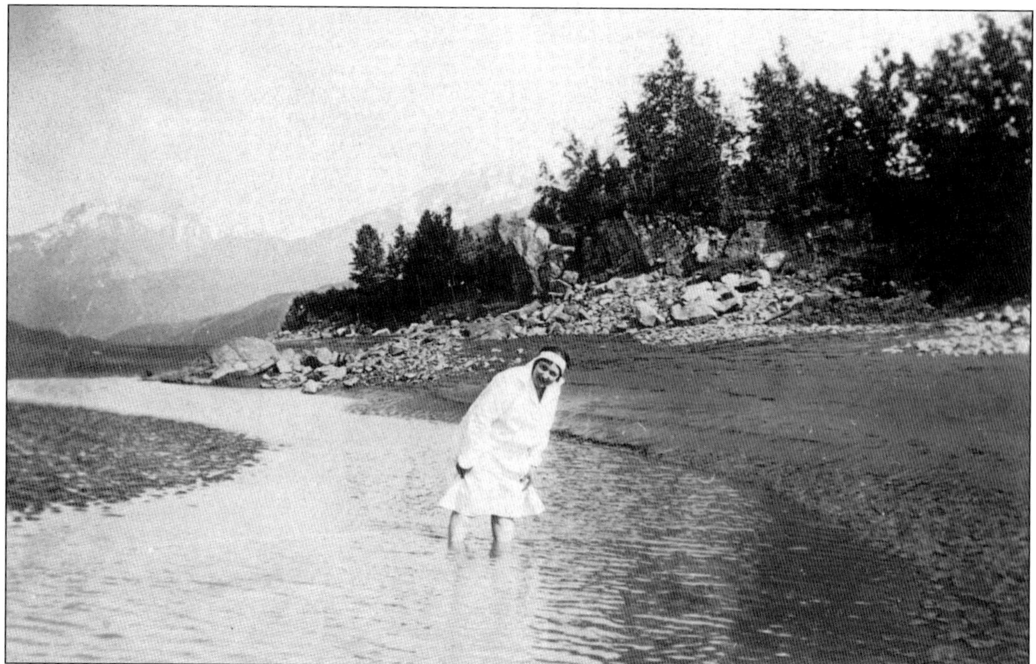

A Dena'ina woman stands in Tikahtnu, also known as Cook Inlet. The Dena'ina have fished in the rivers and streams of Southcentral Alaska for generations. Before the townsite of Anchorage took shape, the Dena'ina used the area as a seasonal fish camp and place of respite.

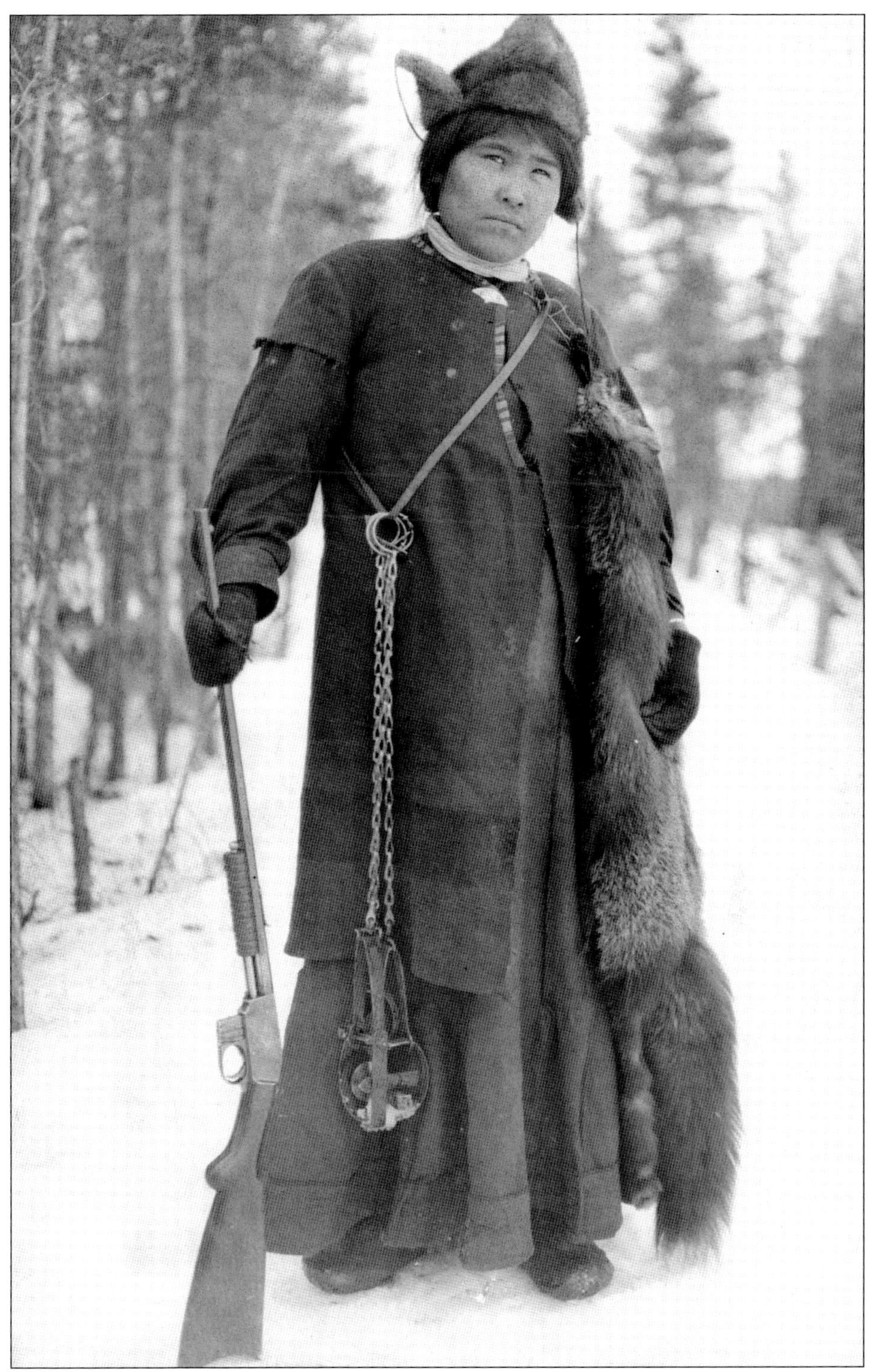

A woman reminds the photographer of the role of subsistence hunting and trapping. Dena'ina people have harvested the bounty of the land around what is today Anchorage for over a thousand years.

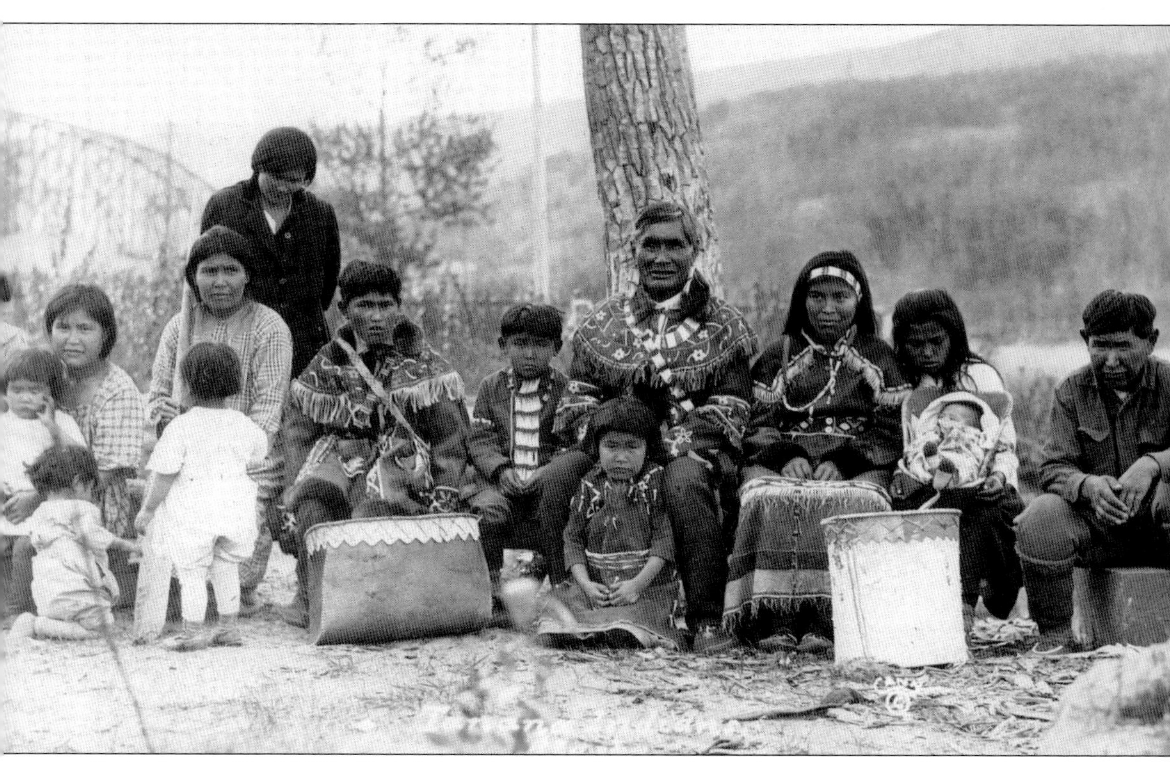

Only during World War II did the white population eclipse the Native population throughout the Alaska territory. The Dena'ina of Southcentral Alaska were outnumbered earlier than this due to the presence of the Alaska Railroad and the rapid growth of Anchorage in the 1920s. However, even as the Dena'ina endured epidemics, violence, and displacement, they have retained a strong cultural heritage and presence in Anchorage and beyond. Today, Anchorage is sometimes called Alaska's largest village. Alaska Native residents continue to shape the community's cultural, economic, and social fabric. Beyond the Dena'ina, Alaska Native people from throughout the state travel to Anchorage to seek medical care, catch a flight out of Alaska, purchase items that are unavailable in more rural communities, and take advantage of the various social and cultural amenities that are offered.

A woman identified only as "Mrs. Esi" stands at attention, adorned in a dentalium necklace and earrings, as she prepares a moose hide. This photograph, taken in the 1920s or early 1930s, may in fact be of the well-known Native elder and matriarch Olga Nicolai Ezi, more affectionately referred to simply as "Grandma Olga." She and her husband, Dena'ina leader Simeon Esia (Ezi), raised and supported five children by harvesting the bounties of the lands and waters of Tikahtnu (upper Cook Inlet). The two also operated a business ferrying supplies up and down the inlet to Dena'ina villages throughout the region. Today, a bronze statue of Grandma Olga, crafted by the artist Joel Isaak, is located near Ship Creek at the small boat launch and depicts her at a fish rack.

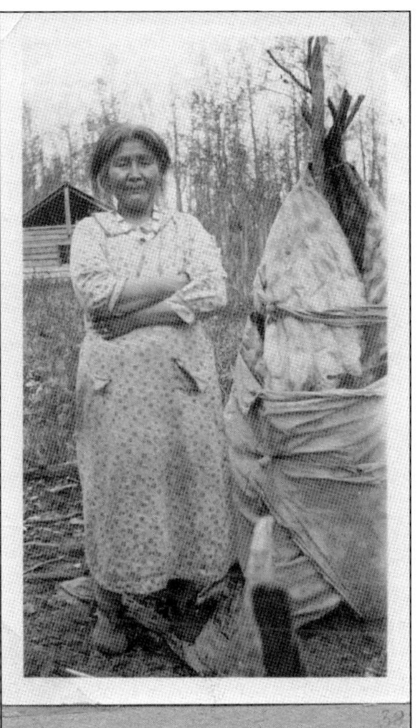

A Dena'ina woman said to be 101 at the time of this photograph in the early 1940s would have seen tremendous changes occur over time. Born in the mid-19th century, when Alaska was claimed by Russia, the Dena'ina of Southcentral Alaska retained much of their land and largely lived free of the colonial influences of the Russians or Americans. That changed during the early 20th century. The children in the photograph would experience a life far different from their elders.

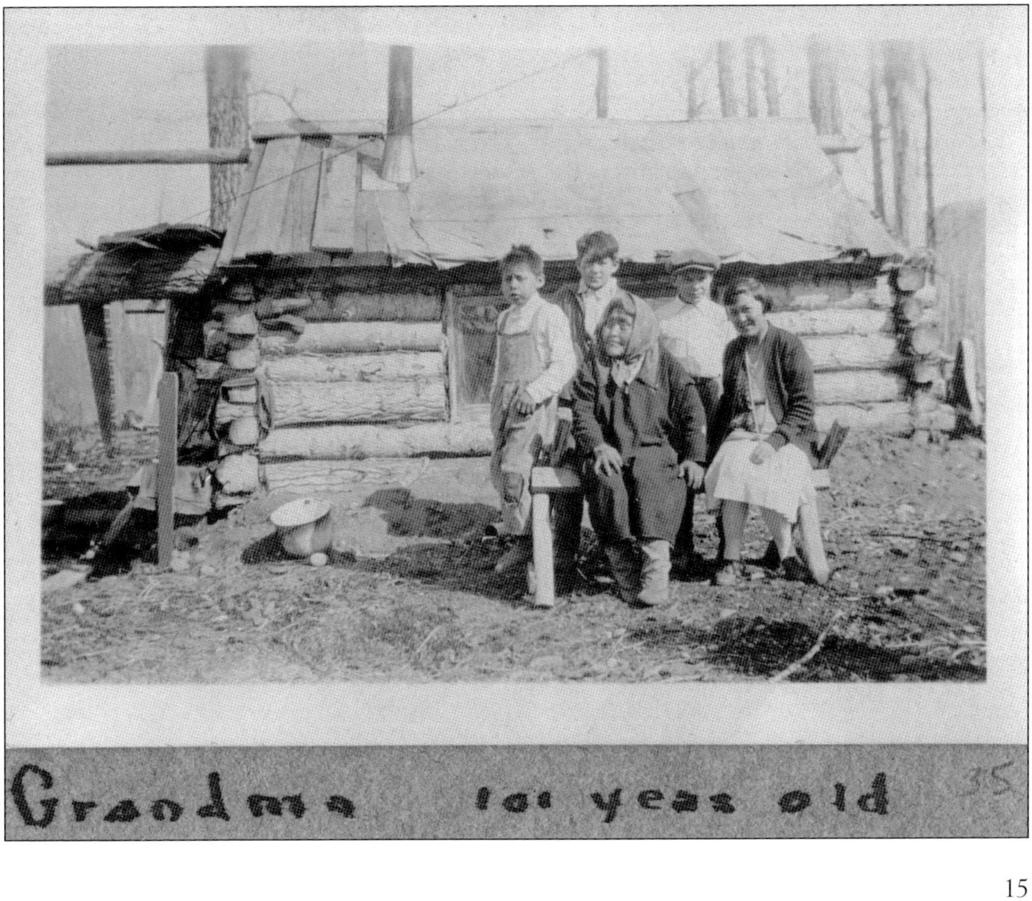

Grandma 101 yeas old

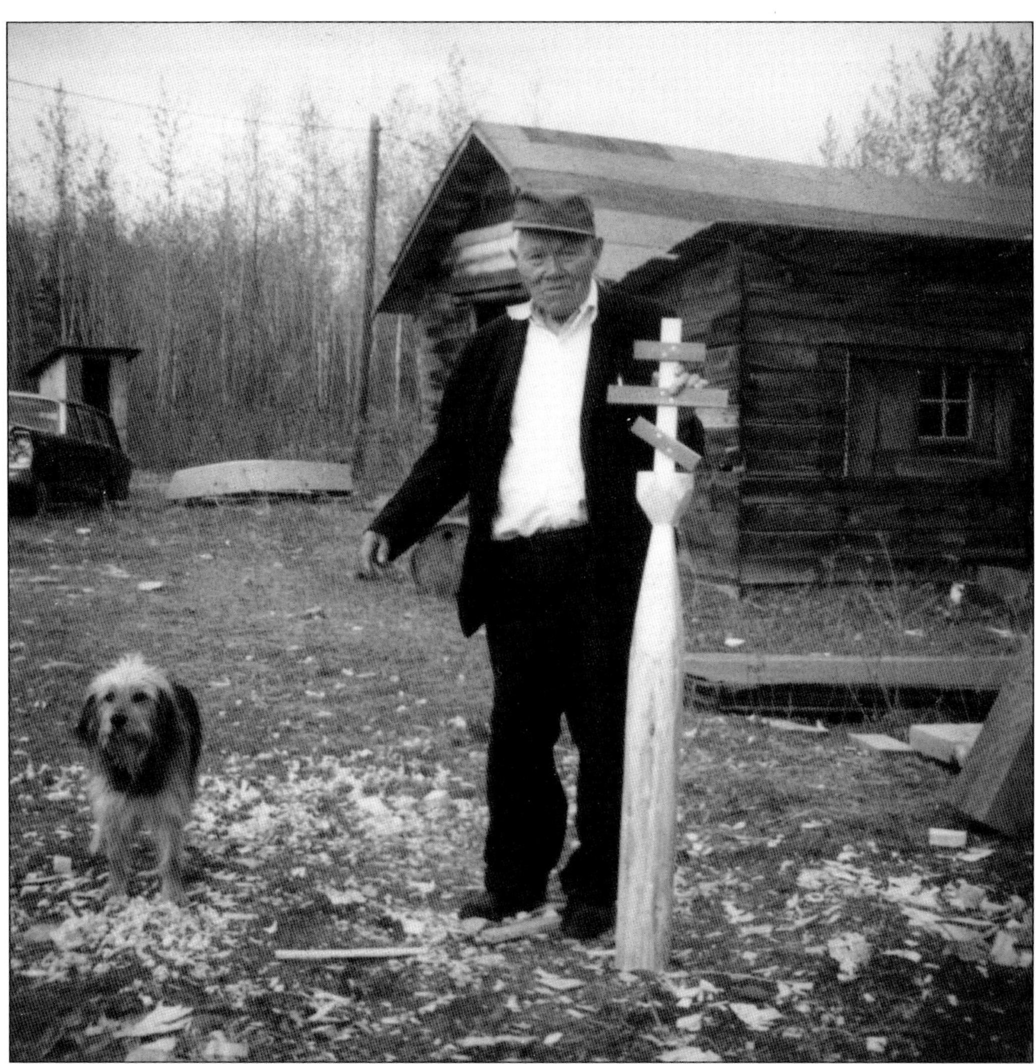

Shem Pete (K'etech'ayuilen), a Dena'ina elder and storyteller, stands outside the Russian Orthodox church in the early 1980s. K'etech'ayuilen, likely born in the 1890s, documented the history of Dena'ina people in the extensive upper Cook Inlet region and provided a critical window into the world of Alaska Native peoples in Southcentral Alaska before the arrival of the Alaska Railroad and during a time of great change and turbulence among Native communities. His knowledge of Cook Inlet's history remains central to understanding how Anchorage and its surroundings have changed over time. K'etech'ayuilen relayed how he and other Dena'ina people subsisted by hunting caribou, moose, and sheep. He endured epidemics of whooping cough and influenza, witnessed the introduction of European religions, and viewed firsthand the wholesale transformation of his ancestral homeland.

Two

The Alaska Railroad Creates a Town

Initially known as the Government Railroad because of the federal government's sizable investment in its construction and operation, the Alaska Railroad put Anchorage on the map and facilitated its settlement. Serving as the hub of a transportation network that extended from Seward in the south to Fairbanks in the north, Anchorage's development as a modern community is directly connected to the establishment of the Alaska Railroad.

In response to the Alaska Railroad Act of 1914, the administration of Pres. Woodrow Wilson directed the newly created Alaska Engineering Commission to select land around the mouth of Ship Creek, known to the Native Dena'ina people of the area as Dgheyay Kaq', to serve as the railroad headquarters. The 1914 legislation "authorized the President of the United States to locate, construct, and authorize railroads in the Territory of Alaska." Within a year, a tent city had sprung up that would double as the construction site for the Alaska Railroad. However, it was not until 1920 that the community was officially incorporated with the name "Anchorage."

Thousands of workers quickly transformed the area around Ship Creek into an industrial work site in clear view of the majestic Chugach Mountains and forests just miles to the east. Those who settled in the newly established community desired the amenities that made life familiar and comfortable. Not surprisingly, nearly as soon as railroad construction began, the markers of modern life followed, from dining and pool halls to laundromats to social clubs and saloons to churches and schools. These new Alaskans quickly identified their favorite local hangouts and built durable community institutions, some of which survive to this day.

While Anchorage is situated in the American West (or, more accurately, the Far Northwest), it never quite resembled a lawless frontier town that still dominates portrayals of turn-of-the-century Alaska in popular culture. In fact, Anchorage was organized and relatively well regulated from its start by the federal government. Indeed, the federal government would play an outsize role in the area's development for the next hundred years.

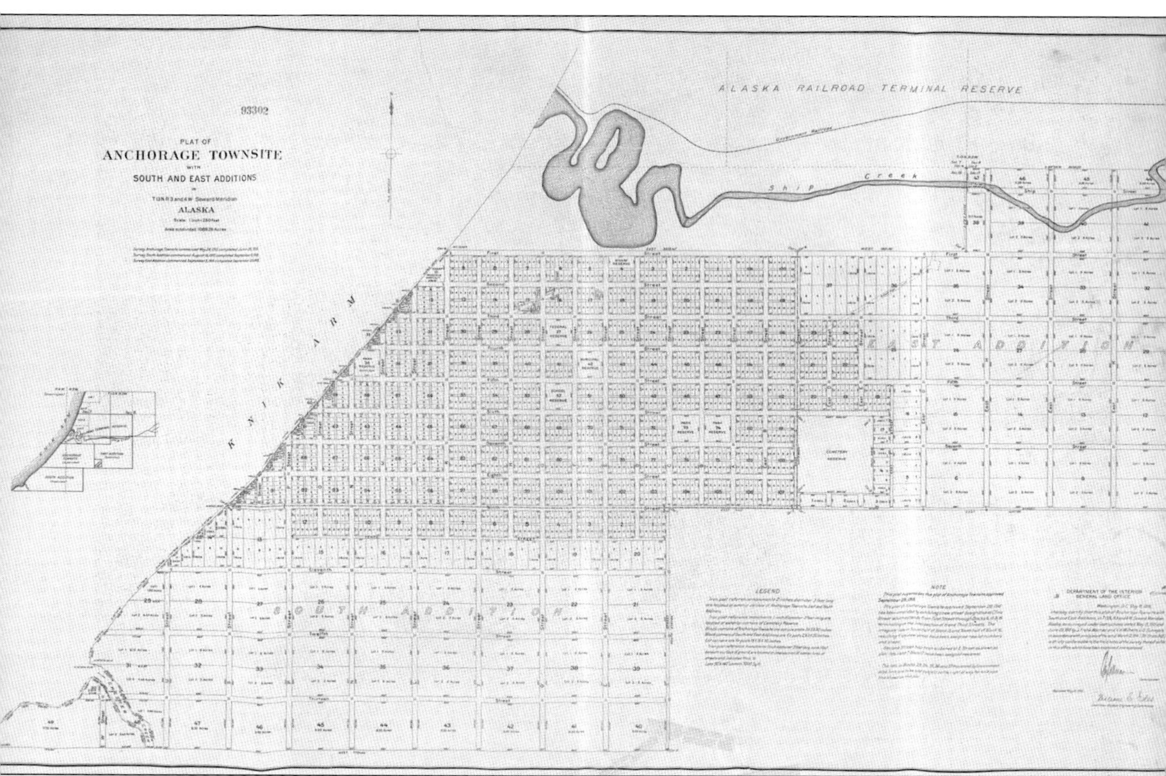

A map of the early Anchorage townsite depicts tracts of land where railroad workers would take up residence and put down roots. Anchorage grew quickly as thousands came north to work for the Alaska Railroad. Under the auspices of the newly created Alaska Engineering Commission, the federal government was intimately involved in planning the community, providing work, and sustaining the region's economic growth. The area around the mouth of Ship Creek was heavily wooded with spruce, cottonwood, birch, and aspen trees, but it had quickly transformed into a center of industrial development and a tent city to accommodate the workforce. The establishment of the Anchorage townsite put tremendous stress on the natural resources of the area and led to the displacement of Native peoples, many of whom relocated farther up the rivers and inlet. (Courtesy of the Library of Congress.)

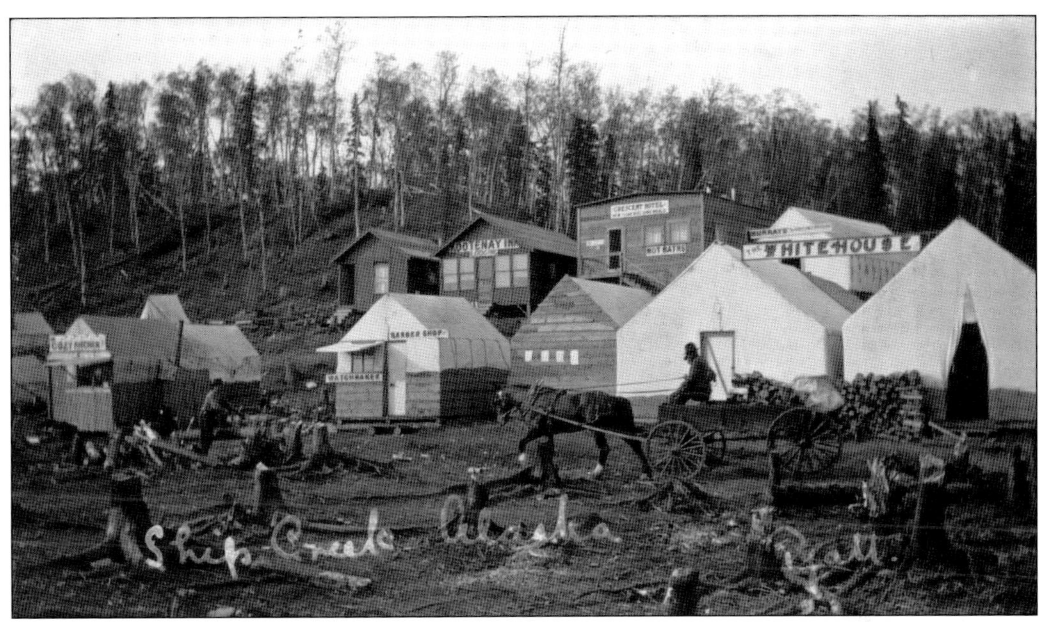

The 1914 legislation known as the Alaska Railroad Act authorized the president of the United States to locate, construct, and maintain railroads in the Territory of Alaska. This led to the establishment of a tent city that doubled as the construction site for the Alaska Railroad. Pres. Woodrow Wilson viewed the construction of the Alaska Railroad partly in the context of national security and possible disruptions to vital domestic energy sources. He and others saw the potential to develop and transport the territory's extensive natural resources. Well-known deposits of coal, for example, existed in the Matanuska Valley north of Anchorage; the railroad would transport the coal to the coast, where it could be loaded on freighters and shipped to markets beyond Alaska.

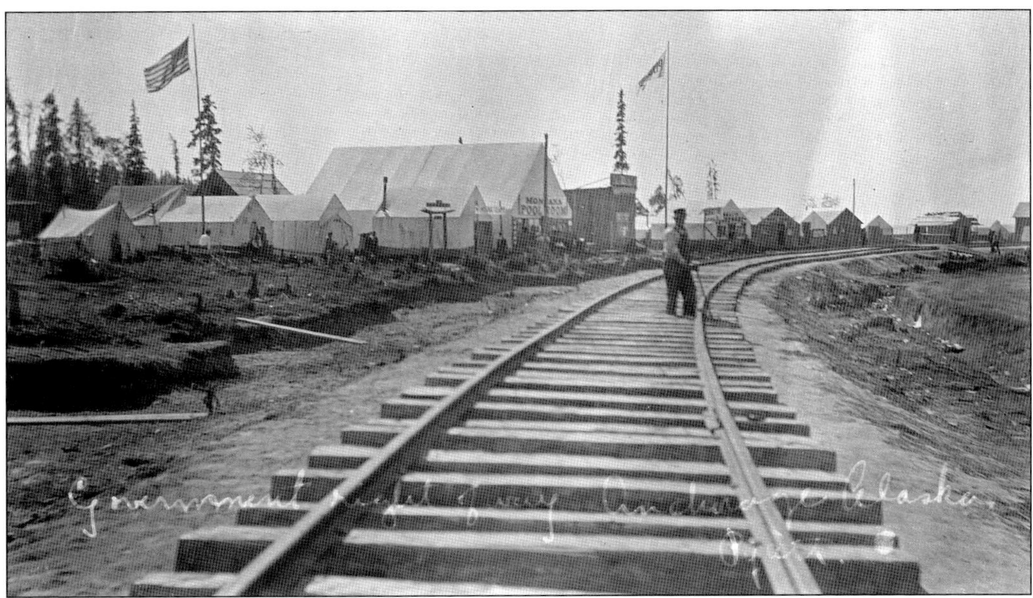

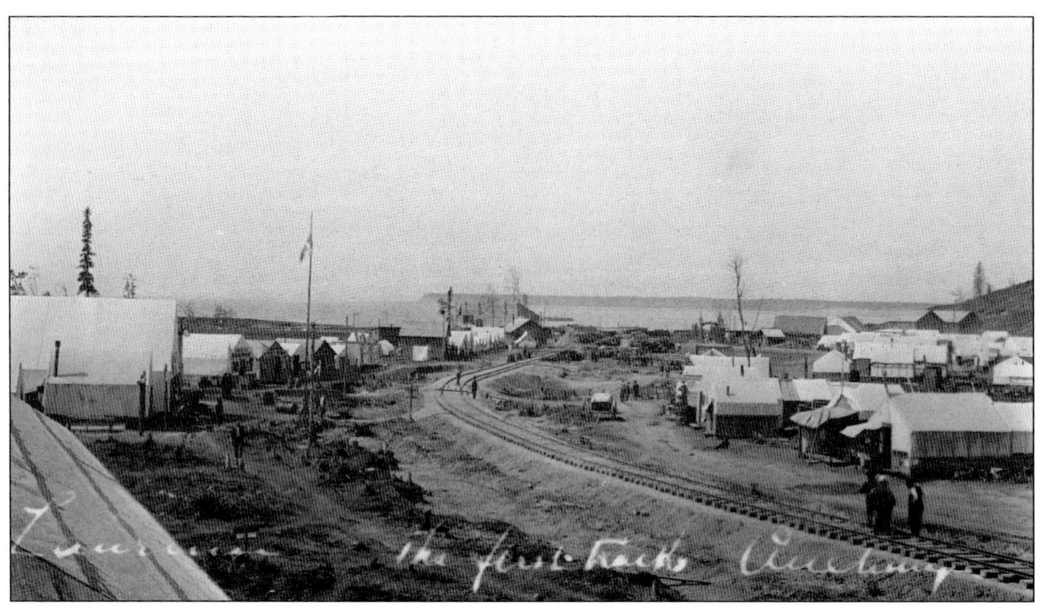

The Alaska Engineering Commission named Ship Creek as the location of the operating hub to build a new federally owned and operated railroad in 1915. But it would be another five years before the community became known officially as Anchorage. Both images, taken between 1915 and 1916, showcase views of the tent city. One is looking north with a view of the Knik Arm and Point McKenzie in the distance. The photograph below depicts the tents up against Chugach National Forest.

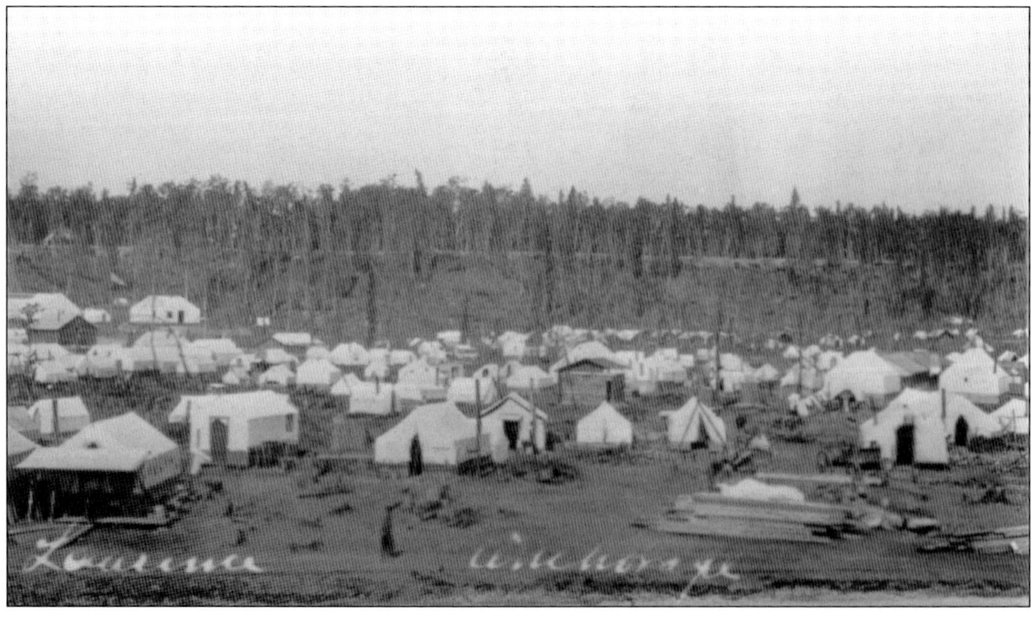

Railroad tracks and tents defined the landscape of the early townsite. Eventually, the tents gave way to permanent storefronts. The large tent in the foreground housed a poolroom. As residents worked hard by day, they looked forward to amusements and entertainment by night.

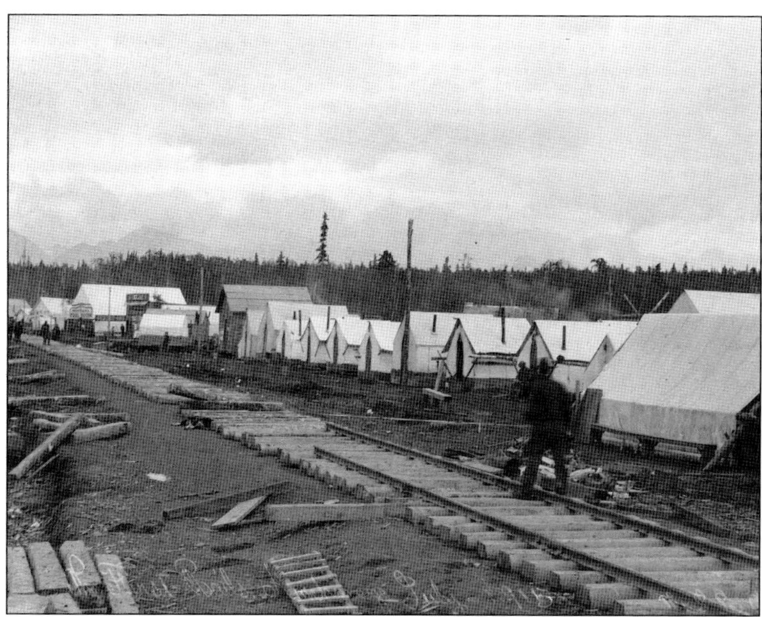

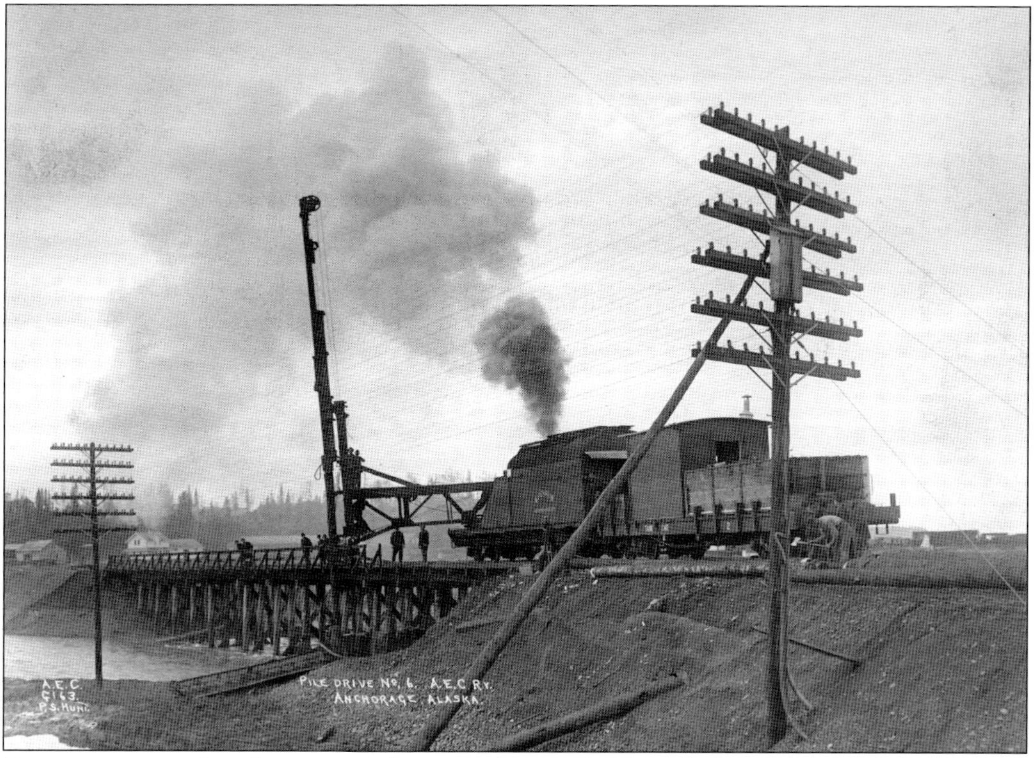

Constructing a railroad across nearly 700 miles of Alaska meant traversing boreal forests and muskeg, the boggy environment found in the Far North. It also required building across rivers and contending with ice, wildfires, and mountainous terrain in one of the world's most seismically active regions. This steam-powered pile driver, photographed in 1915 and manufactured by Bucyrus, pounded long, heavy wooden beams deep into the earth to secure the bridges and shore up track.

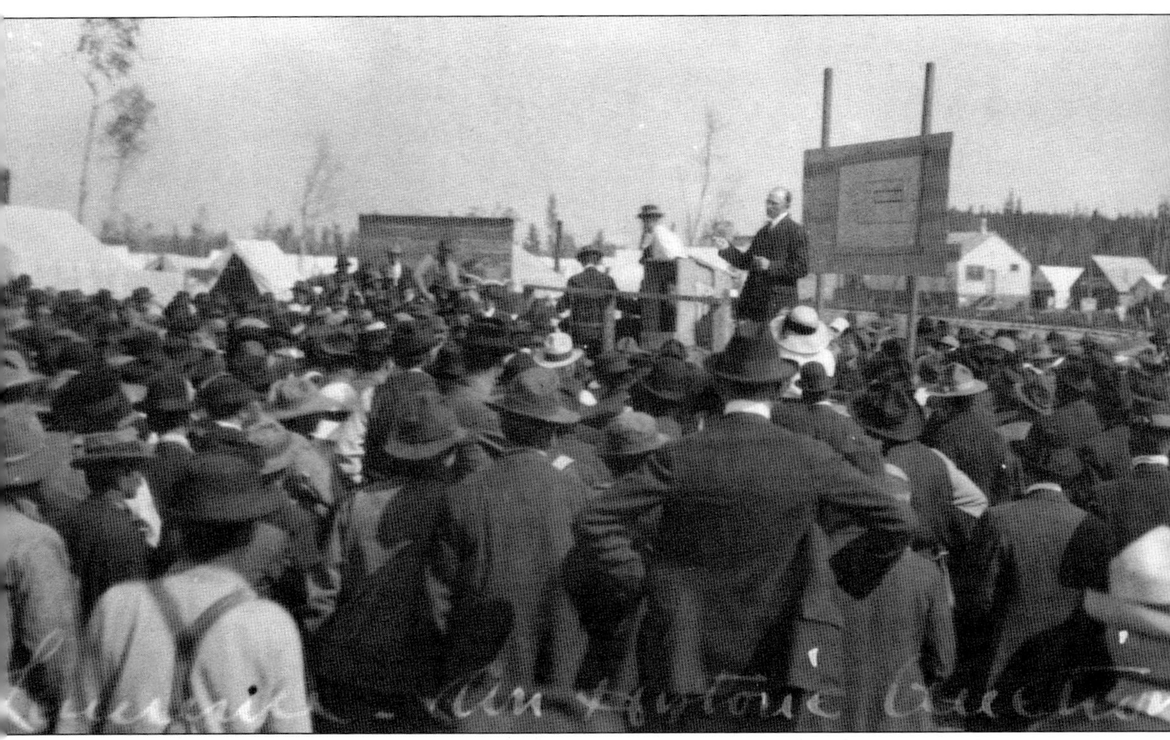

In the summer of 1915, the head of the Alaska Engineering Commission, Andrew Christensen, presided over a crowd of nearly 2,000 people and auctioned off plots of land to the south of Ship Creek. Many of those who bid on land were European immigrants who believed the future in Alaska was bright and the economic fortunes of the town would only increase over time. The lots were priced between $25 and $400, but the bidding led to significantly higher prices, sometimes going for more than four times the initial bid. Christensen recorded an impressive 655 sales on July 10, 1915.

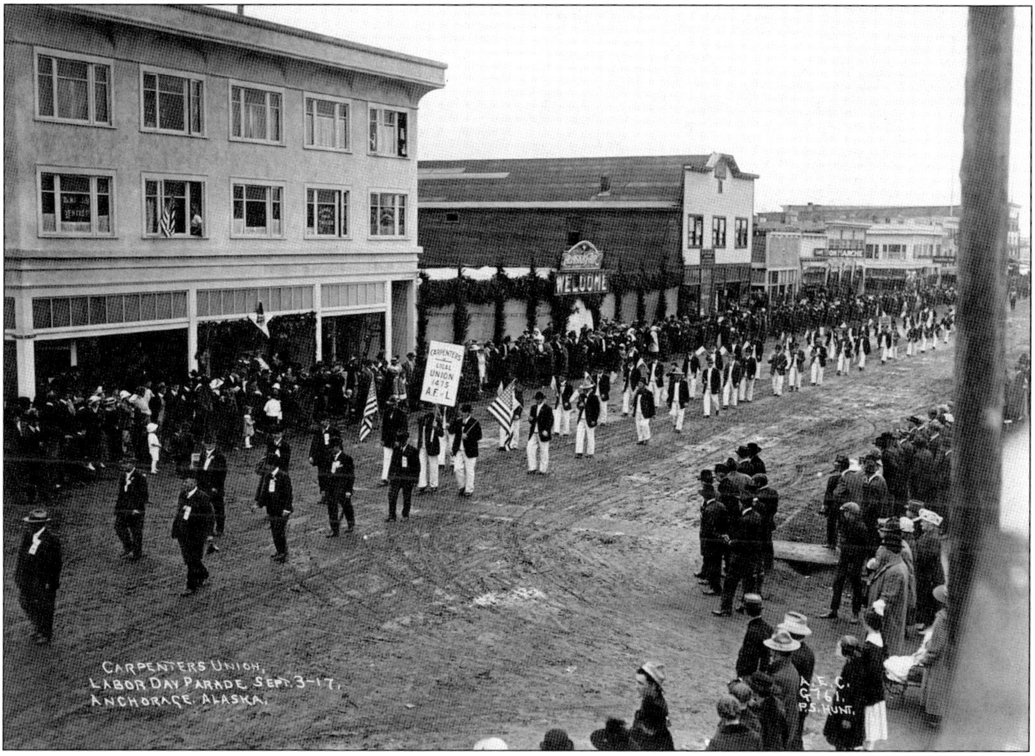

Anchorage had a great demand for workers. Carpenters, teamsters, electricians, plumbers, and others arrived knowing that their trade would be highly valued. Throughout the nation, working people expressed solidarity with one another on Labor Day. Anchorage was no different. The union of carpenters, affiliated with the American Federation of Labor, marched in one of Anchorage's first known Labor Day parades in September 1917.

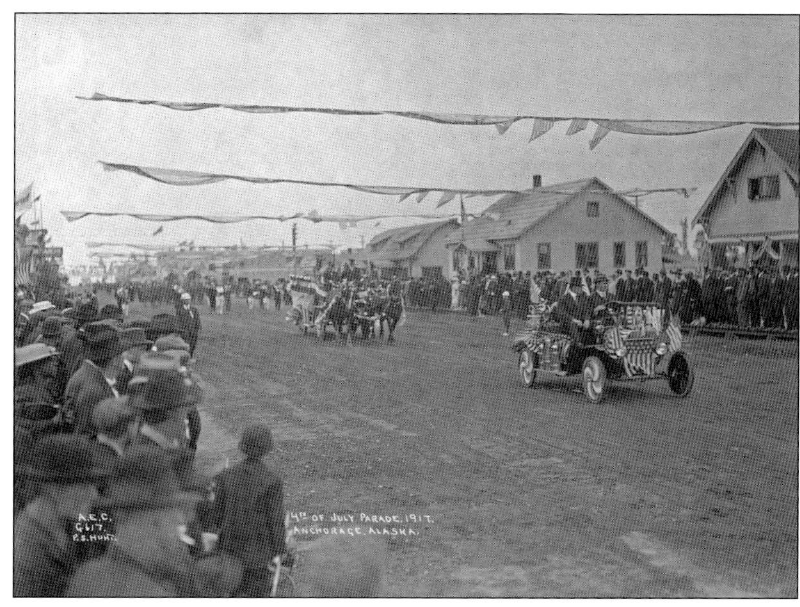

By July 4, 1917, Anchorage had come to resemble a stable town. Residents looked forward to holidays and occasions to celebrate. Independence Day took on special meaning as the daylight exceeded 20 hours and the sun lent its warmth to the festivities.

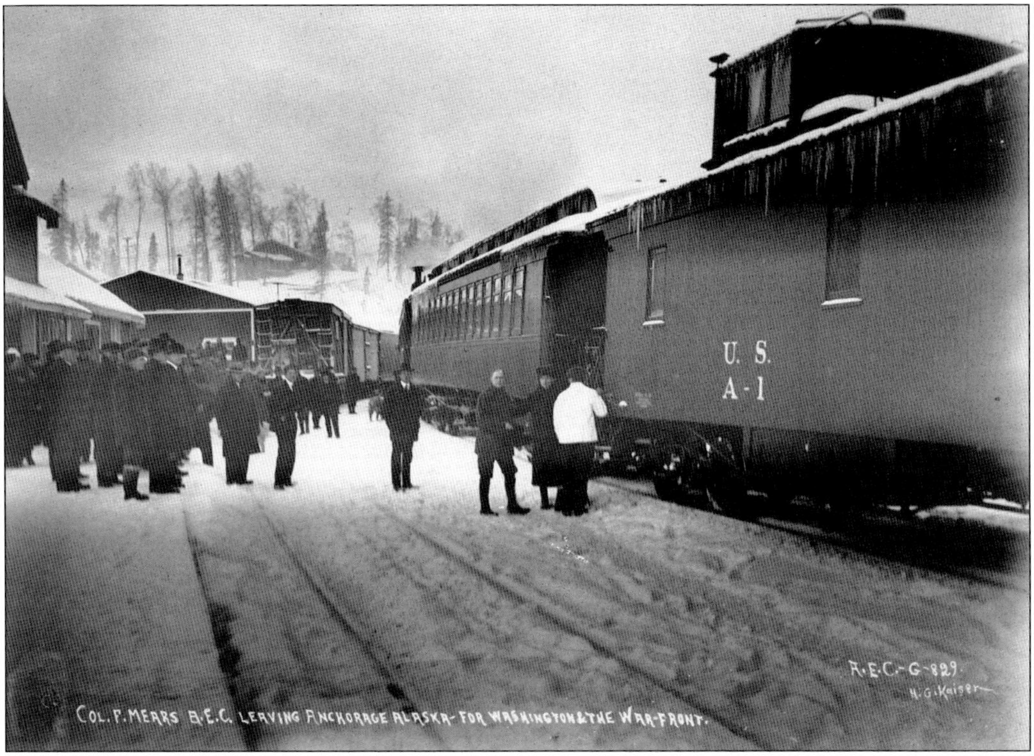

Col. Frederick Mears, seen at the center of this 1917 photograph looking at the camera, served as the principal engineer for the Alaska Engineering Commission. Colonel Mears was a central figure during the earliest days of the railroad construction effort. Pres. Woodrow Wilson appointed Mears to a leadership role in 1914. He was tasked with planning the railroad's central section through 200 miles of wilderness.

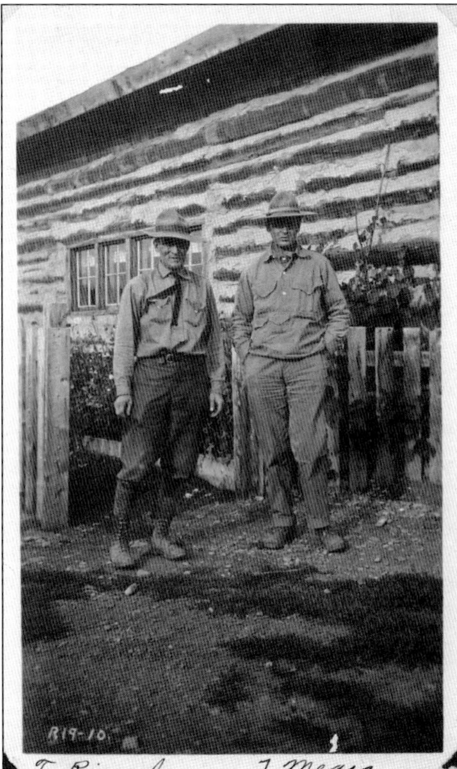

Alaska Engineering Commission leaders Frederick Mears and Thomas Riggs Jr. are seen here preparing for the railroad's construction to begin in 1914. Once the United States joined the war effort in 1917, Mears departed Alaska. He returned after the war to offer additional oversight on the construction before transferring out of Alaska a final time just months before the completion of the railroad in the summer of 1923.

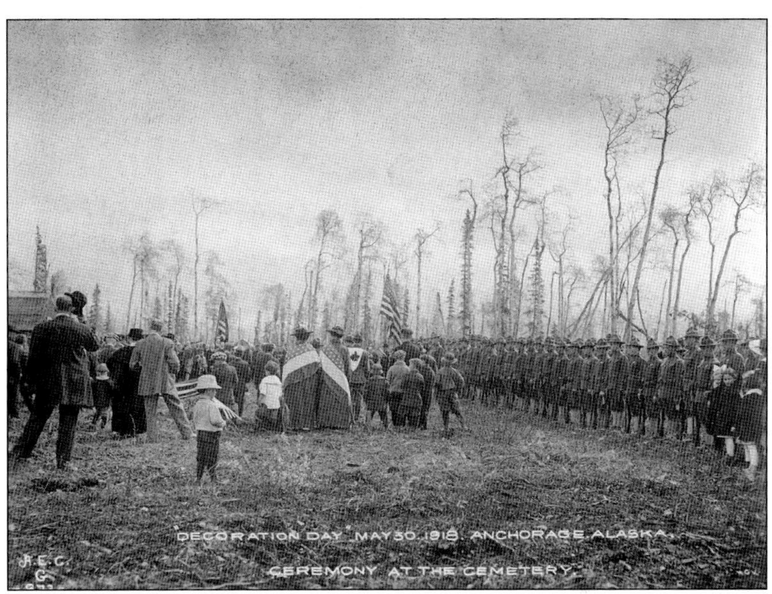

Much of the Alaska Railroad was built during World War I. Alaskans then, as today, honored the flag and fallen soldiers. This image shows Alaskans gathering on Decoration Day in 1918 to remember soldiers who had died in combat during World War I. The holiday has long been known as Memorial Day, though it is still celebrated at the end of May.

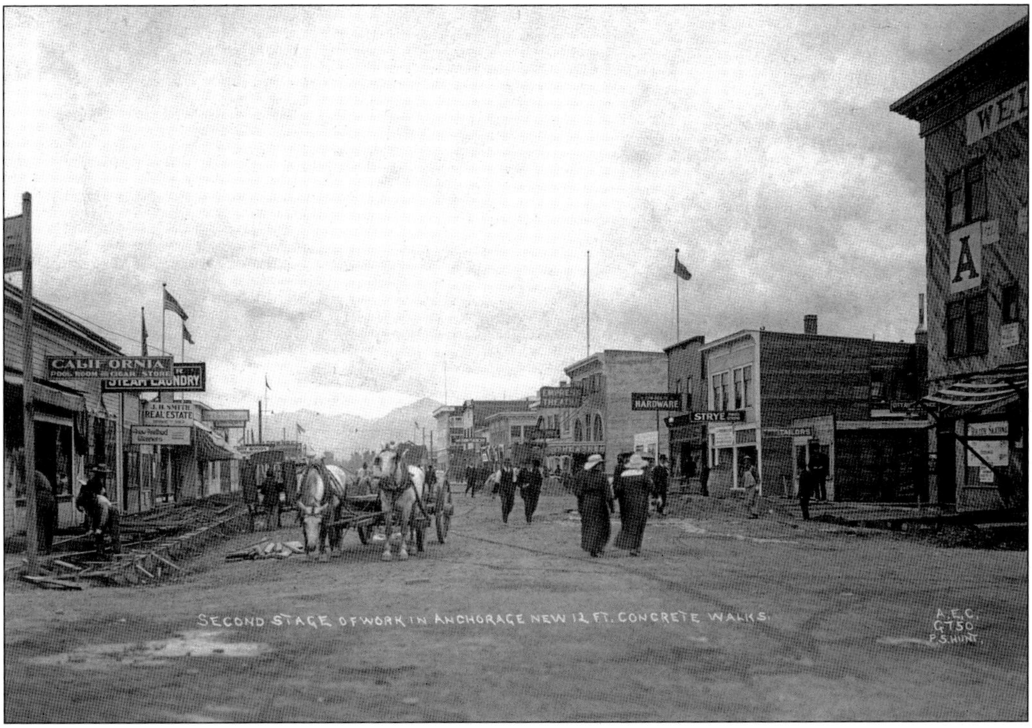

Prominent businesses of early Anchorage included the California Pool Room and Cigar Store, a real estate office, a laundromat, an ice cream parlor, a tailor, a photo studio, a hardware store, a diner, and a theater. Notably absent were saloons and other liquor stores. Alaska was dry before National Prohibition took effect in 1919. But do not be fooled—Anchorage residents creatively worked around Prohibition, as many of the establishments offered bootlegged spirits.

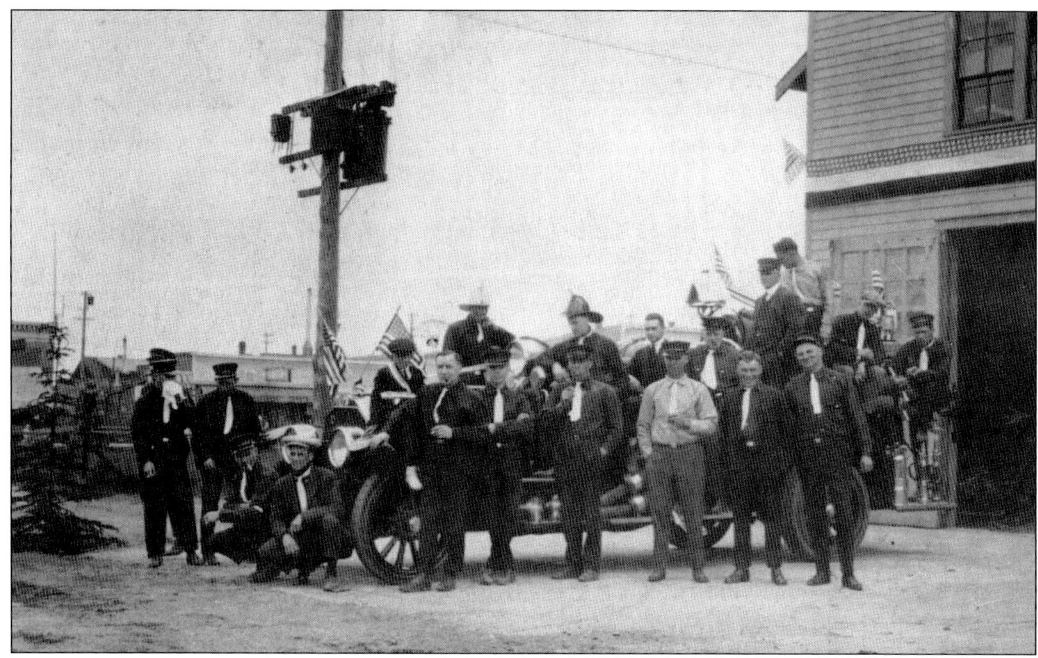

The fire department had its work cut out for it as fire was common in Anchorage, particularly as the townspeople occupied wooden structures. The cold climate led people to heat their homes and businesses in ways that were often not safe by modern standards. This photograph was taken in 1927, the year that the department hired its first paid chief, Thomas Bevers.

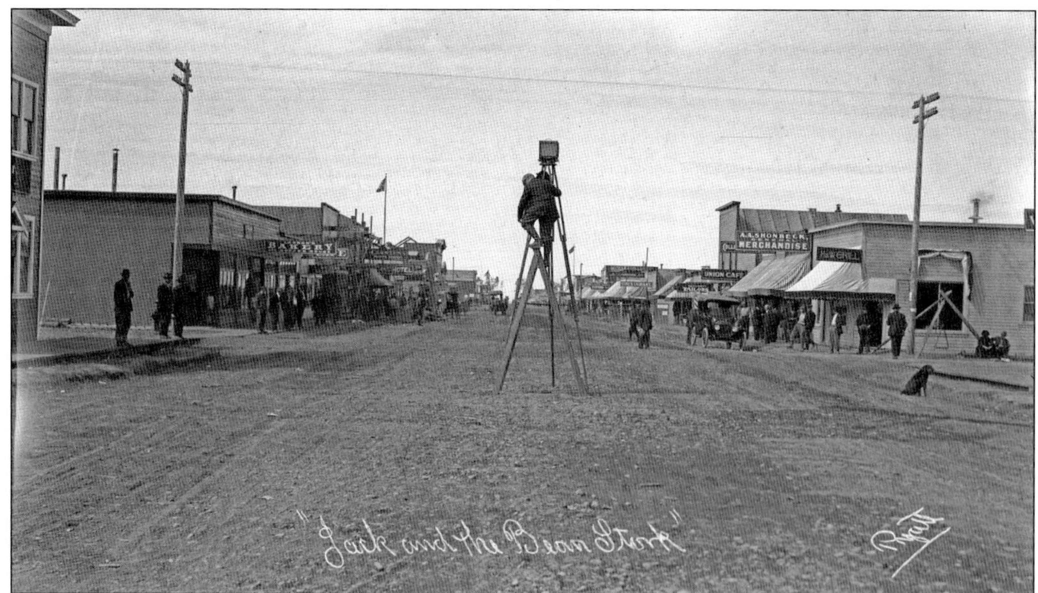

The famous landscape painter Sydney Laurence climbed atop a step ladder to gain a better view of Fourth Avenue. A native New Yorker, Laurence spent considerable time in Alaska and became among the most well-known chroniclers of its scenery and people. His paintings showcased mountains, icy rivers, and the stark beauty of boreal forests in the depths of winter. His photographs typically depicted Alaska Natives donning traditional attire. Laurence's art contributed to the territory's image as the nation's so-called "Last Frontier."

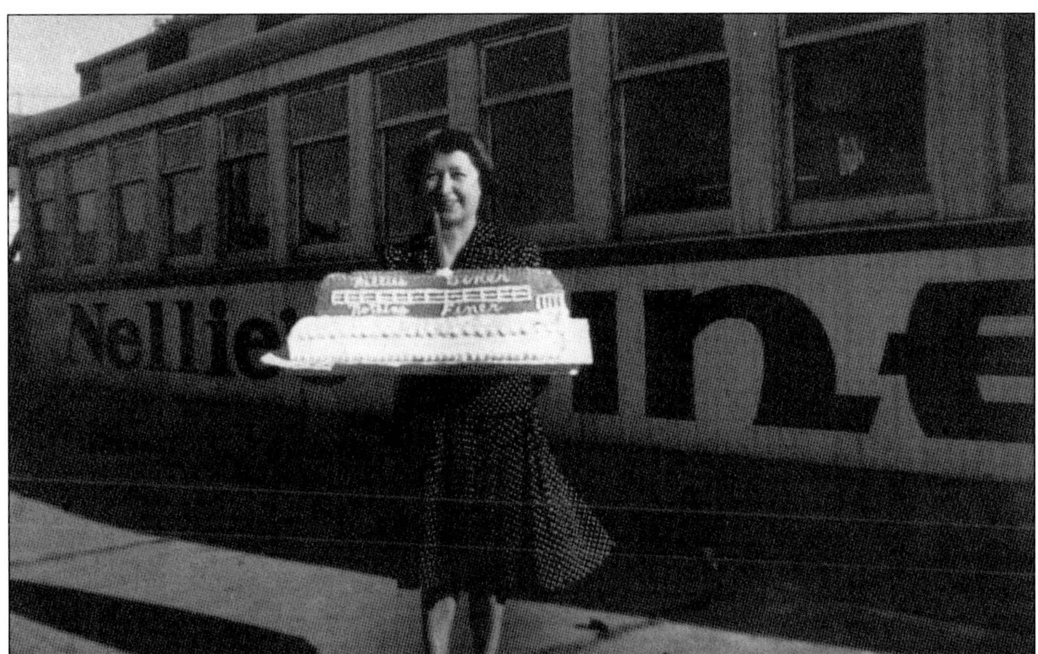

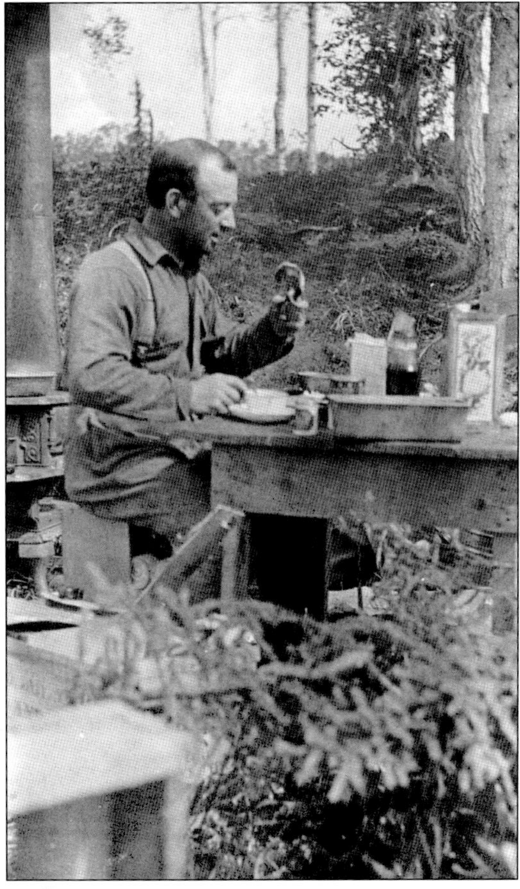

Nellie and John Matthew "Jack" Brown were two of Anchorage's early residents. Nellie Brown (née Shepard) was born in the Alaska Native village of Eyak, near the coast of Prince William Sound. After the railroad displaced many of the Indigenous peoples of the region, Nellie Shepard attended a boarding school in Oregon. She returned to Alaska and met Jack Brown. The two married in 1911 and relocated to the upper Cook Inlet. Jack worked in the newly established Chugach National Forest, where the two lived until moving closer to Anchorage. Soon after, Jack worked for the Alaska Railroad. Nellie had a reputation as a socialite who enjoyed photography and traveling. She also operated a diner out of a surplus railroad passenger car (seen here). Jack and Nellie resided in Anchorage until their deaths in 1972 and 1978 respectively. They became known as Anchorage's first pioneer couple.

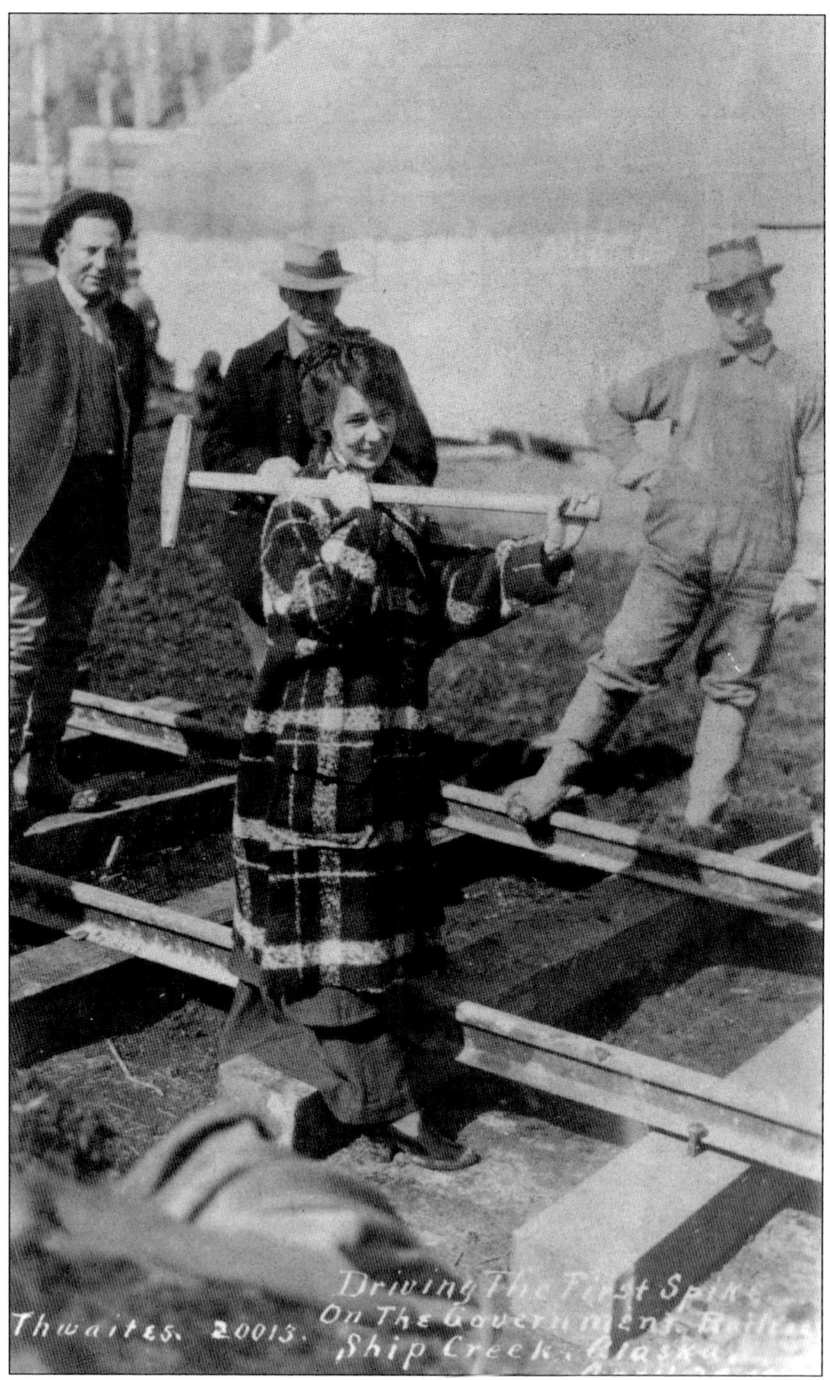

Martha "Babe" White, daughter of Edward and Martha "Mother" White, early Anchorage settlers, drove the first spike of the Alaska Railroad on April 29, 1915. The White family moved to Alaska and started a mercantile trading business in the area around Ship Creek. The construction of the Alaska Railroad occurred primarily between 1915 and 1923. Pres. Warren Harding traveled to Alaska in July 1923 to drive the ceremonial gold spike in Nenana, about 350 miles north of Anchorage. This marked the completion of the railroad.

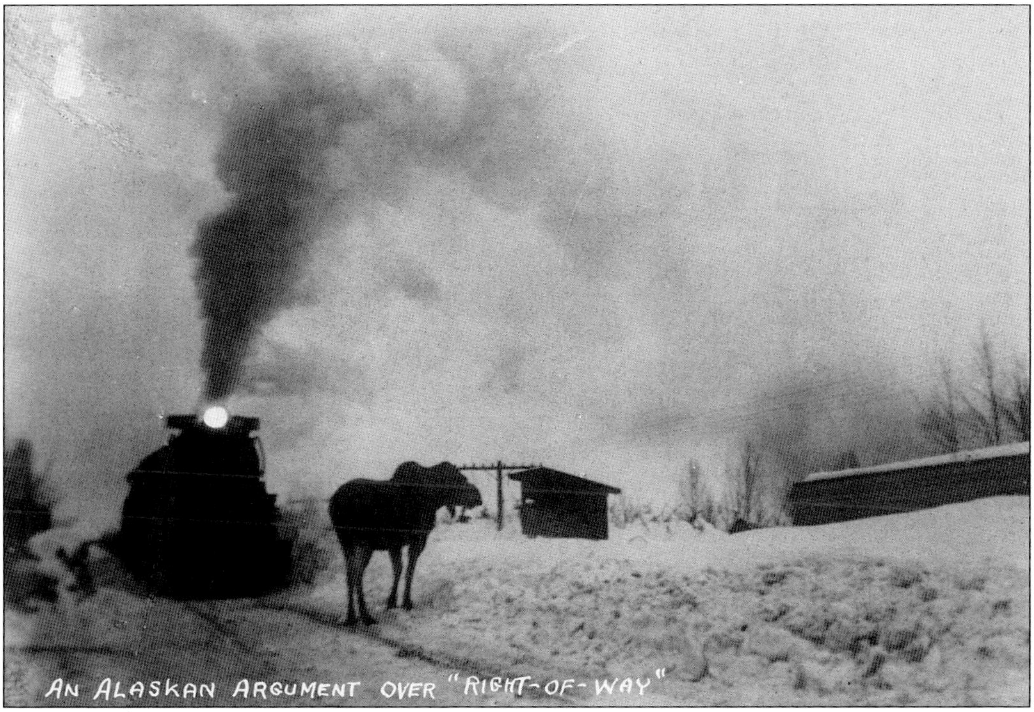

AN ALASKAN ARGUMENT OVER "RIGHT-OF-WAY"

Keeping animals, especially moose, off the tracks of the Alaska Railroad has long been a challenge. During heavy snowfall, moose walk along the cleared tracks. While conductors do what they can to avoid the moose, accidents happen. Alaskans love their wildlife, but they present a unique hazard, even in Anchorage, the state's largest city.

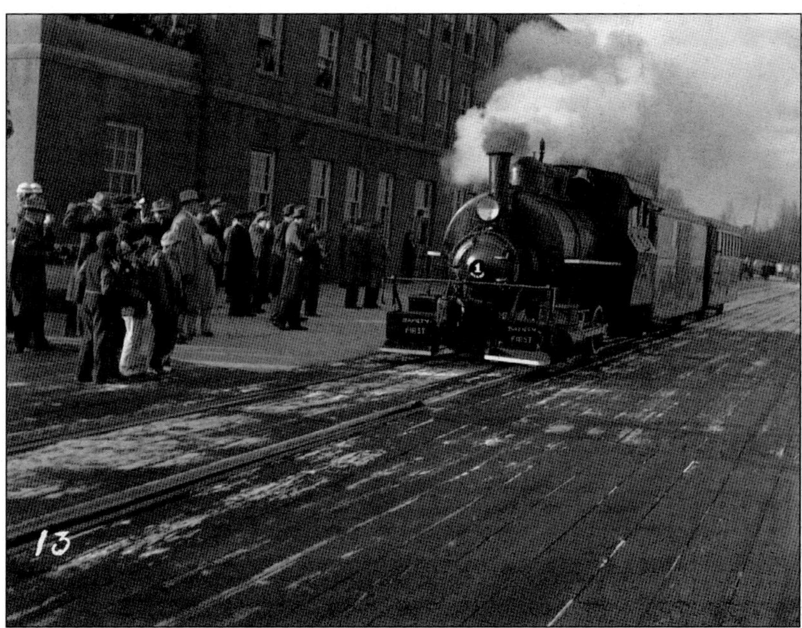

Alaska Railroad locomotive No. 1 steams into the Anchorage depot in 1923 as spectators take it in from the platform. Onlookers are visible peering out from the windows in the Anchorage depot building in the top left of the photograph.

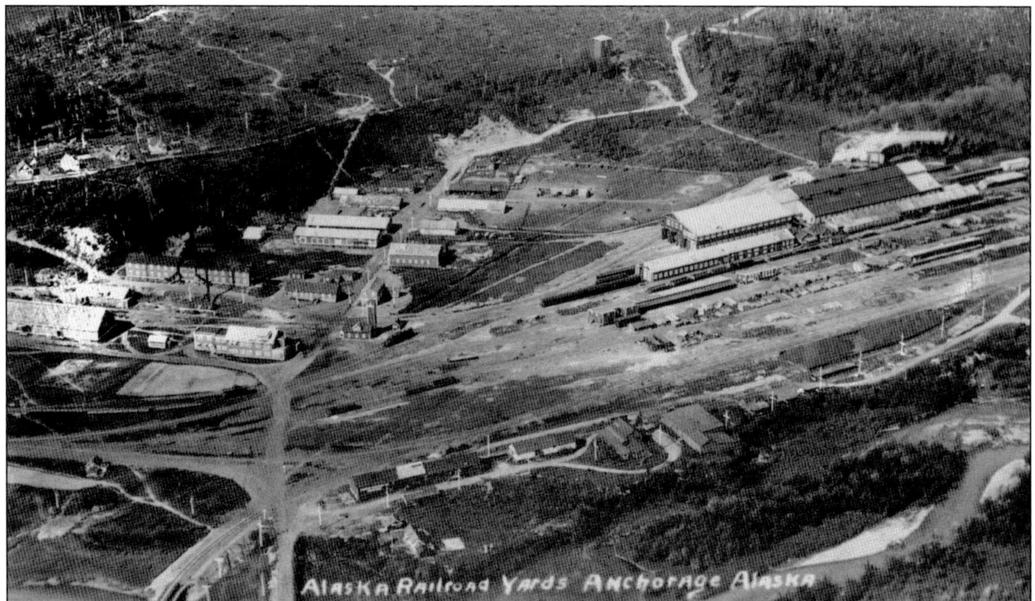

The Alaska Railroad Yards served as the headquarters of the railroad from its completion in 1923 until the 1940s, when the new Alaska Railroad depot was completed. A sprawling complex with mostly wooden structures, the yards had endured fires and costly maintenance. The wear and tear of World War II revealed the necessity of a new, more durable depot.

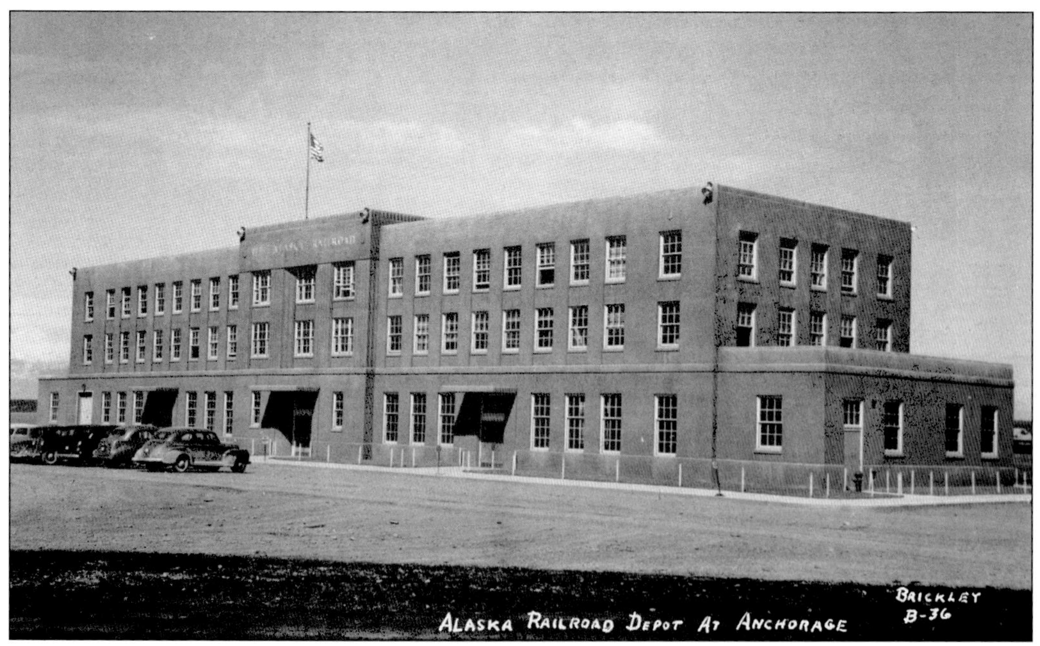

Completed in 1948, the railroad depot took the place of the rail yards. As Anchorage stood poised for growth in the postwar era, the depot became one of the burgeoning community's most recognizable and iconic landmarks. It was listed in the National Registry of Historic Places in 1999.

Three

Life at the Edge of the Forest

As Anchorage transformed from a small and makeshift settlement, largely dedicated to the construction of the Alaska Railroad, to a more stable town, its residents demanded amenities and entertainment found beyond Alaska. With some irony, boosters promoted Alaska as the "last frontier," even as many new residents, it seemed, wanted to live in decidedly nonfrontier conditions. These pioneers of the north evidently wanted to dine in new restaurants, drive down paved streets, attend concerts and movies, and gather at the latest social club.

Sports had proven to be especially popular. In fact, Anchorage developed as baseball had become the nation's pastime. Residents shaped baseball diamonds from the surrounding forest and organized ball games as soon as the snow melted and the ground was dry enough to run the bases. Likewise, the winter freeze-up ensured ample possibilities for hockey, another sport that Alaskans adopted enthusiastically.

Anchorage residents found other creative ways to pass the long summer days and dark winter nights. Amid Prohibition, men and women obtained liquor at the speakeasies. Brothels and prostitution existed with tacit recognition from authorities, though usually on the edge of town. Once Prohibition formally ended in 1933, bars and saloons legally served patrons deep into the night. Live music was played from a variety of venues.

More wholesome destinations sprang up across the landscape, too. Anchorage accommodated a range of churches and faiths. Iconic venues like the Fourth Avenue Theater opened shortly after World War II. Anchorage's premier winter festival, Fur Rendezvous, was popular as residents and tourists took advantage of late February's returning daylight and gathered downtown, mingled in markets, and bartered with trappers who had come to town bearing impressive furs.

By the 1940s and 1950s, Anchorage was imprinted by the segregation that defined other American cities, large and small. African American, Alaska Native, and Asian American residents accessed housing in limited parts of town. One such neighborhood, Eastchester Flats, became an epicenter of entertainment as it accommodated cultural expressions that were deemed "unacceptable" elsewhere. Jazz and blues musicians performed as the entertainment went around the clock. The photographs in this chapter document people on the move and a town on the rise. What began as an industrial settlement on the edge of a forest at the mouth of a creek had become a modern, mid-century community.

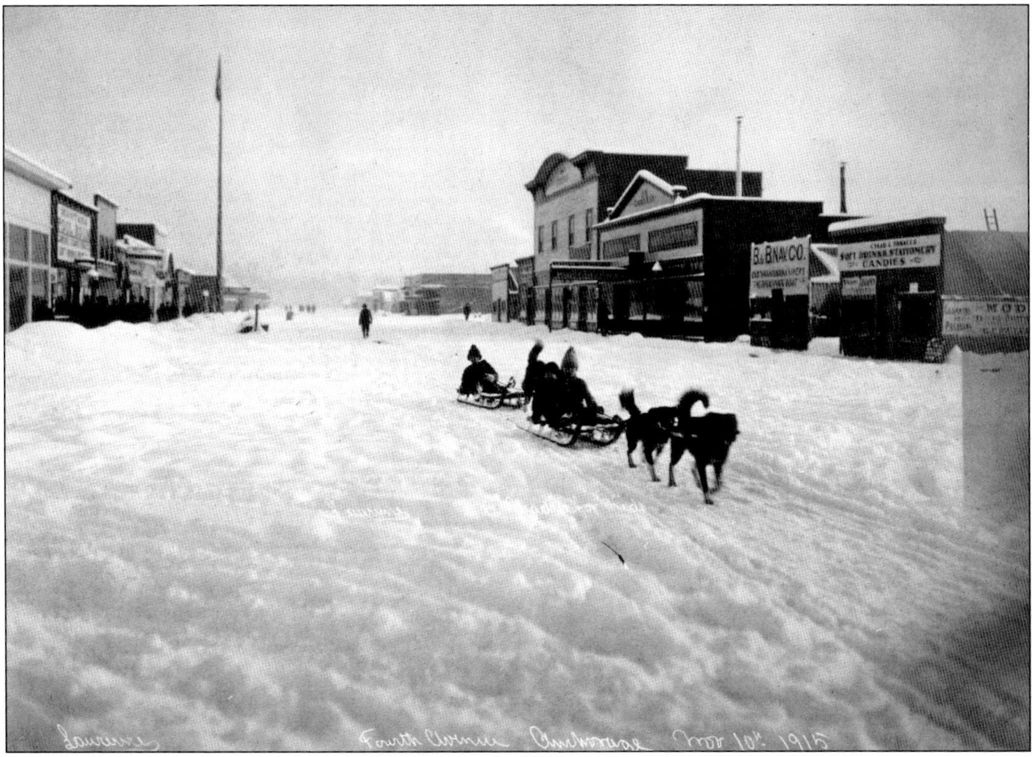

While the storefronts and architecture have certainly changed, contemporary Anchorage residents will recognize snow in the streets and young children playing outside. This photograph, taken by Sydney Laurence on Fourth Avenue in November 1915, reveals a town where children (and adults) often had to make their own fun and adapt to the chilly northern environment where winter arrived early and stayed late.

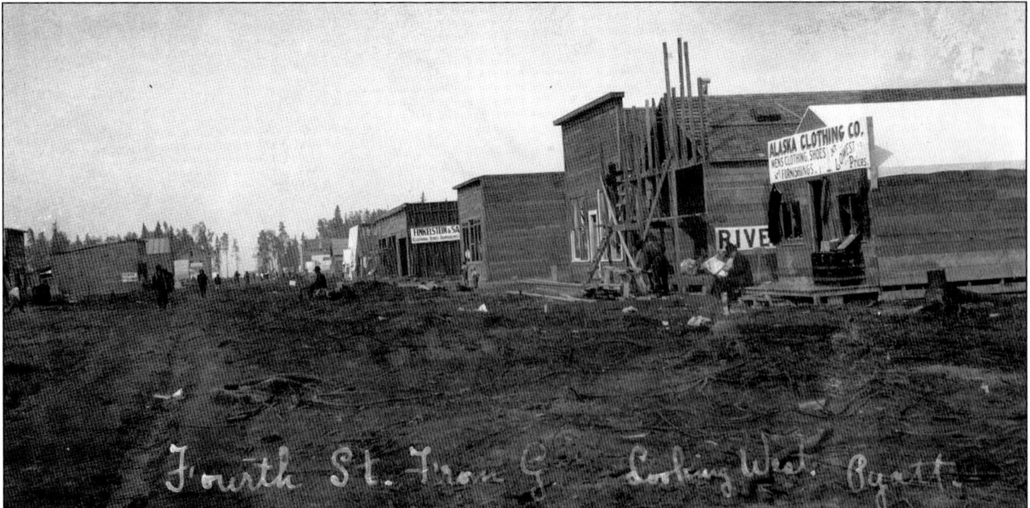

This scene is also from 1915 on Fourth Avenue. The townsite began to take on the appearance of a more permanent settlement with new storefronts popping up on a near-daily basis. Men and women came and went from the railroad construction site to visit a "downtown" that looked a bit different and offered new amenities and temptations with each passing day.

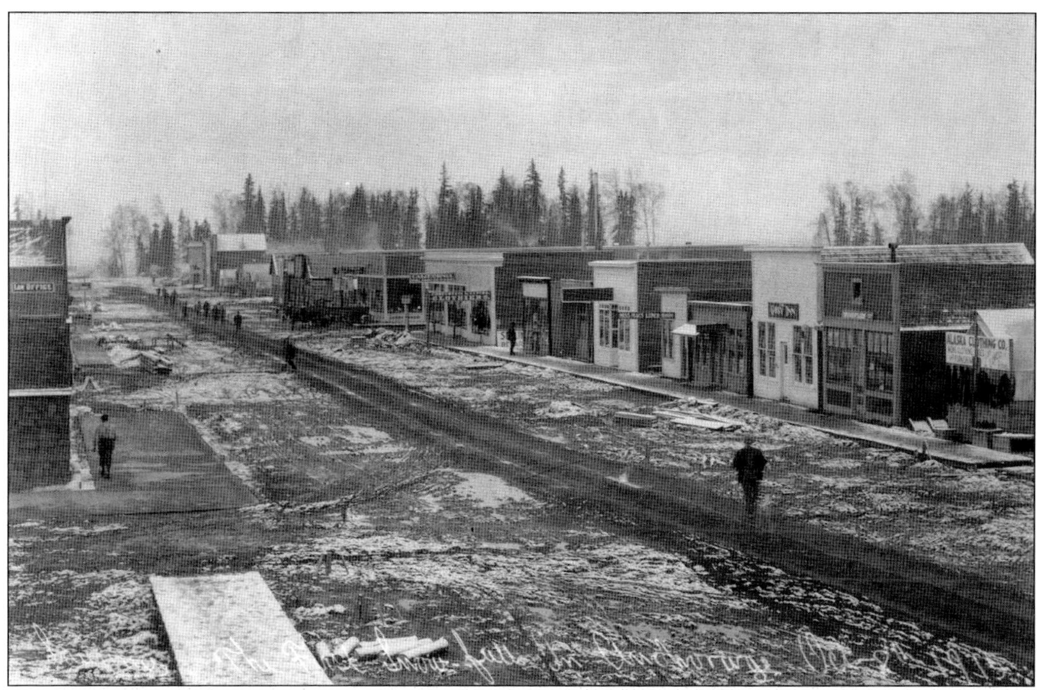

By the late 1910s and early 1920s, Anchorage may have at first glance resembled a frontier town in the Old West. But far from a lawless redoubt, the federal government exerted control in the region and spent copious amounts of money on the railroad. These photographs depict the early development of Anchorage's townsite along the commercial corridor of Fourth Avenue in 1915 and 1916. Fourth Avenue might be considered Anchorage's "main street," serving as the primary hub for entertainment, business, and culture. The street is depicted many times in this book; each photograph demonstrates the ever-changing nature of the growing town. Through good times and bad, Fourth Avenue has remained the heart of downtown Anchorage.

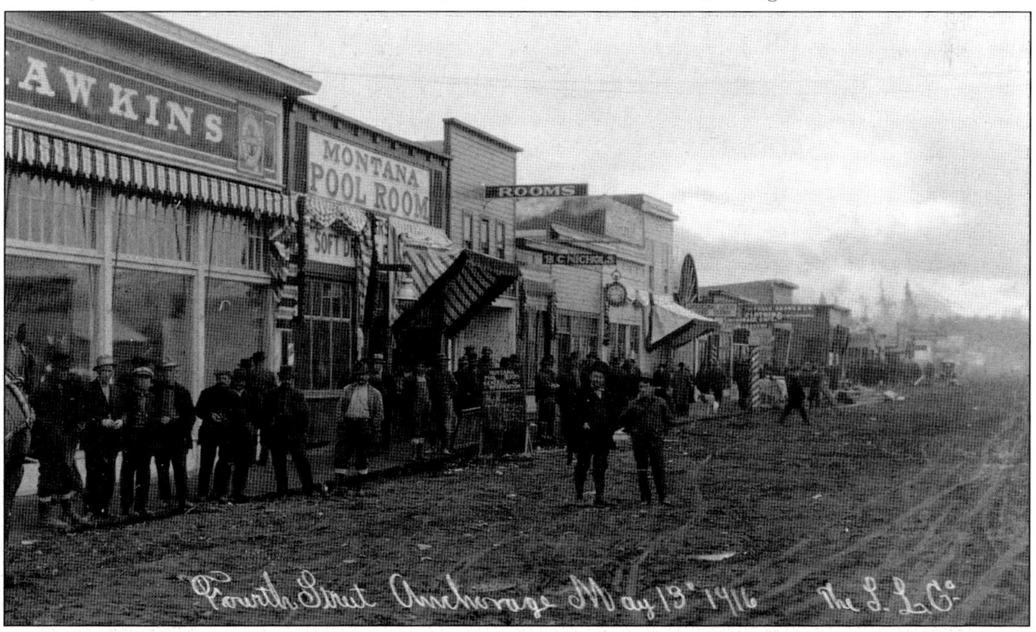

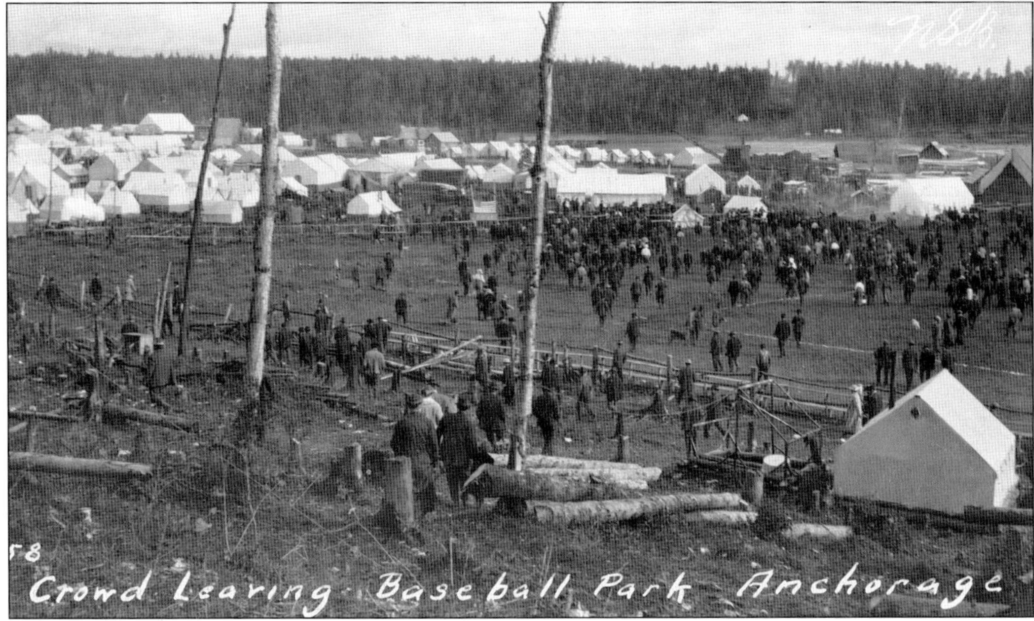

In 1916, amusements, though increasing, were still sparse. Railroad workers, among others who had moved to town, found creative ways to pass the time. Baseball had become popular, and Americans who resided in dense urban environments, rural enclaves, and small towns put together pickup teams to play the game. Anchorage hosted several teams within its first years. The growth and development of Anchorage roughly corresponded to the rise of baseball as the so-called national pastime. Crowds swelled into the hundreds, and pickup games were common. It was, of course, also a great way to get out and enjoy Anchorage's abbreviated summers.

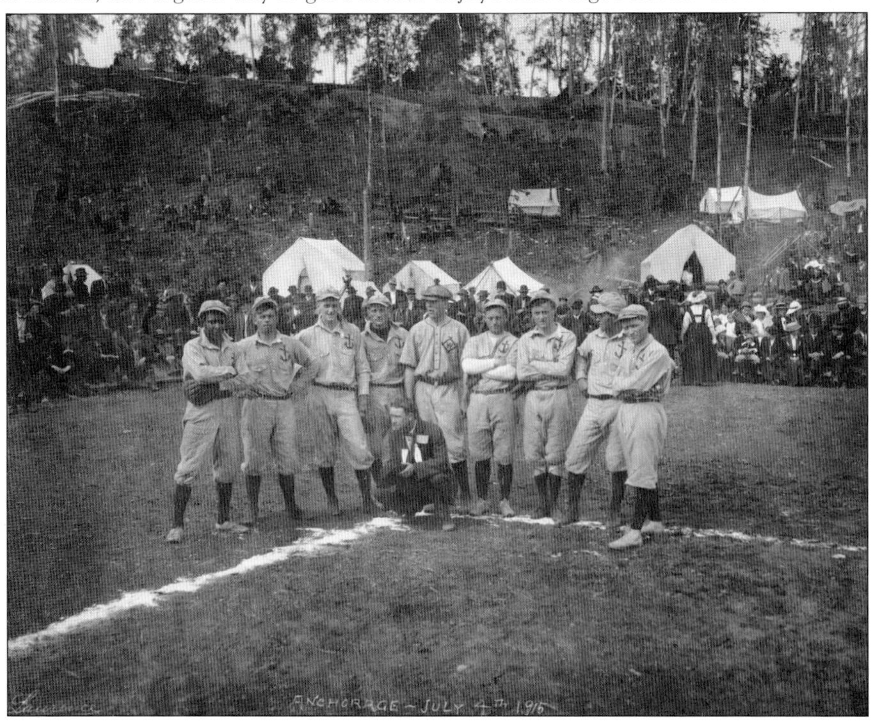

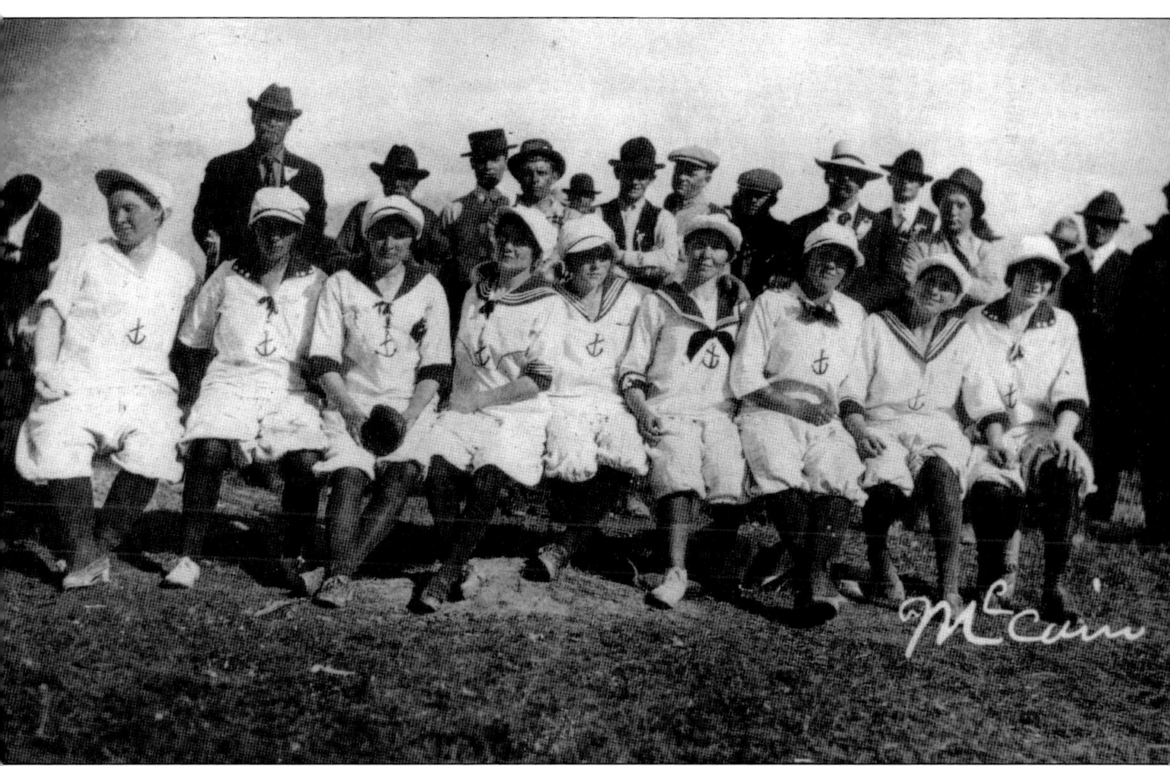

By the 1920s, Anchorage's demographics had begun to even out as more women moved to the area and families grew. Women in Anchorage played as hard as the men, and they, too, fielded teams and played the national pastime. The team depicted here even had an air of professionalism, as evidenced by their uniforms. Sports have long provided opportunities for women to showcase their talents and enter the public sphere. In Anchorage, they also offered an important space to meet up, develop and cultivate social networks, and even organize politically.

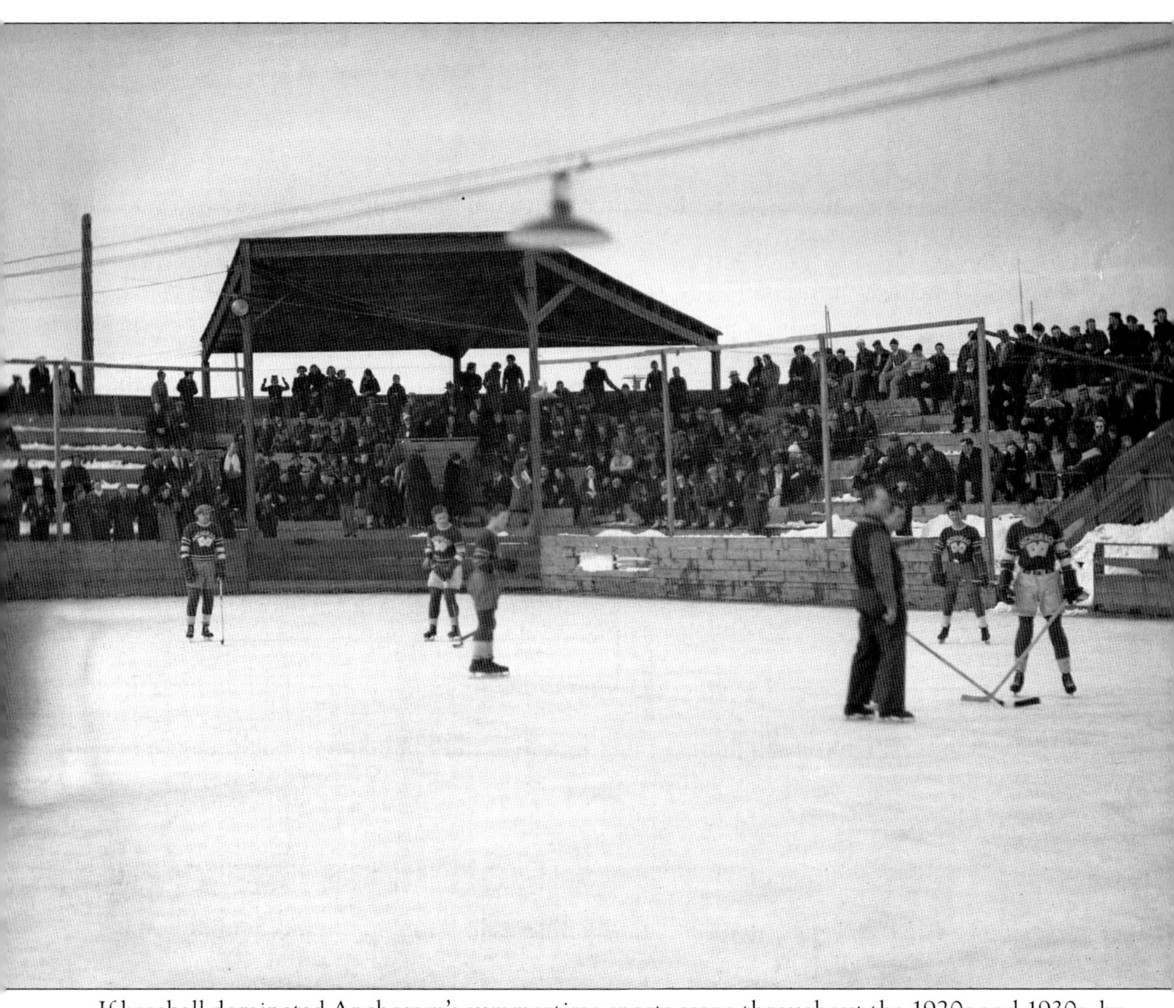

If baseball dominated Anchorage's summertime sports scene throughout the 1920s and 1930s, by late fall and winter, hockey took center stage, or, more accurately, center ice. Since Anchorage's ponds and lakes usually freeze over between the end of October and Thanksgiving, residents had ample time to develop their puck-handling skills. The undated photograph here was likely taken in the late 1920s at an ice rink and featured an organized youth hockey club rather than a pickup game played among friends on a frozen lake. Ice hockey is among several winter sports that Alaskans have long embraced. Cross-country skiing is arguably the most popular.

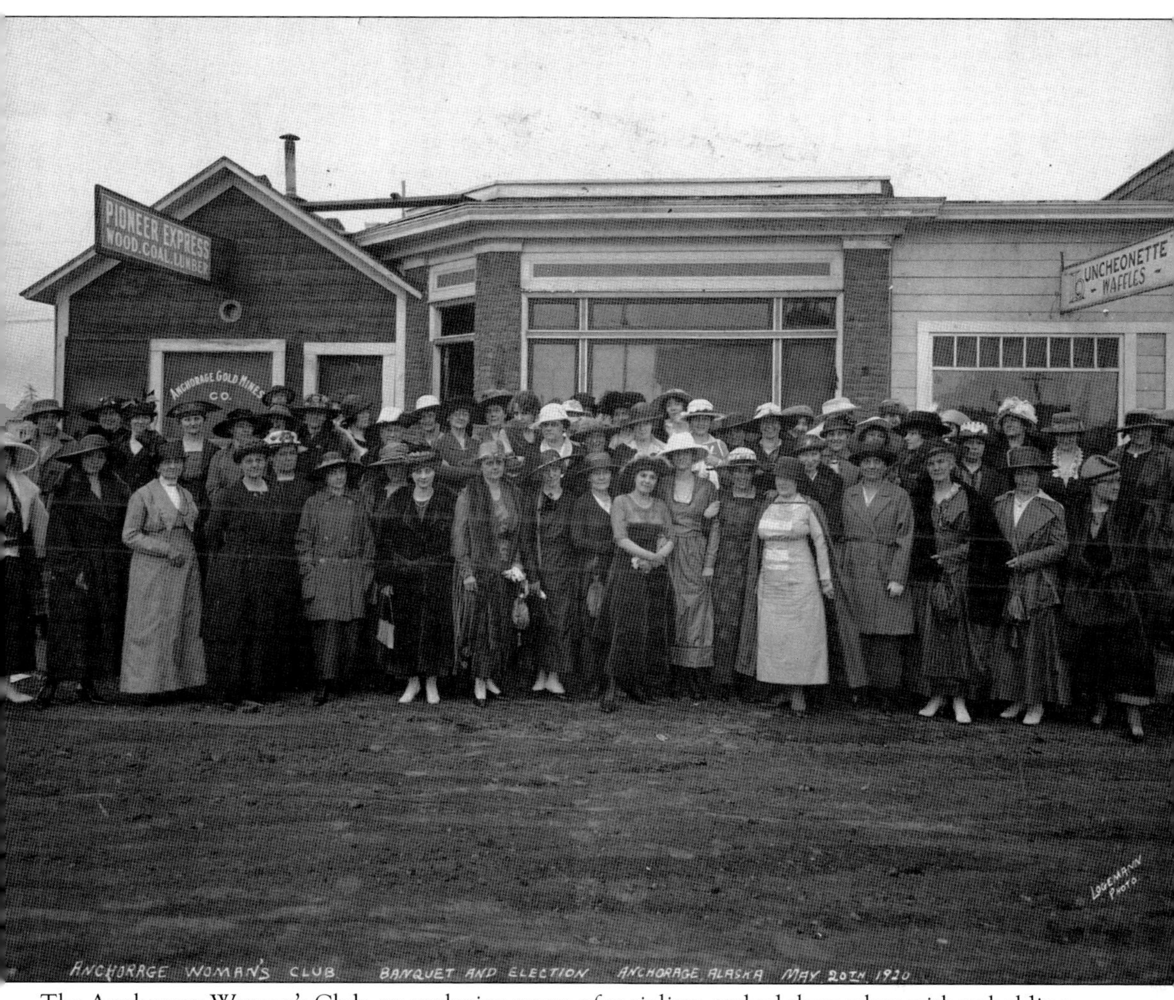

The Anchorage Woman's Club, an exclusive group of socialites, tasked themselves with upholding moral standards and strengthening the community's social and cultural fabric. These women represented a broader movement in the United States during the early 20th century, culminating in the 1920s as white women exercised their hard-fought right to vote and grew more politically empowered. With the ratification of the 19th Amendment, women also took on a greater role in public life, and social clubs became important institutions in many American towns. Anchorage was no different. The photograph here was taken in May 1920 on Fourth Avenue looking north. Railroad cottages on Third Avenue are visible in the background to the far left. One of the cottages was repurposed in 1979 and became a beloved Anchorage fine dining establishment, Marx Bros. Café.

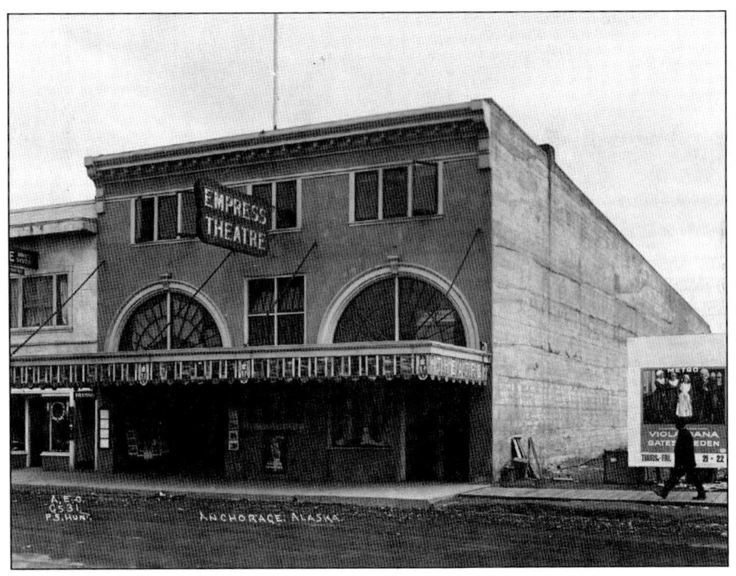

The opening of the 450-seat Empress Theatre in 1916 marked an important milestone in Anchorage's young history. As the population demanded contemporary entertainment, the Empress delivered a steady schedule of major motion pictures. Alaska entrepreneur Austin "Cap" Lathrop financed the theater. In 1941, the Fourth Avenue Theatre opened and largely supplanted the Empress, which closed its doors in the early 1950s.

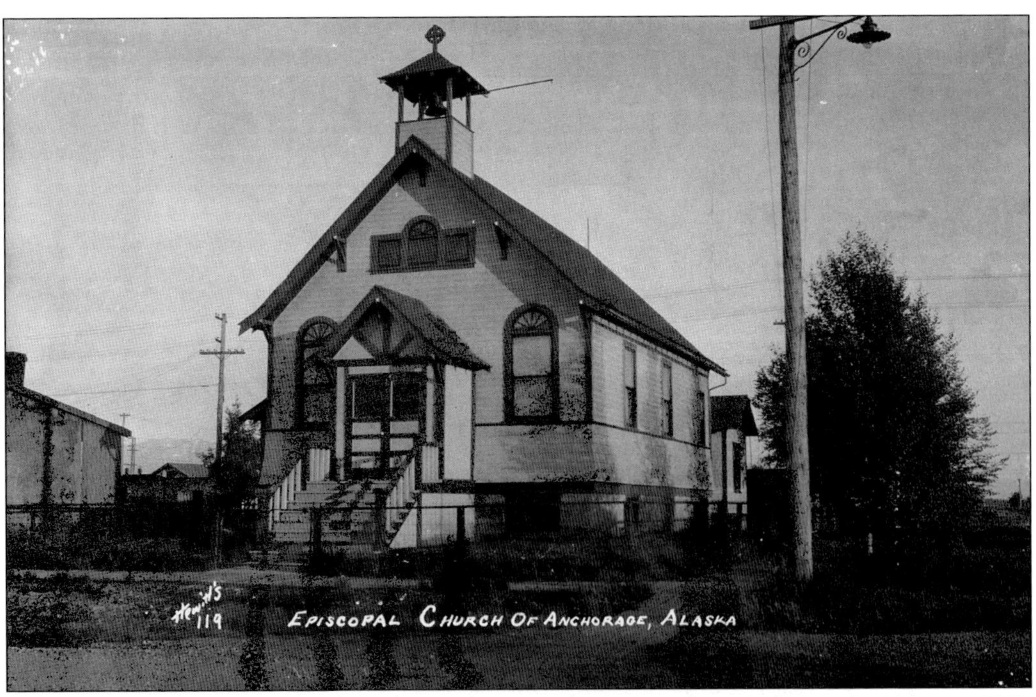

The All Saints Episcopal Church held its first service in the summer of 1915 in Government Hill, Anchorage's first neighborhood. The sanctuary opened in 1917, making the Episcopal church one of Anchorage's earliest permanent structures. The church was later relocated south of Ship Creek, where it remained until the early 1950s. It was replaced by the church of the same name at the corner of Eighth Avenue and F Street.

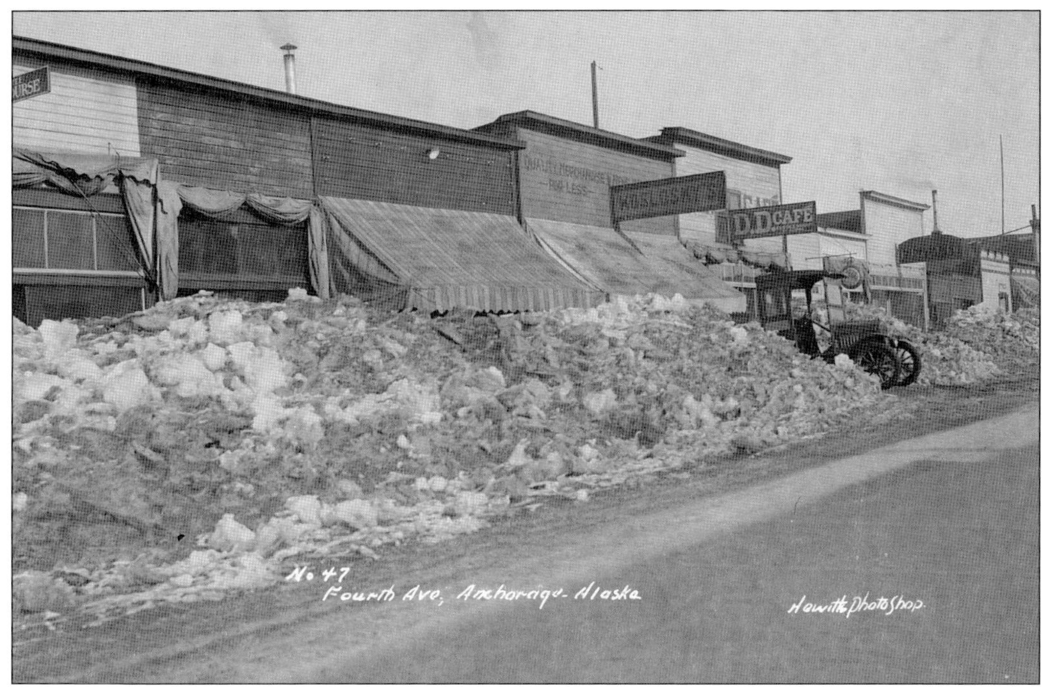

An Anchorage winter street scene from the 1920s bears a striking resemblance to the modern era. High snow berms and impassable roads were barriers to travel during Anchorage's long winters 100 years ago, just as they sometimes are today. It became clear to community leaders early on that they would need to invest in the latest snow removal equipment. Few matters animate local politics more than effective (or ineffective) snow removal.

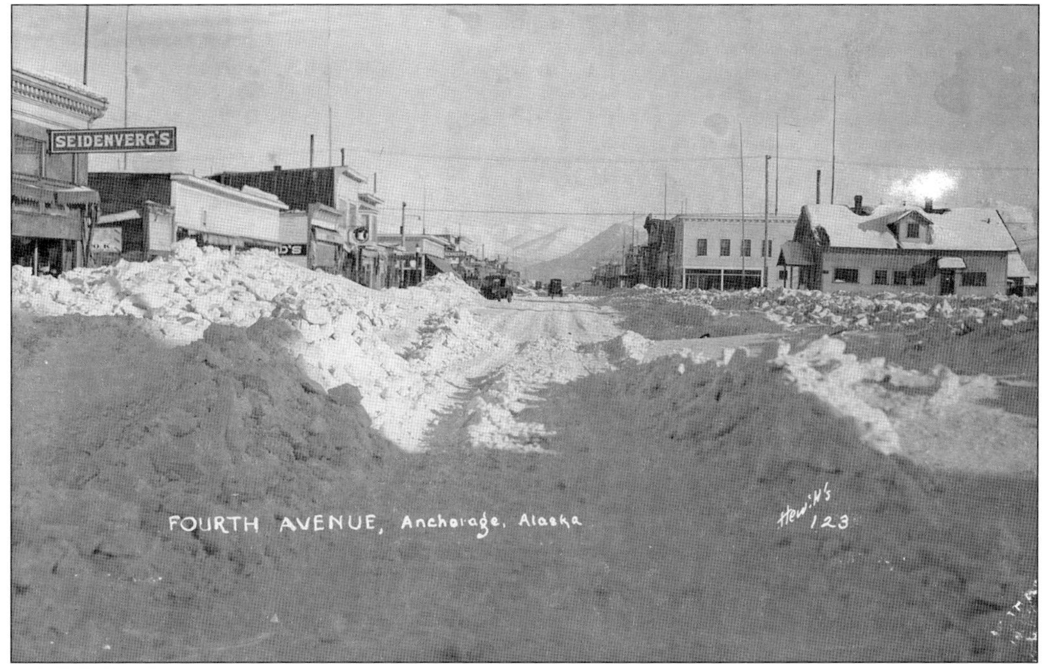

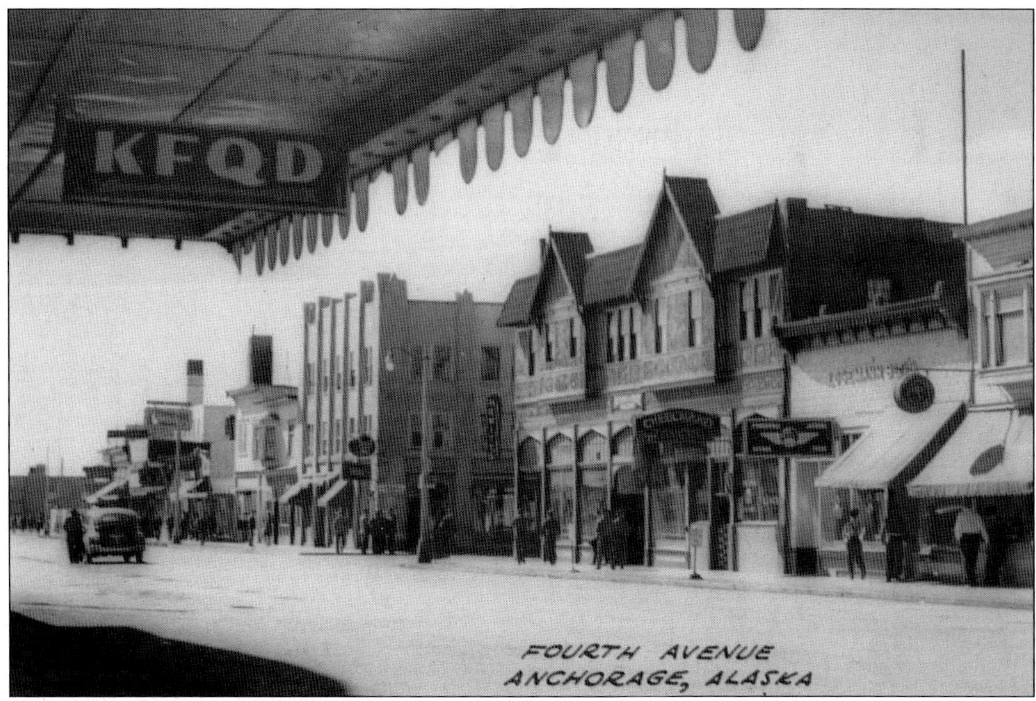

Dubbed "the voice of the golden north," KFQD was a leading source of news and entertainment in Anchorage throughout the 1920s and 1930s. Located on Fourth Avenue between E and D Streets, the station's familiar exterior is viewed in these two photographs. Looking west from under the KFQD awning, the Logemann Building, Cheechako Tavern, Hewitt's Drug Store, and Rexall Drugs are visible across the street. KFQD was an early Anchorage radio station that gained its license in 1924. The station retains its call letters today. Radio was a central means of communication and the primary way that Alaskans could stay up to date on the news around their vast territory as well as the broader world. To this day, many rural Alaskan communities rely on radio to receive news and updates about the weather, public safety, and more.

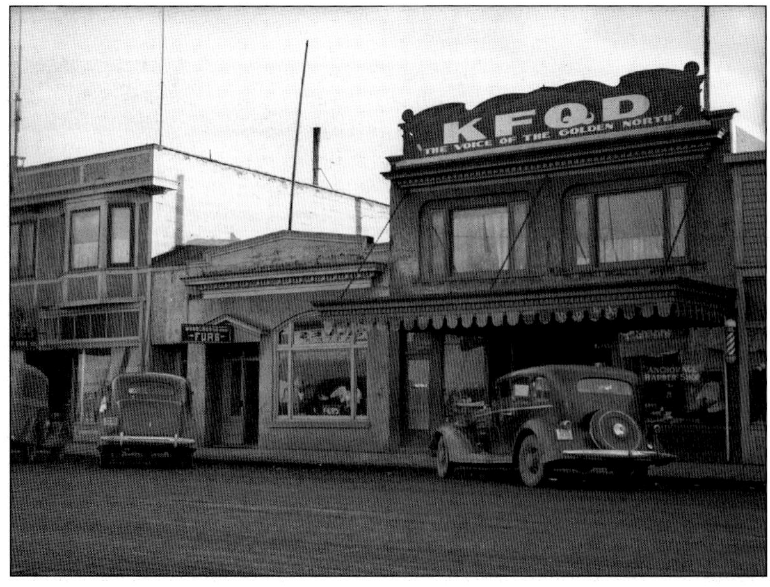

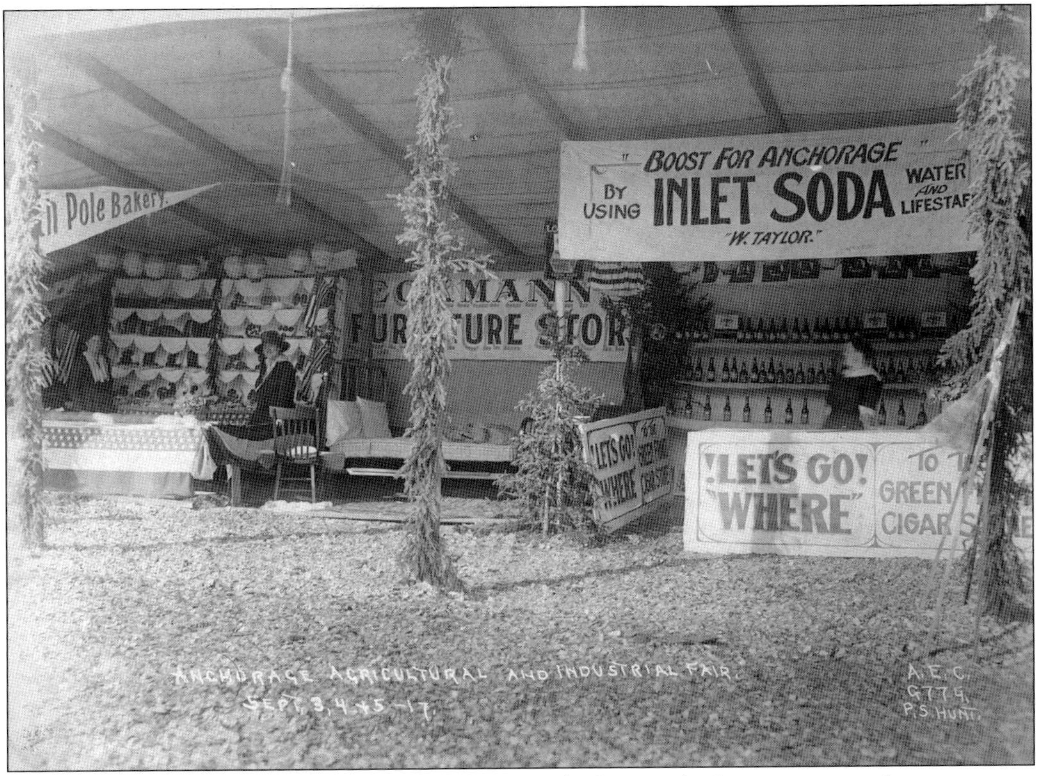

The Anchorage Agricultural and Industrial Fair took place in the late summer and was among a few fairs that occurred in Alaska during the 1920s and 1930s. Here, three women pose at their respective stalls, selling mineral water, furniture, and baked goods. Today, tens of thousands of Alaskans gather in Palmer at the Alaska State Fair, which has its roots in the agricultural and industrial fairs of this earlier era.

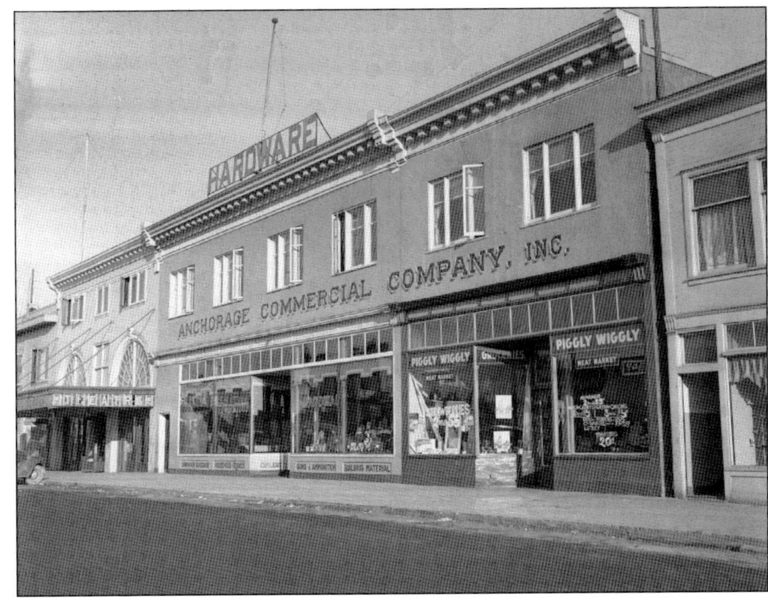

In this view of Fourth Avenue near H Street in the late 1930s, the Empress Theatre is visible to the left, easily identified by its marquee. The Anchorage Commercial Company and Piggly Wiggly were two popular retail outlets that early residents of Anchorage relied upon for dry goods and other essential provisions.

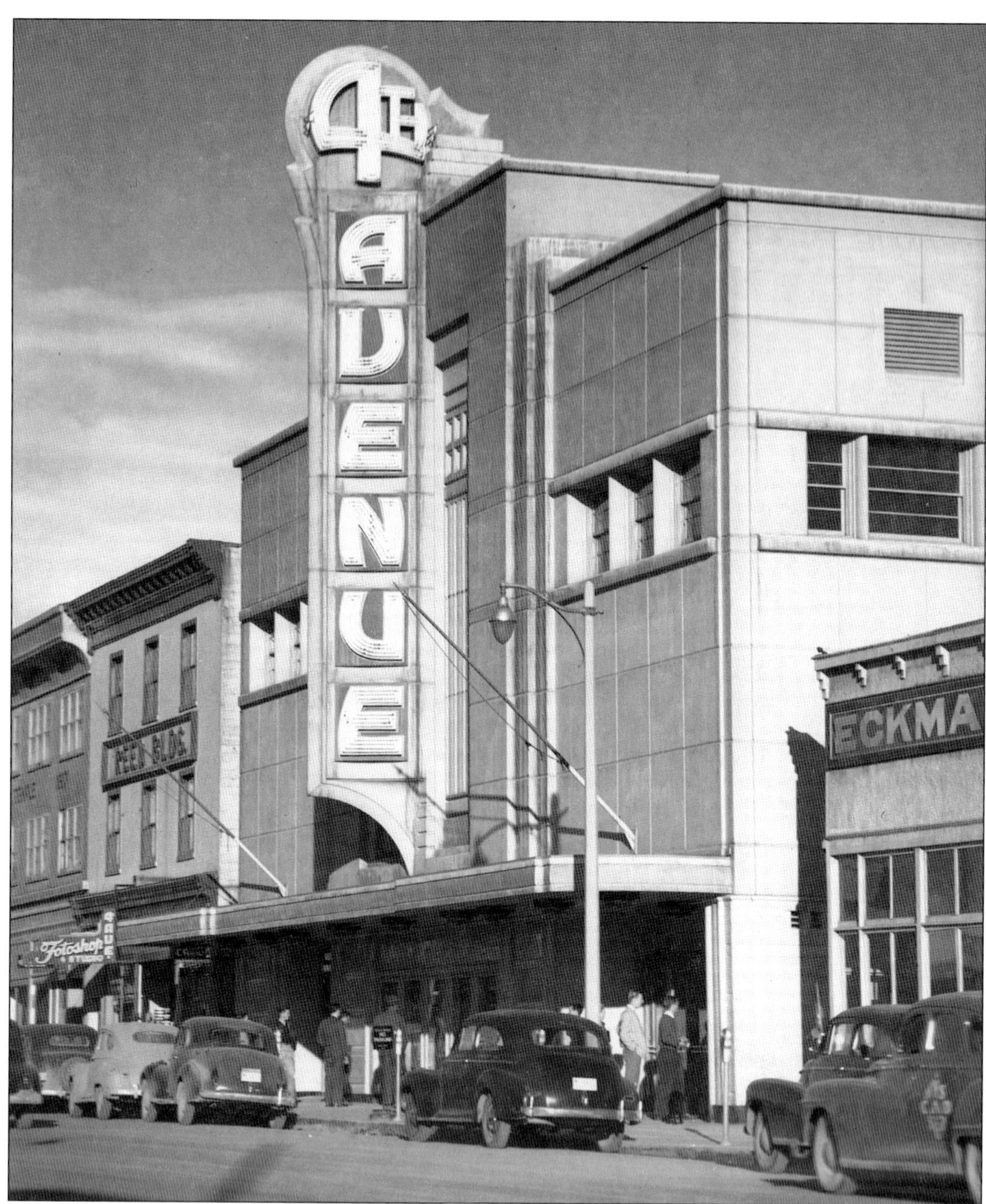

One of the most recognizable buildings in Anchorage for several decades, the Art Deco–style Fourth Avenue Theater sat majestically along the south side of the street on which it was named. Cap Lathrop, a wealthy Alaskan businessman and political figure, financed its construction, just as he had the Empress Theatre before it. Workers broke ground in 1941, but the Second World War delayed the theater's completion until 1947. During its heyday in the 1950s and 1960s, the theater presented major motion pictures to sold-out crowds of over 900 people. Its interior featured a mural of Mount McKinley (now Denali) with gold accents, among other handcrafted artistic flourishes. While the theater was beloved and in use for decades, it fell into disrepair by the 1990s and 2000s. After considerable debate over the future and possible repurposing of the theater, it was demolished in 2022.

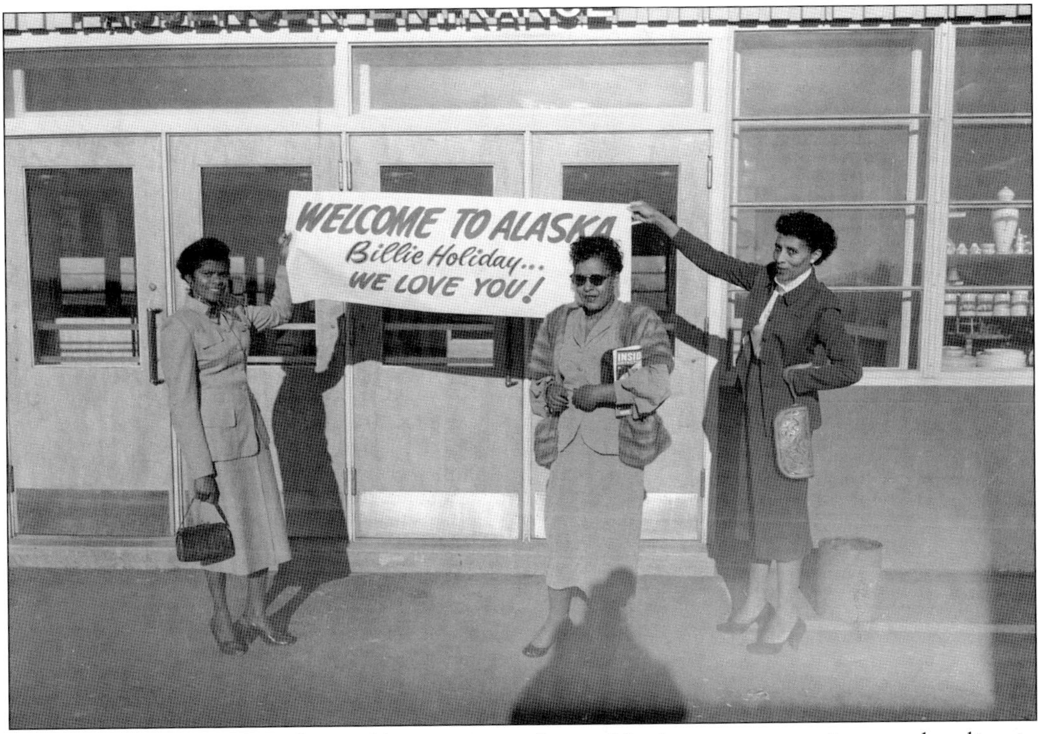

Anchorage has hosted its share of live music, and arguably the town was at its most bustling in the postwar decades. The sound of music came from Anchorage's wealth of bars, restaurants, and theaters. As one example, jazz legend Billie Holiday visited Alaska in 1954, a time of rapid growth in Anchorage largely due to the expansion of the military during the height of the Cold War. Holiday was among many iconic Black entertainers who performed in the territory during the postwar decades. Other jazz and blues greats included T-Bone Walker and Jimmy Rushing, both of whom played deep into the night to sold-out crowds.

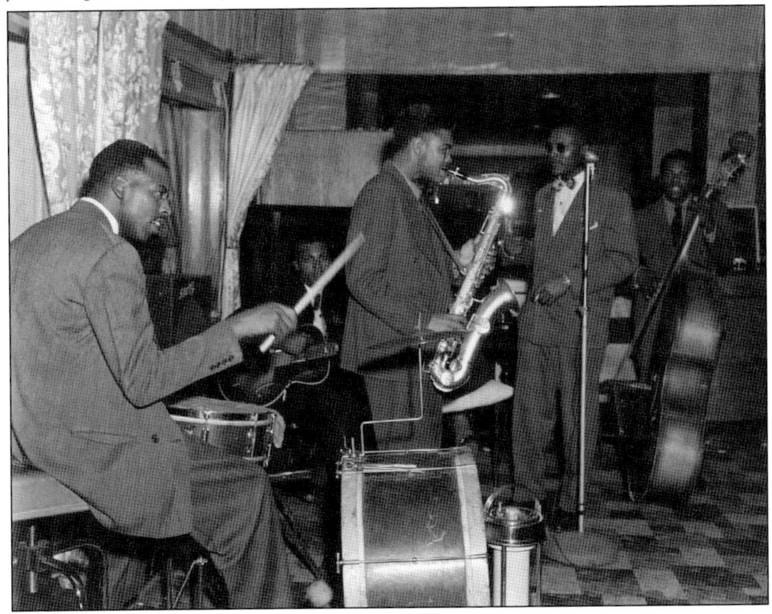

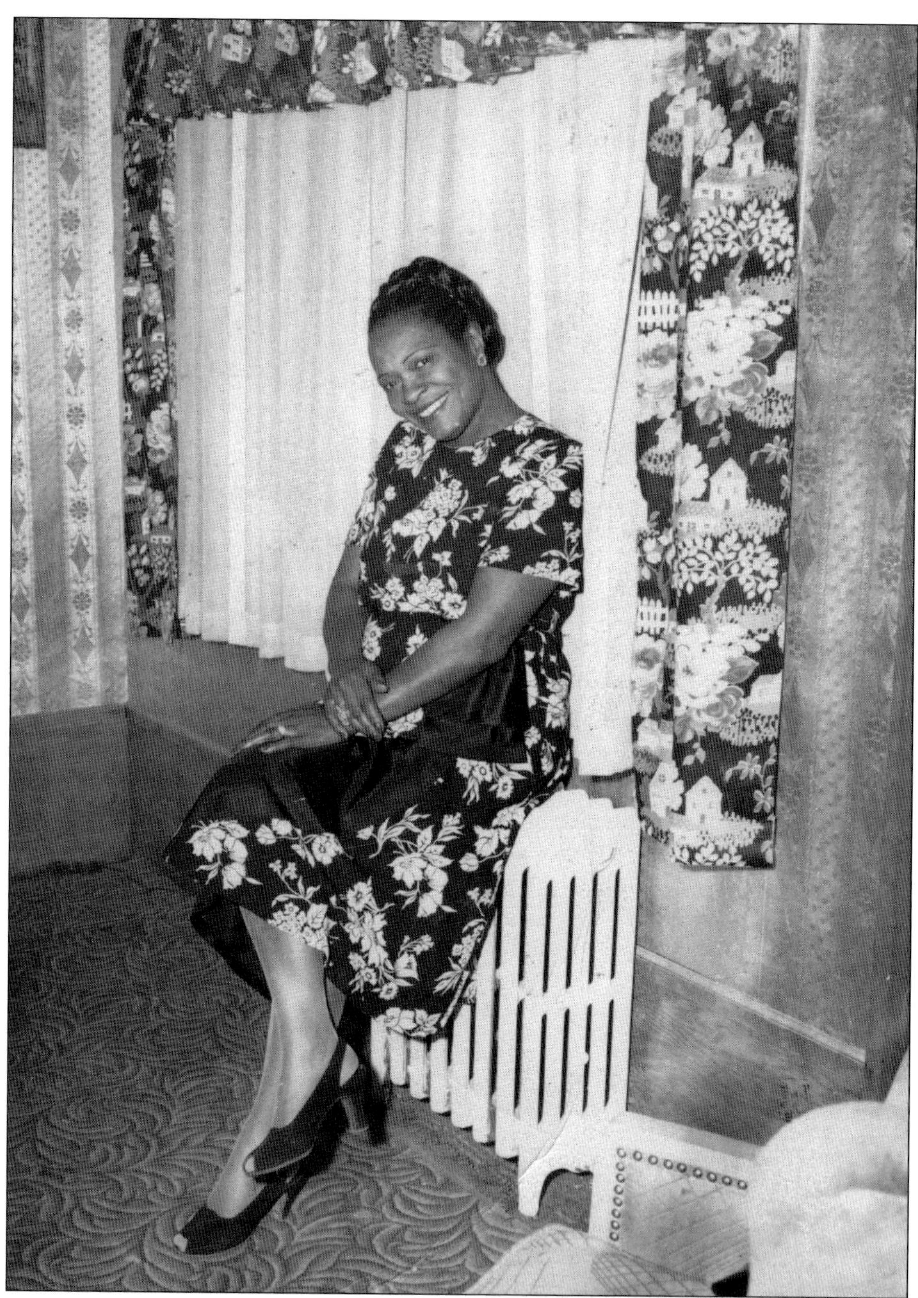

Zula Swanson was born in Alabama in 1891 and escaped an impoverished upbringing in the Deep South to make her way to Anchorage in 1929. Swanson worked as a madam, bootlegger, and real estate investor and eventually amassed large savings and extensive tracts of land. By the 1950s, she had become one of the wealthiest real estate investors in Alaska. In 1962, she sold land on what is now Fifth Avenue to JCPenney for an estimated $250,000, a handsome sum at the time. Zula Swanson remained active in Anchorage's civic affairs throughout her life. She was a founding member of the Anchorage chapter of the National Association for the Advancement of Colored People (NAACP) in 1951 and served in various community clubs, including the Daughters of the Elks. Swanson passed away in 1973 at the age of 82.

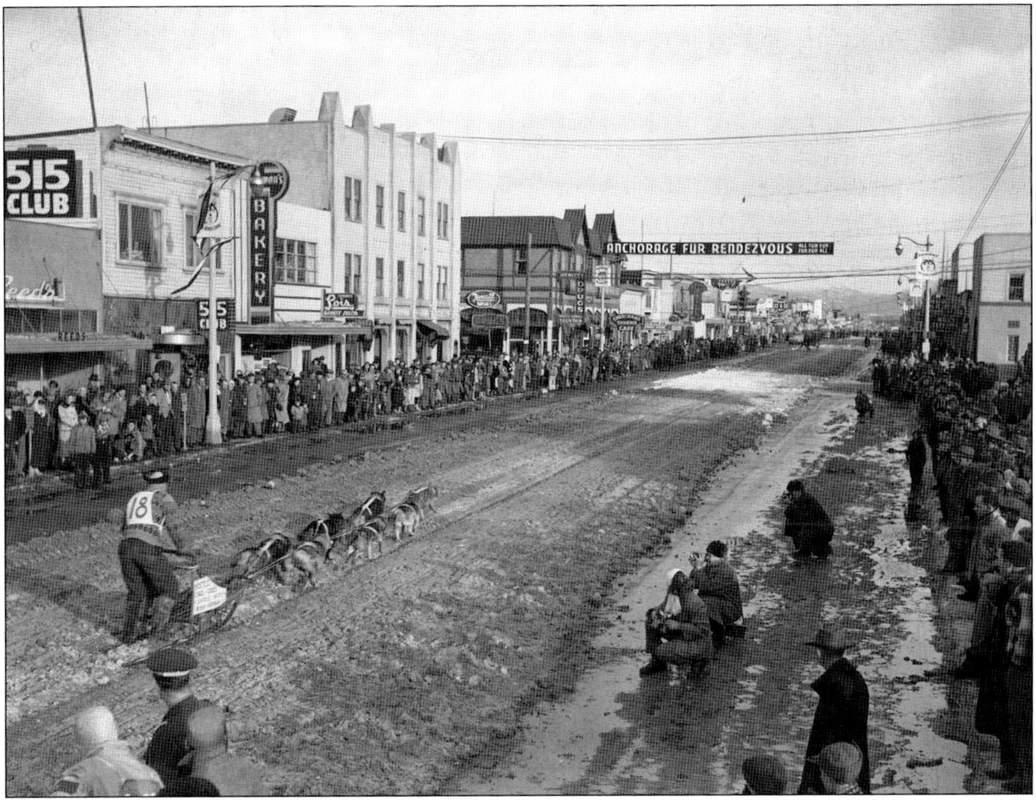

These photographs depict Anchorage's most well-known and celebrated winter tradition, Fur Rendezvous (or "Fur Rondy" to locals). The festival dates to 1936, when it began as a swap meet where fur trappers and traders sold and bartered their wares. Over time, it has become a 10-day celebration that marks Anchorage's transition from the long winter into spring. By late February and early March, daylight begins to noticeably increase, and residents are ready to celebrate. While Fur Rondy continues to celebrate the history and heritage of fur trapping, it has become more akin to a carnival with rides, games, and family entertainment.

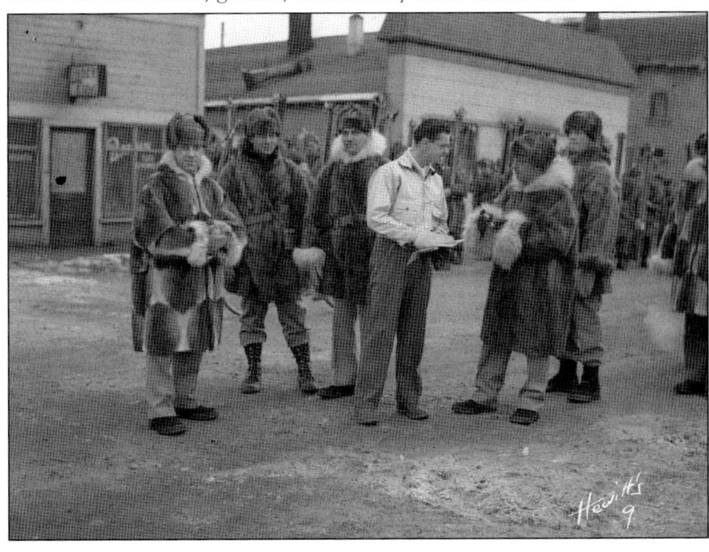

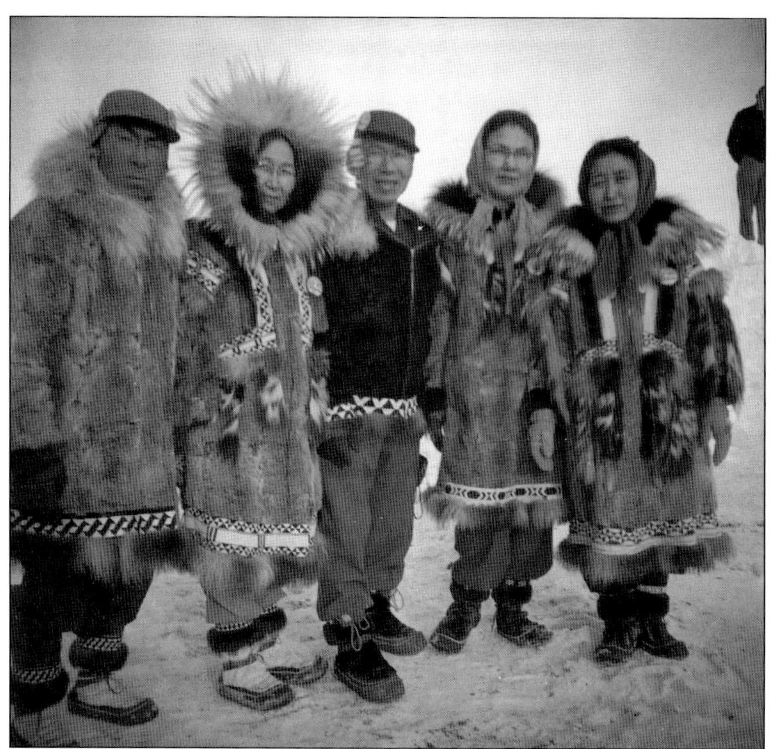

Much of downtown Anchorage is dedicated to the festivities with Fourth Avenue serving as one of the centers of the action. By the 1950s and 1960s, Fur Rondy assumed its modern character, featuring dog mushers, parades, and a carnival-like atmosphere in addition to its roots as a gathering place for trappers, traders, and fur aficionados. This photograph, taken in the 1950s, shows Alaska Native participants proudly decked out in parkas (atkuk) and boots (mukluks).

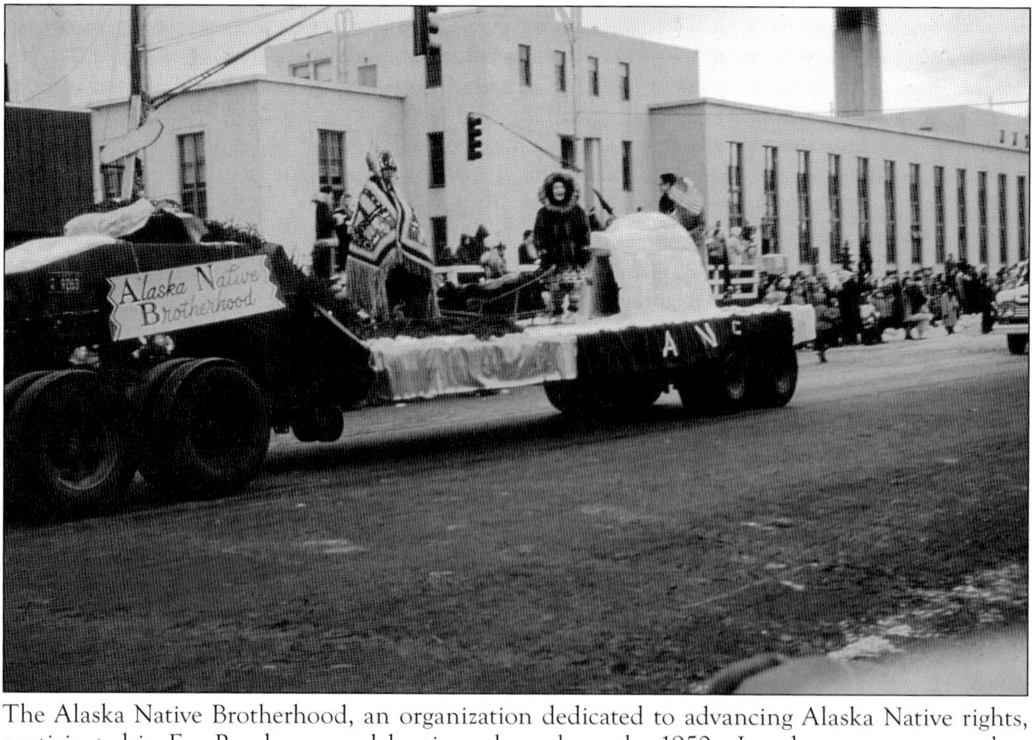

The Alaska Native Brotherhood, an organization dedicated to advancing Alaska Native rights, participated in Fur Rendezvous celebrations throughout the 1950s. Its advocacy was central to ensuring civil rights and Native land claims.

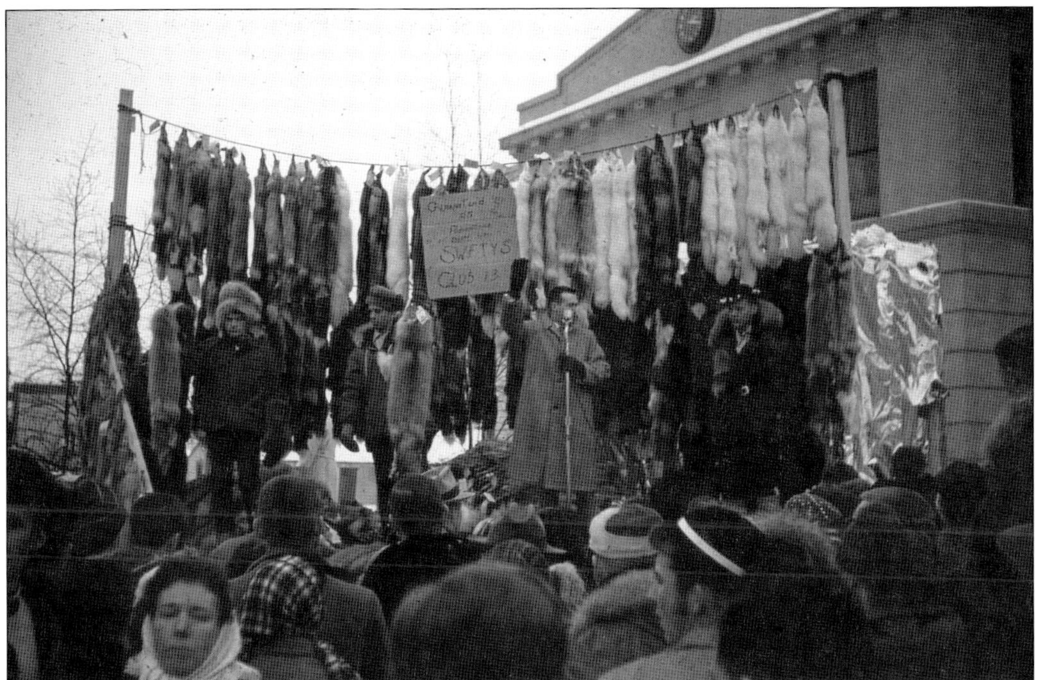

This photograph, taken in 1956, depicts a scene from an auction and harkens back to the roots of Fur Rendezvous as a modest gathering for trappers and traders to unload their furs and secure a livelihood. Even as tastes and traditions change over time, one can still attend Fur Rondy and secure some of the most impressive and well-preserved furs.

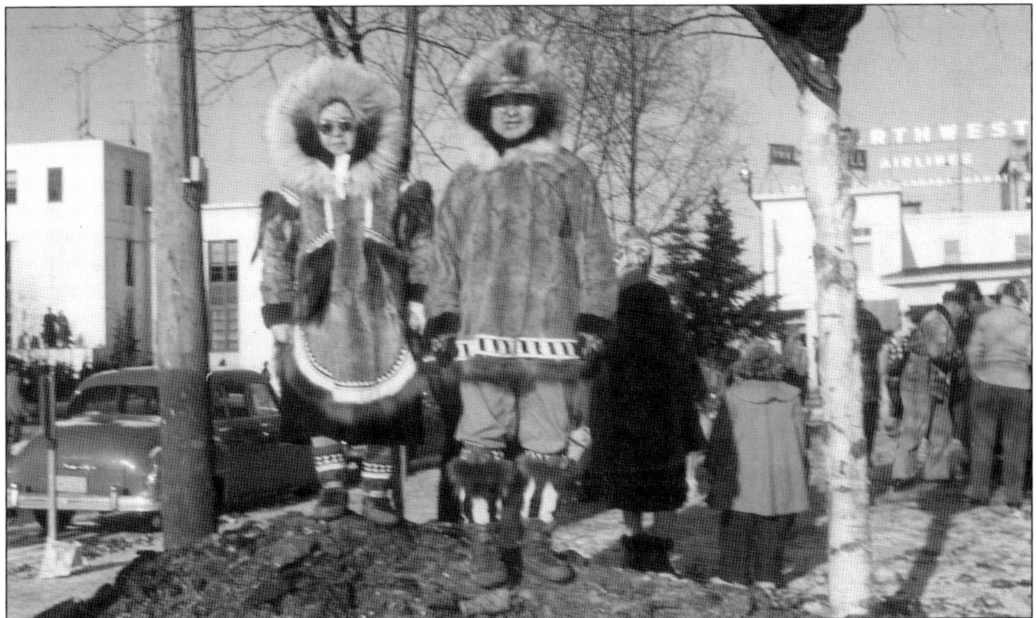

A couple showcases their wares at the Rendezvous. Fur parkas and boots are not only fashionable and culturally significant, but they are also necessary winter gear in Alaska. These garments may consist of the skin of seals, reindeer, bears, foxes, or other mammals found in the Circumpolar North and are uniquely well suited to the cold environment of the Arctic and sub-Arctic.

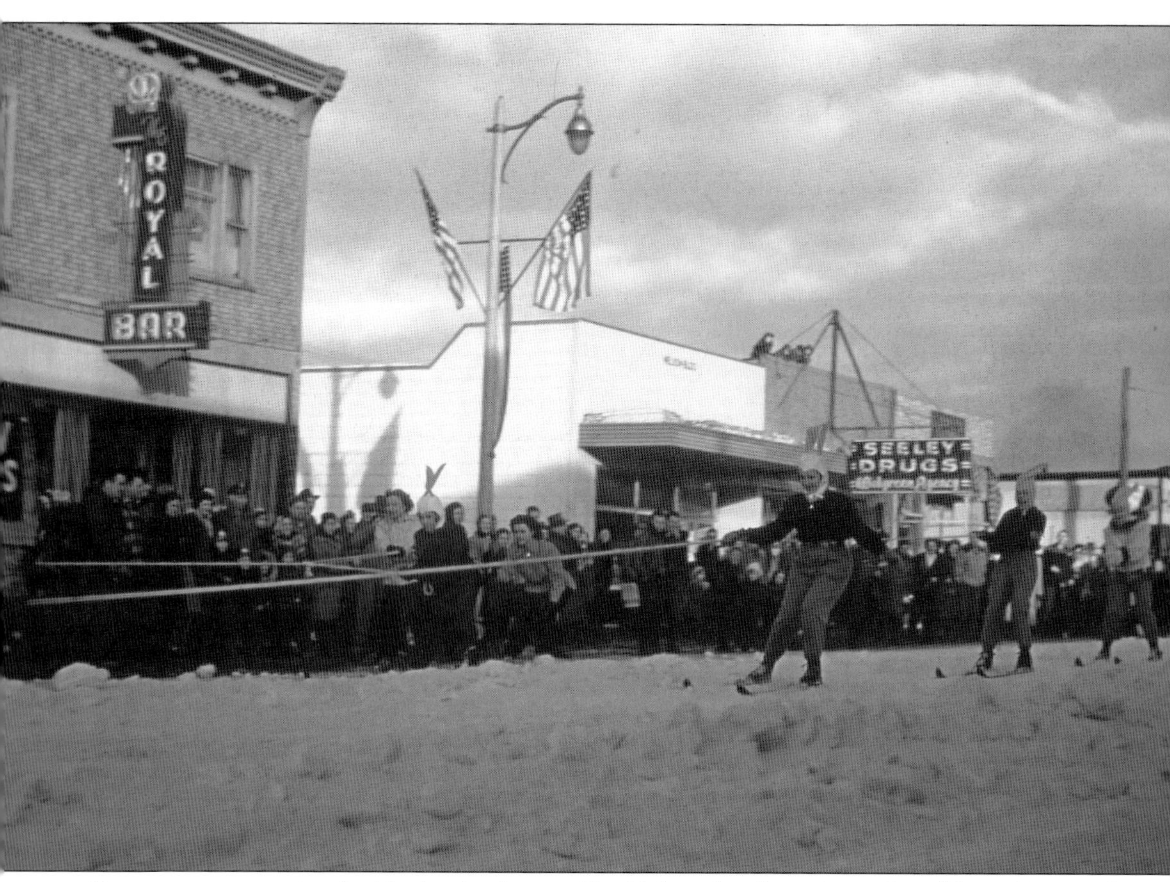

Four women, associated with the Anchorage Ski Club and calling themselves "Snow Bunnies," are pulled down Fourth Avenue during a Fur Rendezvous in the late 1950s, much to the delight of onlookers. Fur Rendezvous is known for its many quirky traditions, competitions, and games. In addition to these "Snow Bunnies," some participants elect to race down Fourth Avenue with reindeer, an Anchorage take on the famous tradition in Pamplona, Spain, of running with the bulls. Other activities include outhouse races, a snow sculpture competition, blanket tosses, the Fur Rondy melodrama, and the ceremonial start to the world-famous Iditarod Trail Sled Dog Race, or more simply, the Iditarod.

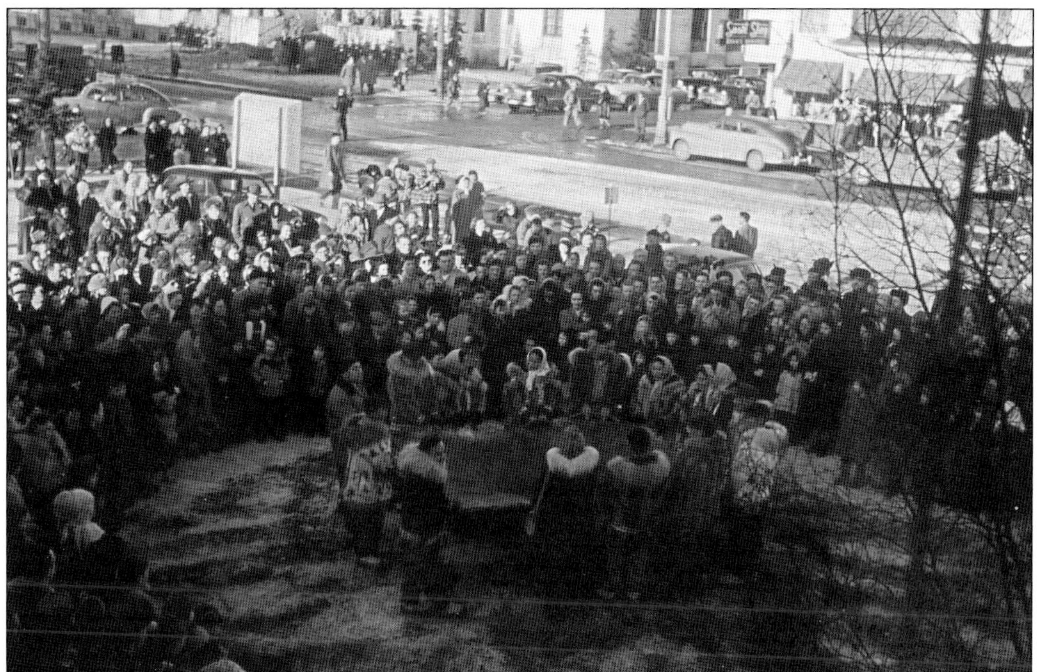

Alaska Native residents gathered at Fur Rendezvous for a blanket toss. Seen here in 1950 and 1956, respectively, the event typically occurred on the grounds of Anchorage's city hall. Blanket toss is a game where someone is tossed into the air and caught on a blanket held by a large group of at least eight to ten people. The blanket is usually made of seal, walrus, or bison skin. One person is tossed into the air by having the group pull the blanket taut and release it in unison. The goal is to land on the blanket safely while jumping higher into the air. Skilled jumpers may pull off flips and kicks in midair. The blanket toss is a traditional part of several Alaska Native communities.

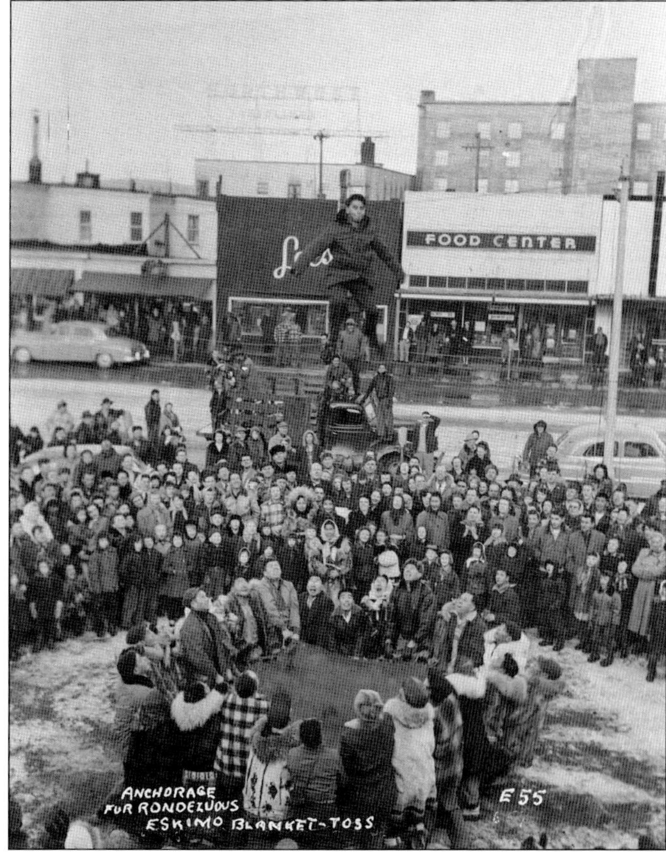

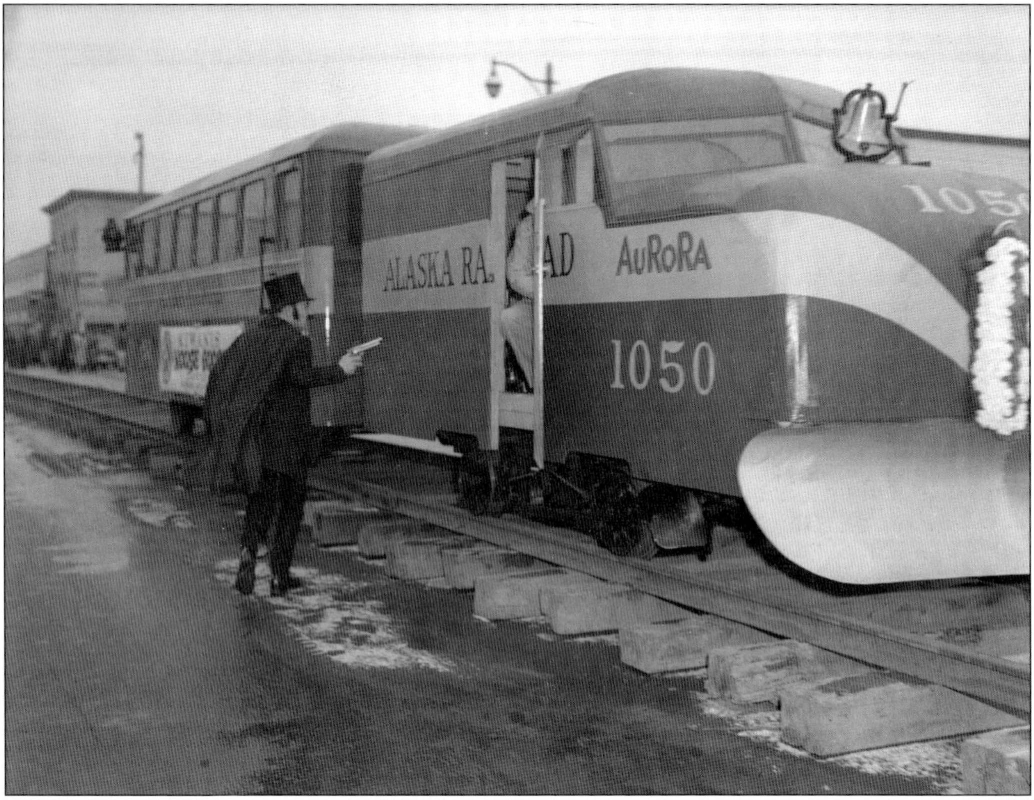

The Alaska Railroad unveiled its Aurora train in 1947. The blue and gold streamliner, which improved and upgraded its passenger service between Anchorage and Fairbanks, was also a handsome showpiece for the railroad. At the 1952 Fur Rendezvous, the Aurora was the site of a mock train robbery to the amusement of attendees. Rendezvous planners worked with the Alaska Railroad to put temporary tracks along Fourth Avenue to show off the impressive 1050 engine, cutting-edge railroad technology in its day. The Aurora train anticipated the Alaska Railroad's transition into passenger service and tourism. Today, thousands of tourists board the Alaska Railroad each summer to see the scenic stretch of the state from Seward to Fairbanks.

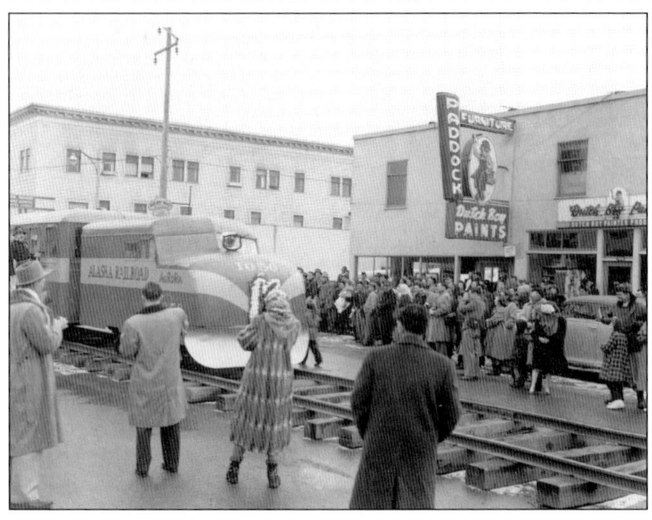

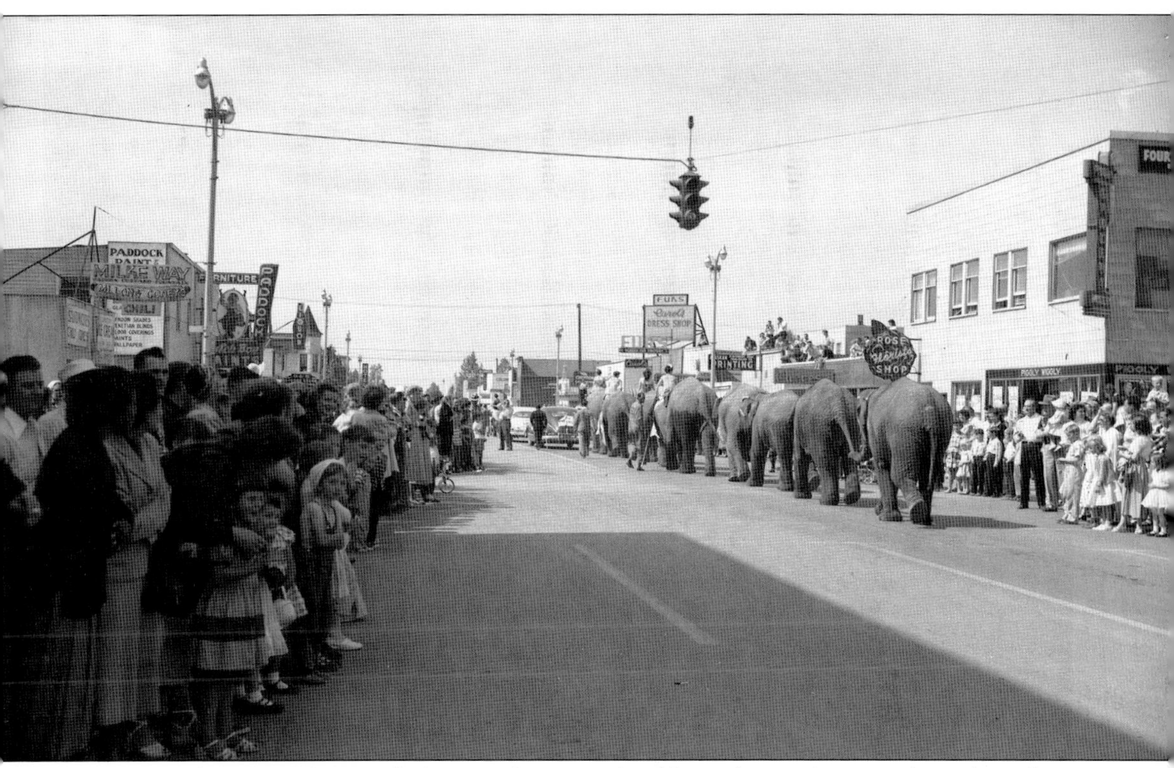

Although Anchorage is deservedly known for icy and cold weather and winter festivals such as Fur Rendezvous, the community has long made the most of its short summers, from swimming in one of Anchorage's many lakes to playing baseball to the circus coming to town. In July 1954, the Cristiani Brothers Circus made a considerably long trip north up the Alaska Highway. A parade of elephants marked their triumphant arrival, stomping down Fourth Avenue to the joy of the thousands who gawked at the world's largest land animals. The Cristiani Brothers were the first national circus act to perform in Anchorage. Without a direct rail link from the lower 48 states, one could imagine the logistical challenges of bringing the circus to town via truck and tractor-trailer. Not surprisingly, Anchorage residents appreciated the trouble and attended the circus with great enthusiasm.

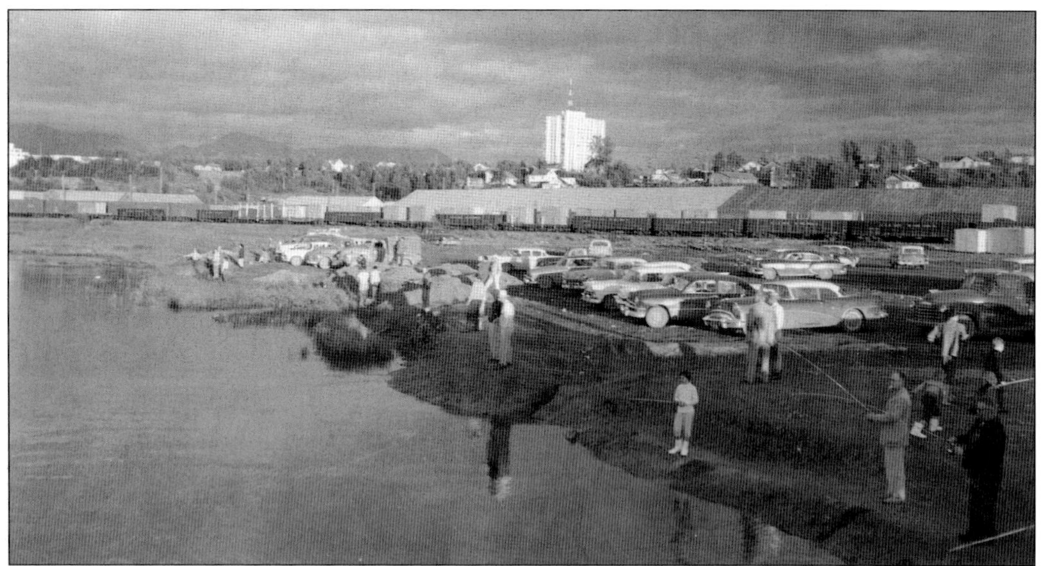

Anchorage is perhaps the only American city that affords the opportunity to fish for chinook (king) salmon in the shadow of its downtown. Alaskans and tourists alike have taken to Ship Creek to fish for salmon for as long as Anchorage has existed. In the 1950s and 1960s, Anchorage residents pulled up in their vehicles within feet of the water. The Alaska Railroad depot is on view in the background. Anchorage waterways host all five species of wild Alaska salmon: king, red (sockeye), pink (humpy), silver (coho), and chum (sometimes called "dog").

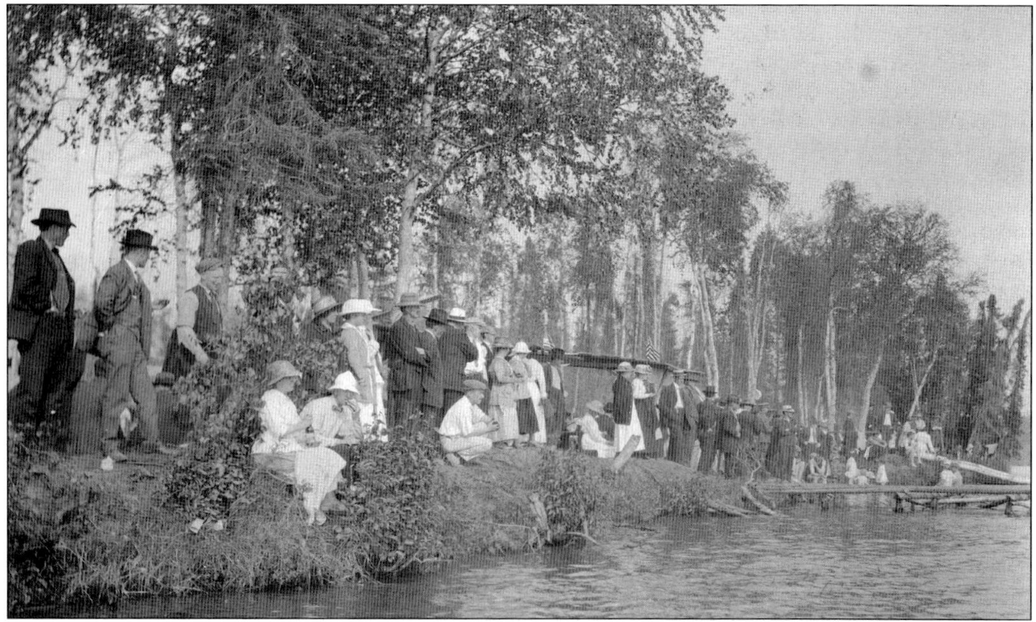

Spenard Lake is named after Joseph "Joe" A. Spenard, an ambitious Canadian-born settler who arrived in Anchorage with his wife, Edith, in 1916. But it was originally known as Jeter Lake after the homestead of Thomas Jeter. Located four miles south of Anchorage's downtown, the lake was a retreat and a business venture for Joe Spenard during Anchorage's early years. Residents swam, sunbathed, and with a bit of luck, avoided the mosquitos. The lake and its surrounding homesteads would eventually be incorporated into the Anchorage municipality in 1975.

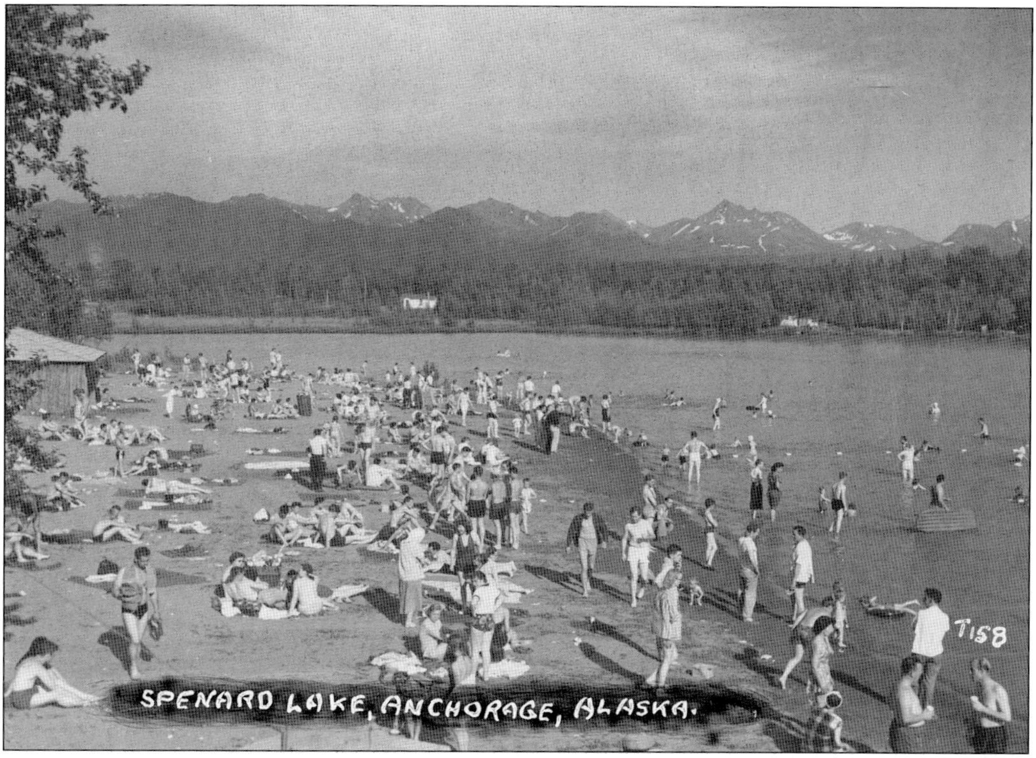

T158

SPENARD LAKE, ANCHORAGE, ALASKA.

When the sun shines for nearly 20 hours during Anchorage's summer solstice, it can warm up the area and entice nearly everyone outside. While temperatures may not typically exceed 75 degrees, Anchorage's summer revelers will find any number of lakes and ponds suitable for a swim or simply resting by the water (trying, if possible, to avoid the swarms of mosquitoes that are also a hallmark of summer in Alaska). Lake Spenard was a popular choice for swimming in the 1940s and 1950s. Today, the lake is on the property of the Ted Stevens International Airport, and swimming is no longer permitted.

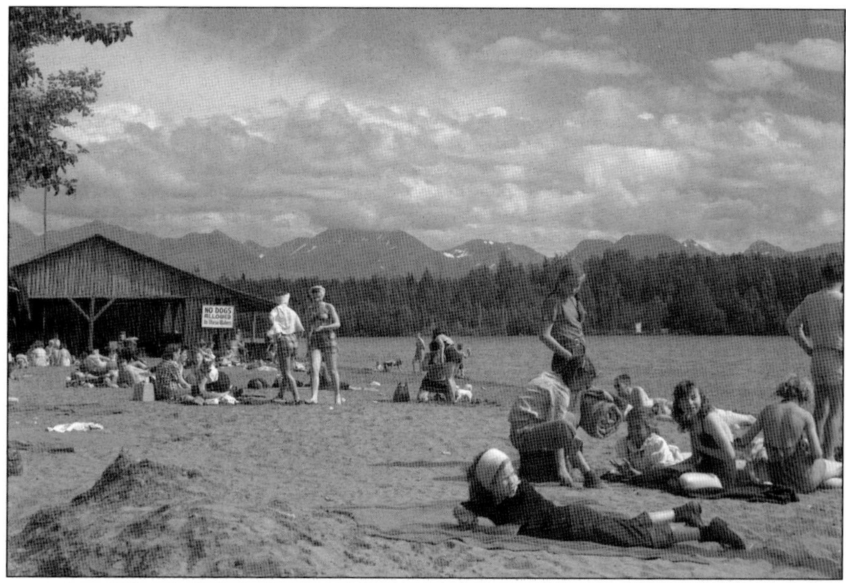

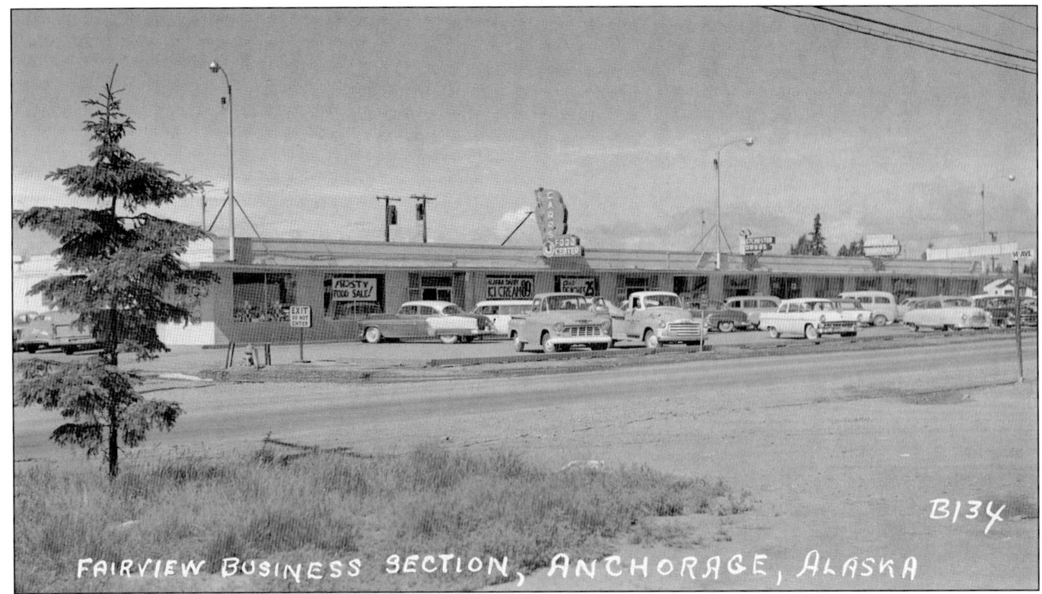

Carrs Food Center (now known as Carrs-Safeway) was among the earliest full-service supermarkets in Anchorage. The first Carrs opened in 1950 in a Quonset hut along Gambell Street in Fairview. It soon moved into the facility seen here. Carrs maintains a grocery store in the same location today. The road sign to the far right of the photograph contains the identifier "Fairview" just below Fourteenth Avenue. This, along with the style of vehicles in the parking lot, indicates the photograph was taken in the 1950s. The Fairview community remained independent from Anchorage until 1959.

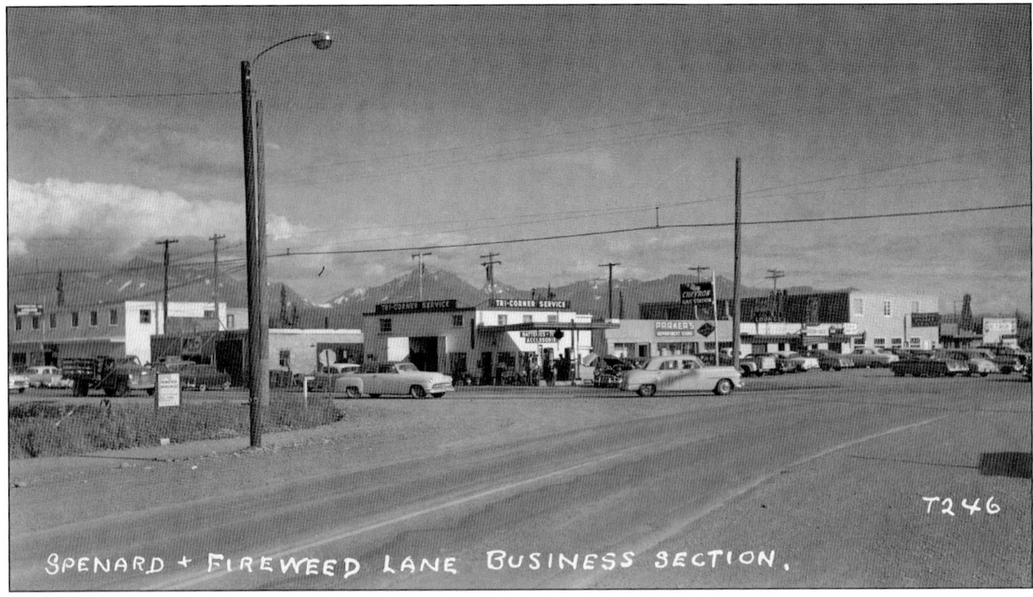

Throughout the 1940s and 1950s, the primary commercial corridor of Anchorage was its downtown. However, the community expanded southward. This view is the intersection of Spenard Road and Fireweed Lane with Tri-Corner Auto Service, Parker's Department Store, and the Fireside Lounge visible. Today, the area is occupied by one of Anchorage's most famous spots for nightlife, Chilkoot Charlie's.

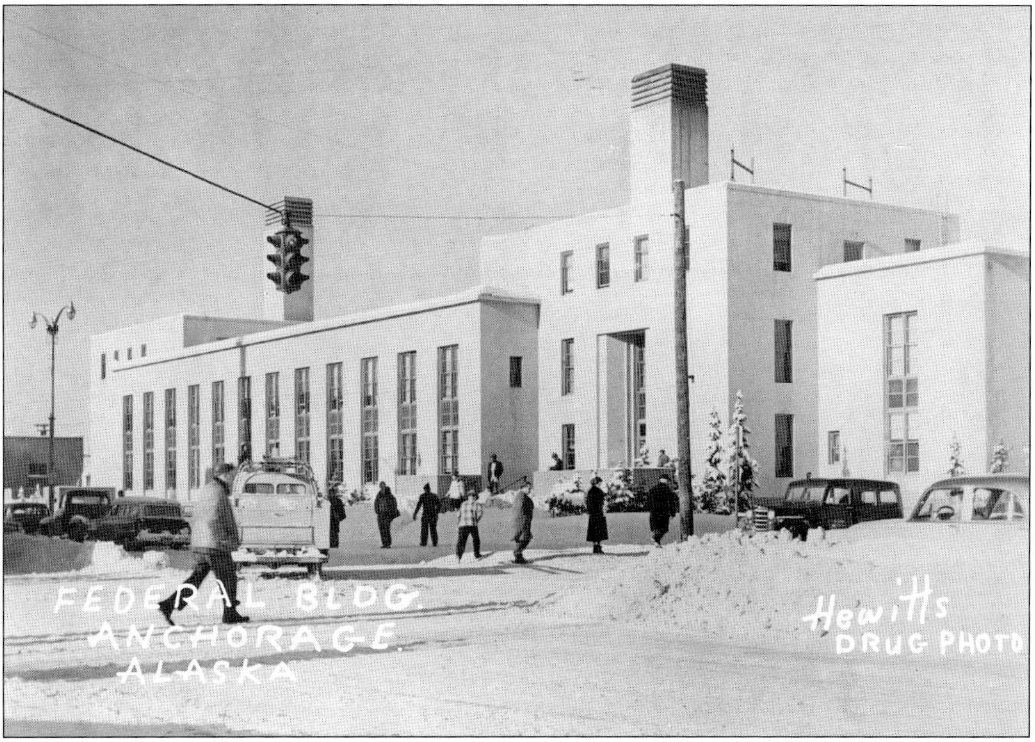

This scene outside of the Anchorage Federal Building on Fourth Avenue was taken in the 1940s. Since the construction of the Alaska Railroad, the federal government has maintained a strong presence in the community. The building remains one of the centerpieces of Anchorage's downtown.

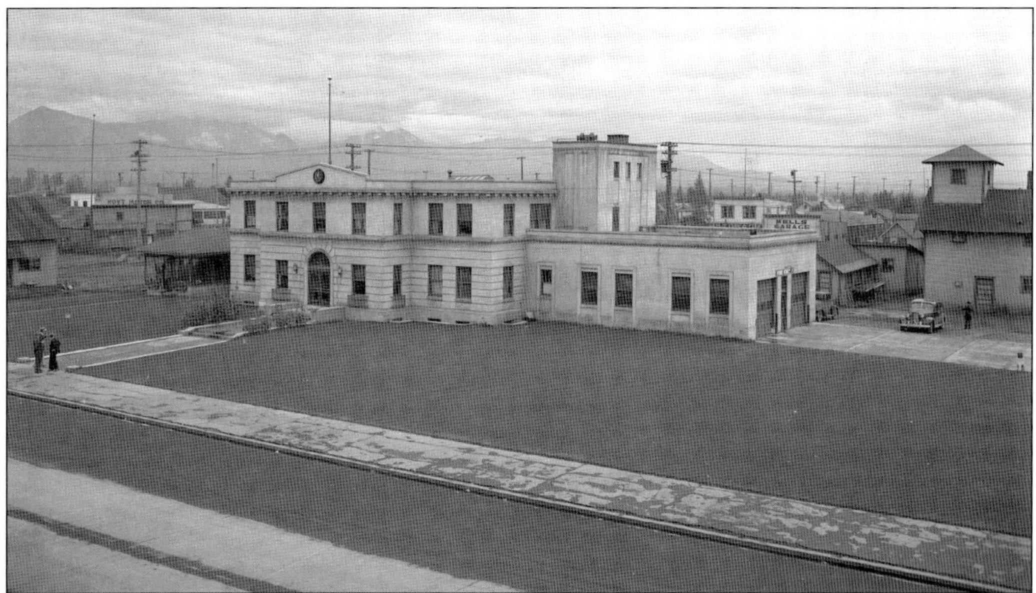

Along with the federal building, Anchorage's historic city hall conveys civic pride and anchors the downtown core. Although the current city hall lies two blocks to the south, the historic city hall, photographed here in 1939, remains a popular spot for tourists and residents alike to stroll by and linger on the grounds, often enjoying a hot dog or ice cream cone on a warm summer day.

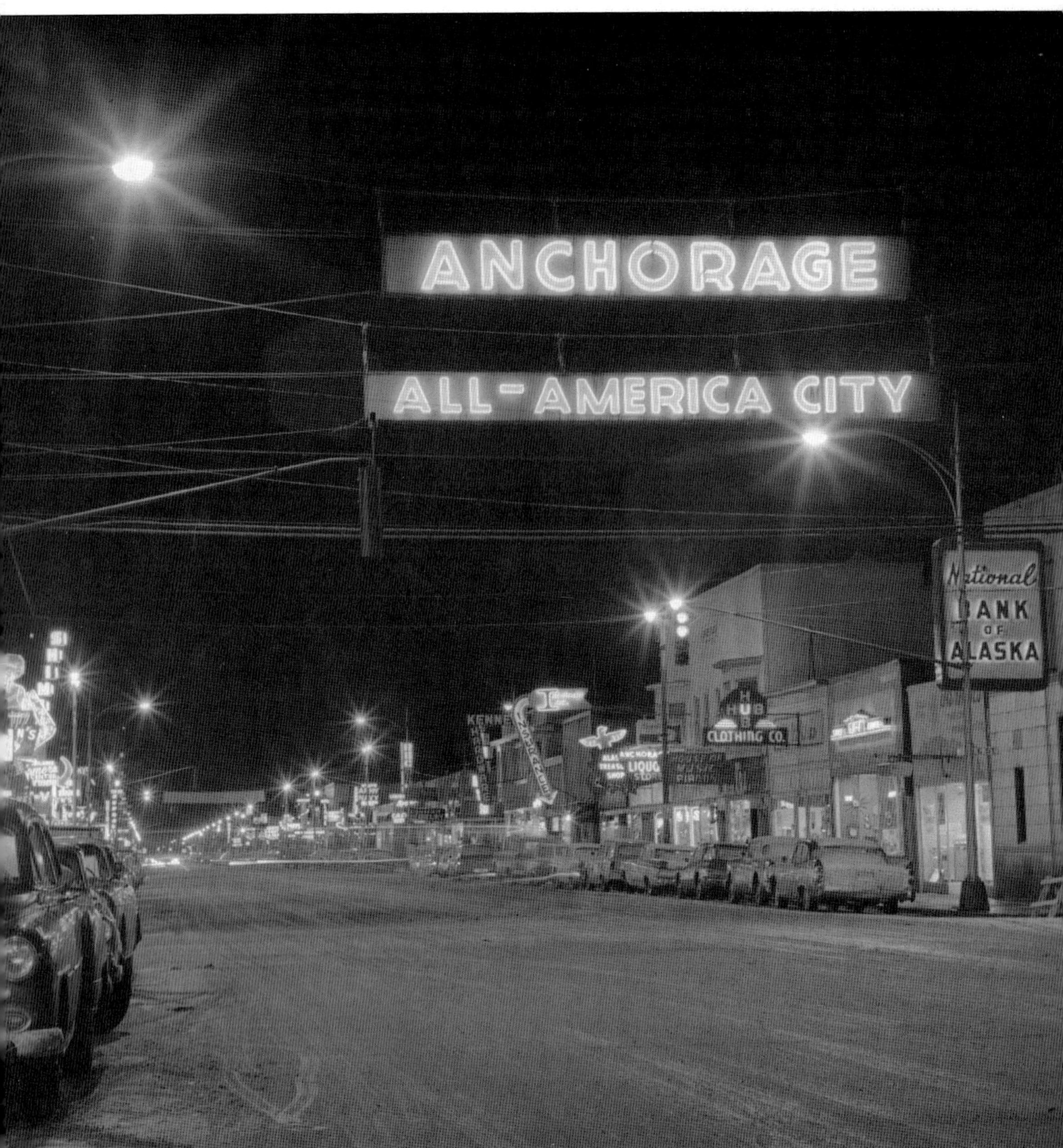

Anchorage has been recognized as an "All-America City" by the National Civic League in four separate years: 1956, 1965, 1985, and 2002. This photograph, taken after the first recognition in 1956, captures downtown Anchorage after the sun has gone down on a crisp fall evening. Dozens of neon signs showcase the vibrancy of the young, confident community. Throughout the 1950s, the military expanded its presence as the nation entered the peak of the Cold War. With thousands of military personnel, a growing economy, and the buzz of statehood, Anchorage had entered something of a golden era.

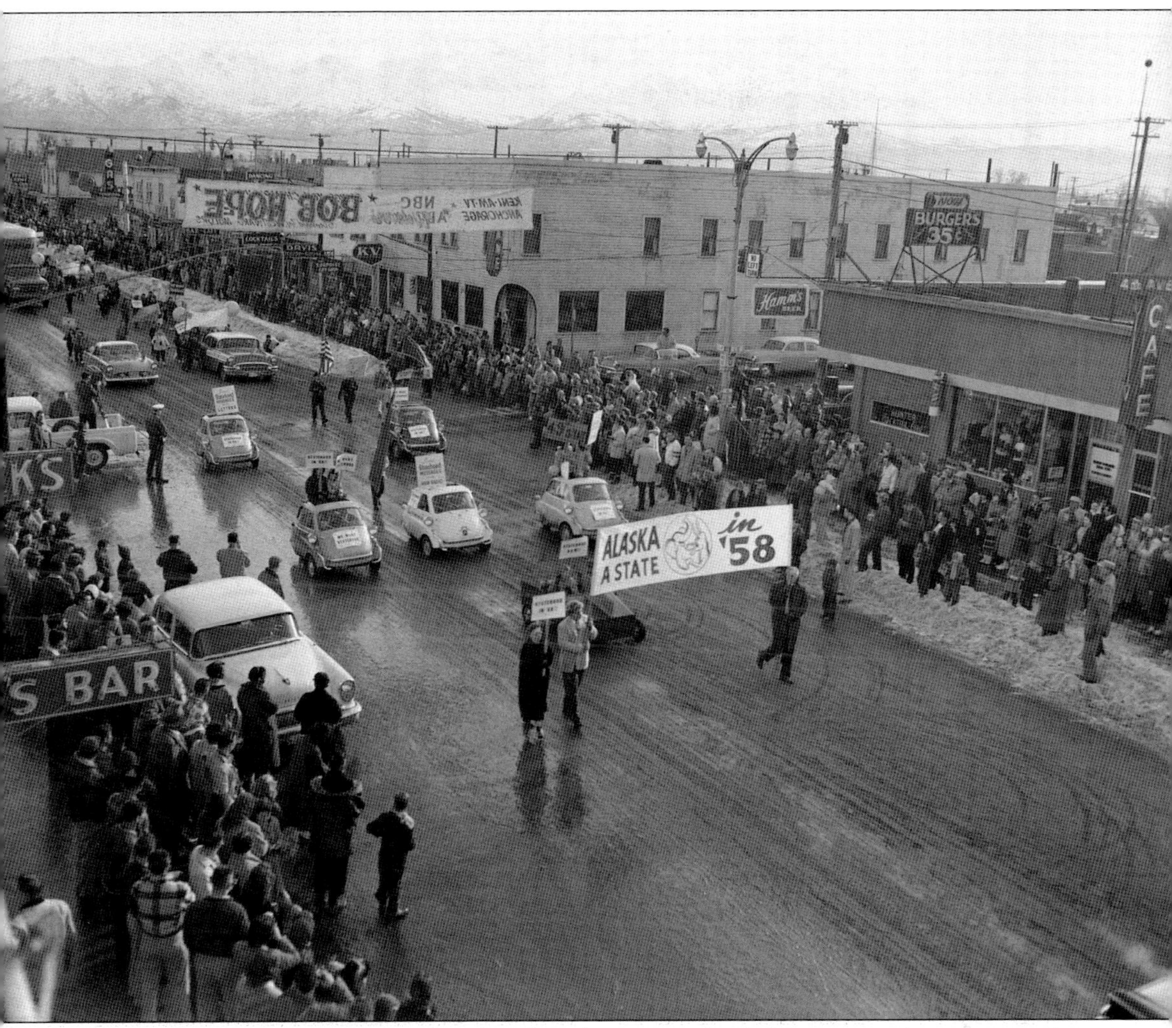

Anchorage had grown from a small railroad settlement in the 1920s to a modest town in the 1930s and 1940s to an emerging city in the 1950s. Residents of the Territory of Alaska had also become impatient with what many perceived as their status as second-class citizens, and they demanded statehood. A parade of Alaskans marches down Fourth Avenue holding signs to make their case. While Alaska did not technically join the union as the 49th state until January 3, 1959, those who demanded "Alaska a State in 1958" had victory in their sights. Even today, many longtime Alaskans fondly remember the statehood era as one of community solidarity and years where just about anything seemed possible. Indeed, Alaska's official state motto became "North to the Future" in 1967.

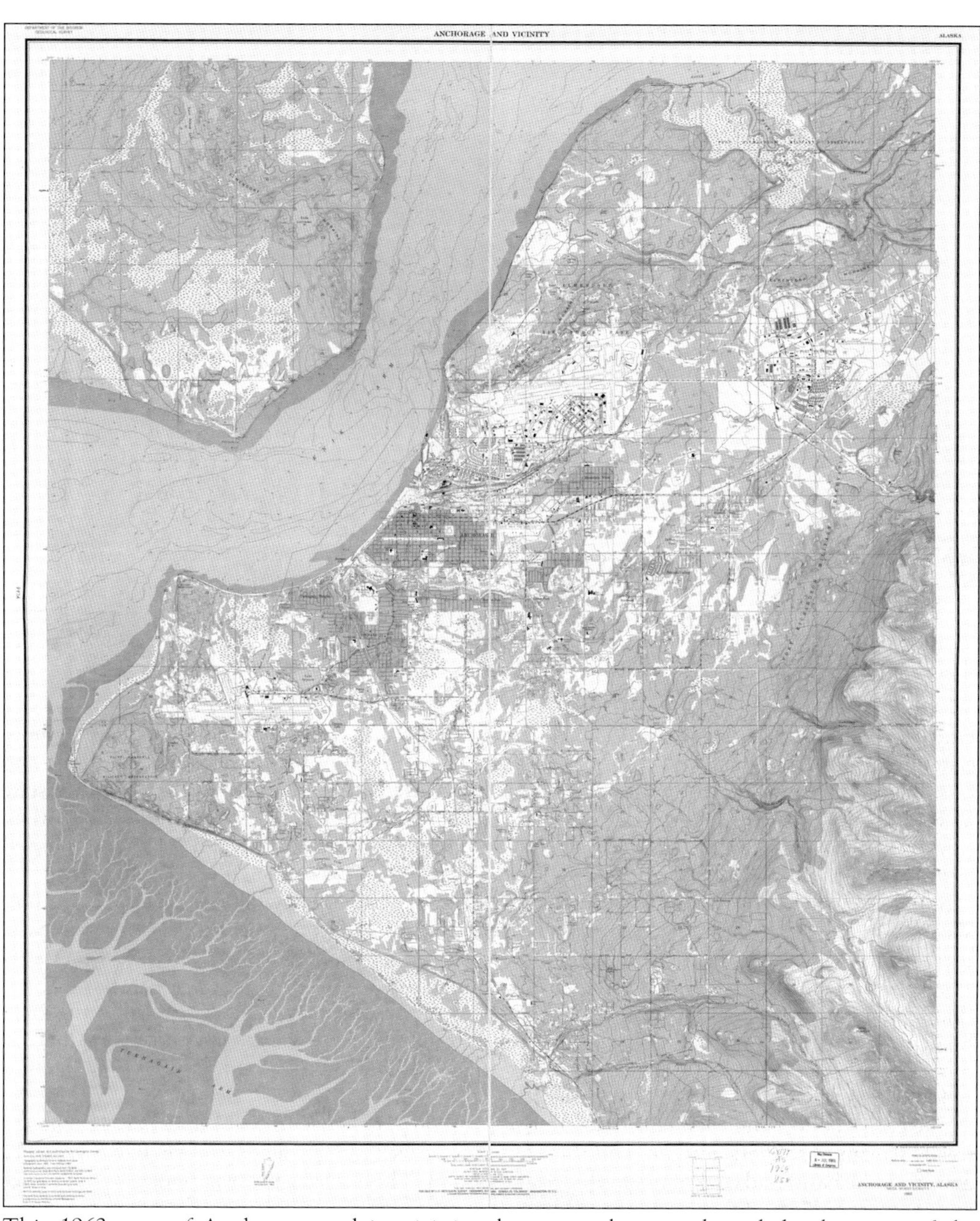

This 1962 map of Anchorage and its vicinity showcases the growth and development of the region or what is known as the "Anchorage Bowl." By 1951, an international airport opened, and Anchorage's limits stretched beyond Chester Creek. Spenard and Mountain View remained independent of the city, but not for too much longer. The modern definition of the municipality of Anchorage, formed by merging the city and borough, dates to 1975. The two sprawling military bases, Fort Richardson and Elmendorf Air Force Base, are visible just to the north and northeast of Anchorage. The map also depicts the extensive amount of water, mostly lakes and wetlands, that existed throughout Anchorage. Developing housing in many parts of the municipality required mitigating or draining the boggy land, known as muskeg. (Courtesy of the Library of Congress.)

Four

A Military Community

During World War II, Anchorage took on greater significance for the US military. Alaska, more generally, had become particularly strategic as it straddled the North Pacific and the Arctic and was geographically closer to Northeast Asia and the Soviet Union than any other American state or region. Not surprisingly, the military's presence greatly increased during the war and then continued to expand amid the Cold War. In Anchorage, the Army and Air Force both established bases, Fort Richardson and Elmendorf Air Force Base, respectively.

Built primarily in 1940 and completed in 1941, the two bases predate American entry into World War II by mere months. However, the decision among military commanders to locate the bases just outside of Anchorage reveals the critical role that American leaders envisioned Alaska would play in global affairs during the second half of the 20th century. At the end of the Cold War, there was a discussion of shrinking the military footprint in Alaska. In 2005, the Base Realignment and Closure Commission (BRAC) decided that Fort Richardson and Elmendorf Air Force Base should consolidate their operations. In 2010, the two merged into what is known today as Joint Base Elmendorf-Richardson (JBER).

The construction and then expansion of these military bases in the 1940s and 1950s ensured a steady stream of soldiers, airmen, and their families, as well as contracted and civilian workers to maintain the bases and contribute to the local economy. This fueled a postwar boom in Anchorage and its surroundings. Military families relied on Anchorage as a social and cultural outlet as well as for the everyday conveniences that a growing city could provide. Likewise, Anchorage relied on military personnel to participate in the economy, engage in civic life, and even put down roots. In fact, Alaska has per capita among the largest active duty and veteran populations in the United States. By mid-century, Anchorage had truly become a military town. It remains so to this day.

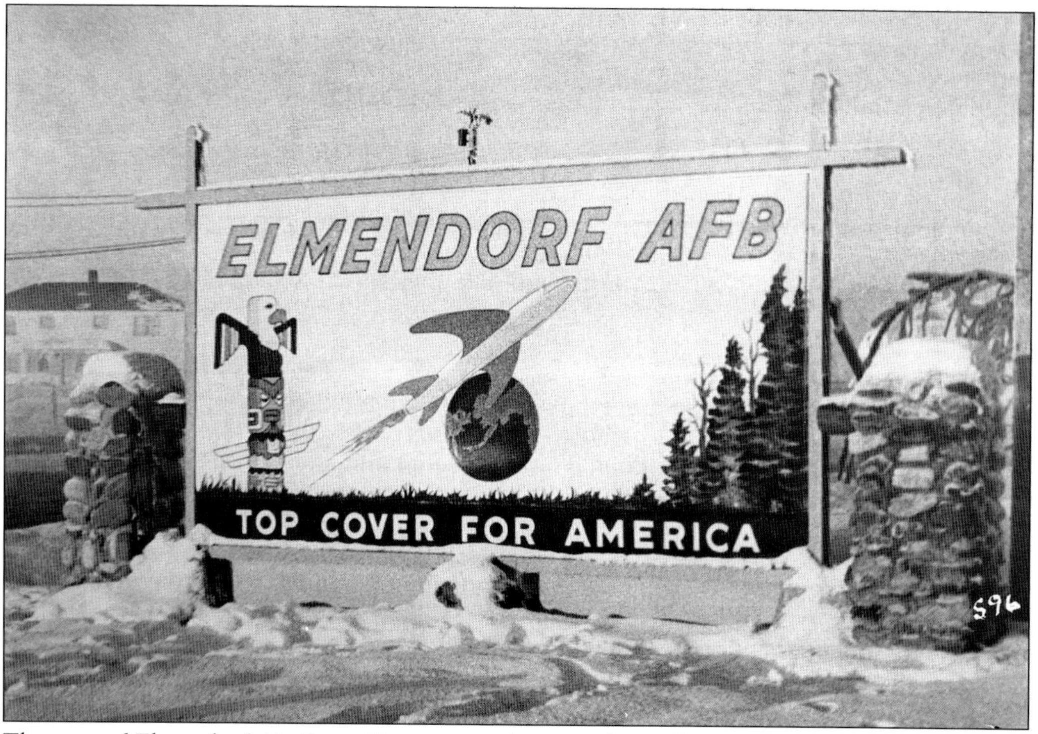

The gate of Elmendorf Air Force Base is seen here in the early 1950s. The base was a critical staging ground and strategic location as the United States and the Soviet Union ramped up their Cold War rivalry. The base hosted fighter and cargo jets as well as bombers.

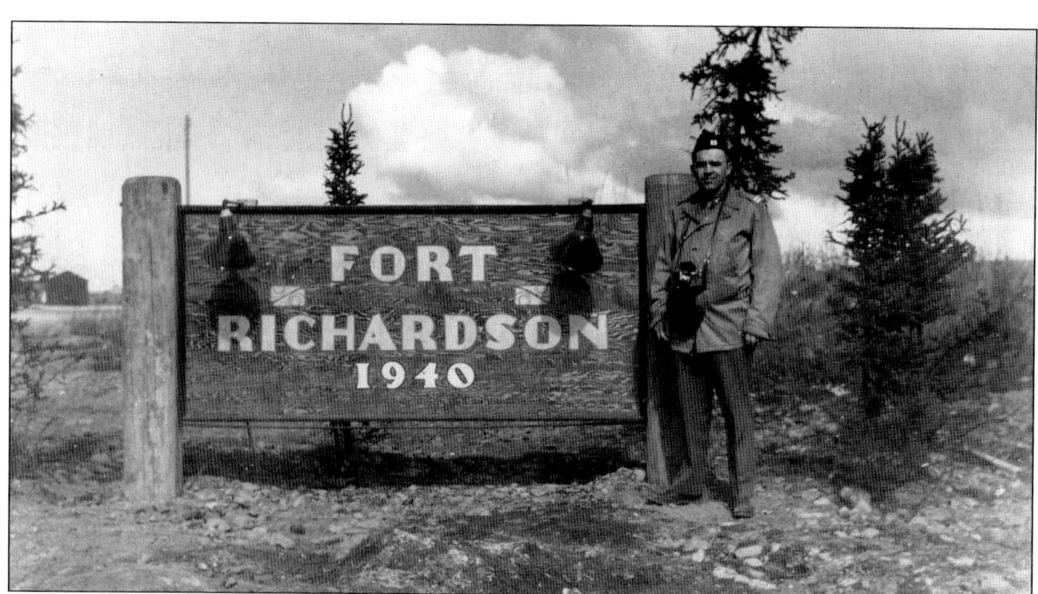

A soldier stands at the newly placed sign for Fort Richardson in 1940. The base has played an integral role in the defense of Alaska and the broader Circumpolar North. It has also become central to Anchorage's identity as a military town.

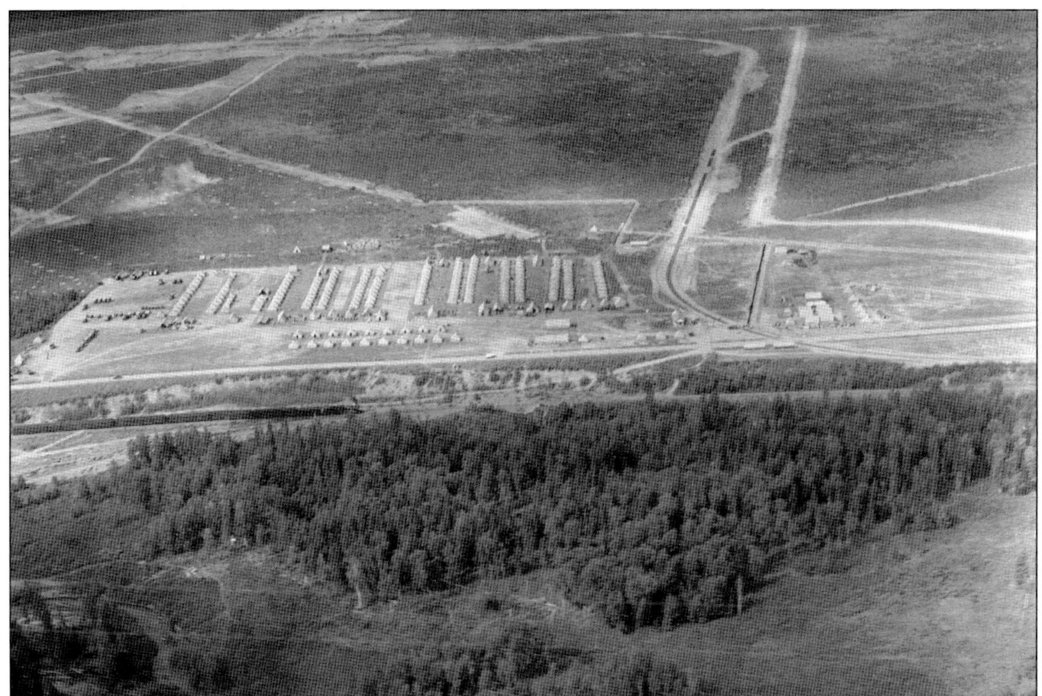

In this early image of Elmendorf Field, likely taken in the summer of 1940, tents are visible at the center, and the airfield is to the upper right. The Alaska Railroad snakes through the airfield just below the tents, delivering provisions. The Alaska Railroad has long served as a partner of the military and has served the bases since they first opened.

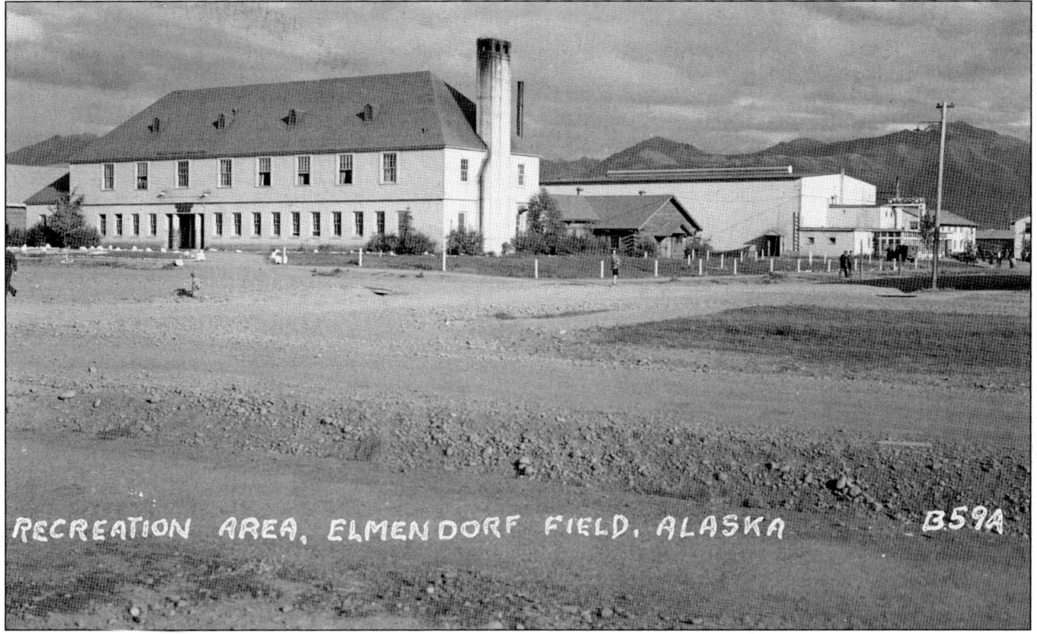

Before 1947, Elmendorf Field was an airfield under the command of the US Army. This photograph depicts the recreation area on-site where airmen and soldiers went bowling, maintained their physical condition, and socialized with one another as they prepared for war.

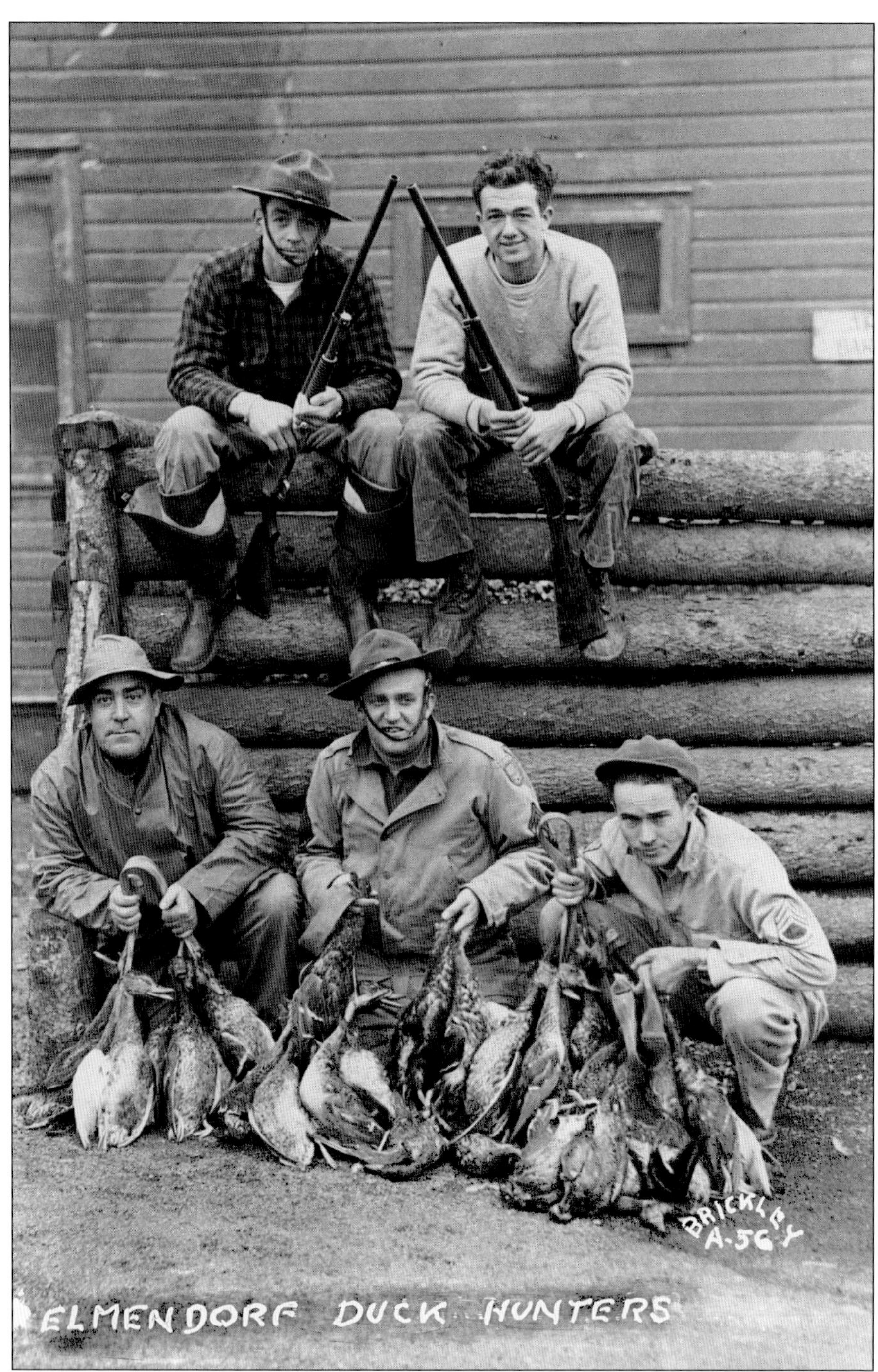

The men who served in the armed forces in Alaska during the war passed the time in several ways. Like soldiers stationed elsewhere, they encountered downtime and forged common bonds with one another. Here, young soldiers pose after a duck hunting trip. Anchorage's access to the wilderness has afforded opportunities to hunt, fish, and recreate in some of the most remote and stunning environments in the country. Not surprisingly, many service members and nonmilitary residents alike have taken advantage of all that Anchorage and its surroundings have to offer.

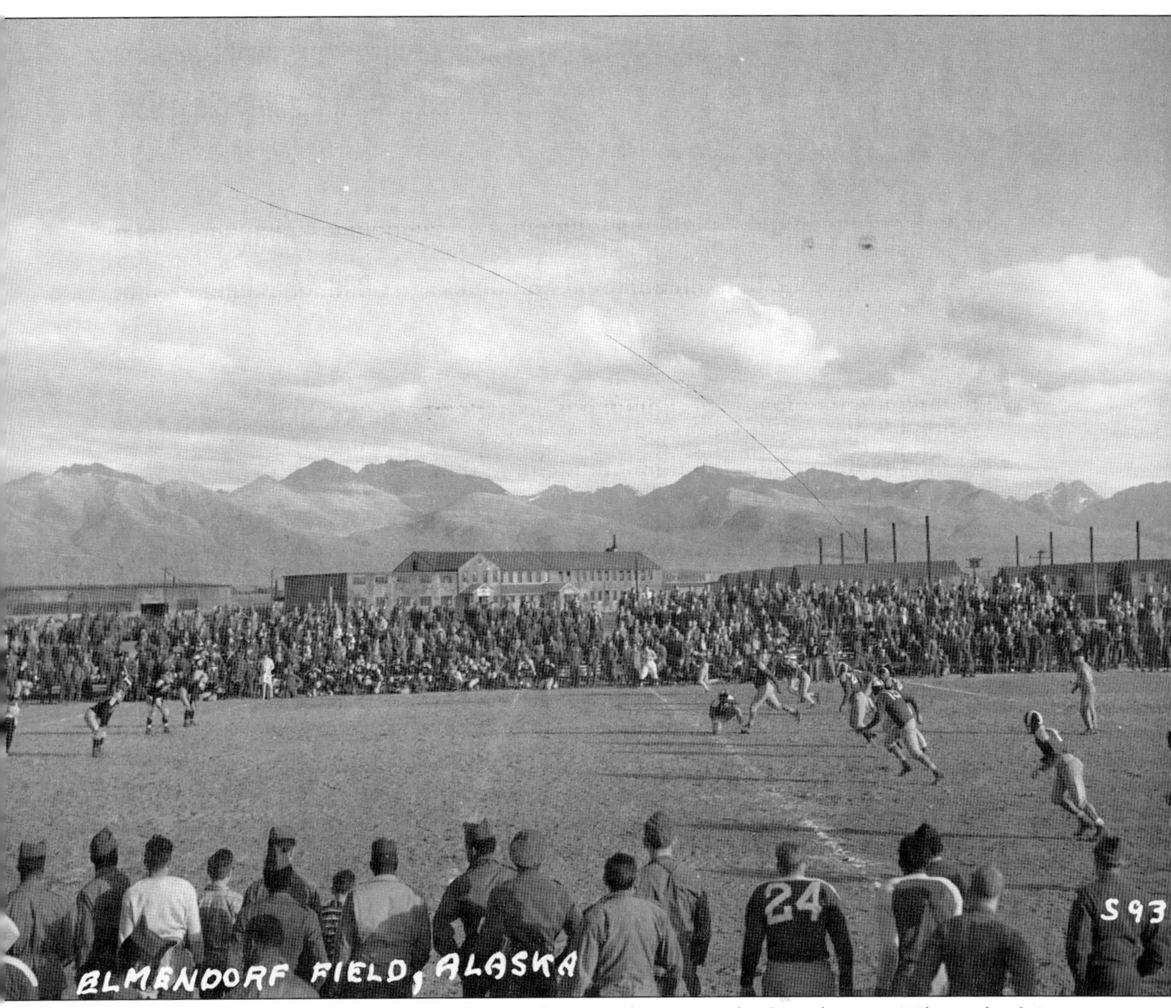

As the military expanded its presence in Anchorage during and after the war, Elmendorf Air Field and Fort Richardson accommodated the soldiers and provided various outlets for leisure and entertainment. Notably in this photograph, Black soldiers (seen among the kicking team and in the foreground along the sidelines) participated in the game. While the military remained segregated through World War II, thousands of Black soldiers nonetheless served in Alaska. They were instrumental in constructing the Alaska Canada Highway and retaking islands in the Aleutians from the Japanese in 1942 and 1943.

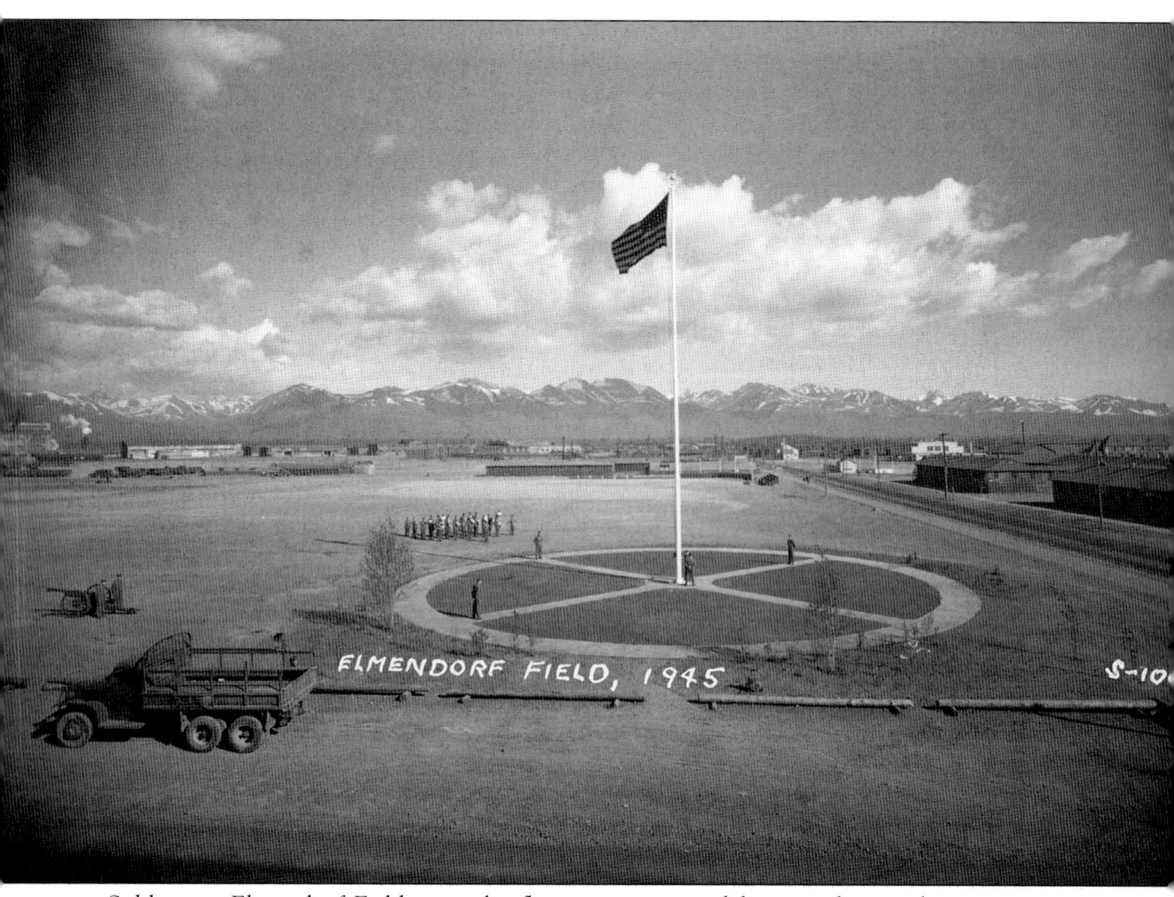

Soldiers at Elmendorf Field raise the flag at a victory celebration during the summer of 1945 at the conclusion of World War II. A military band plays as two men prepare the cannon for a ceremonial firing. The barracks are visible to the right, and the Chugach Mountains rise to the east of the base.

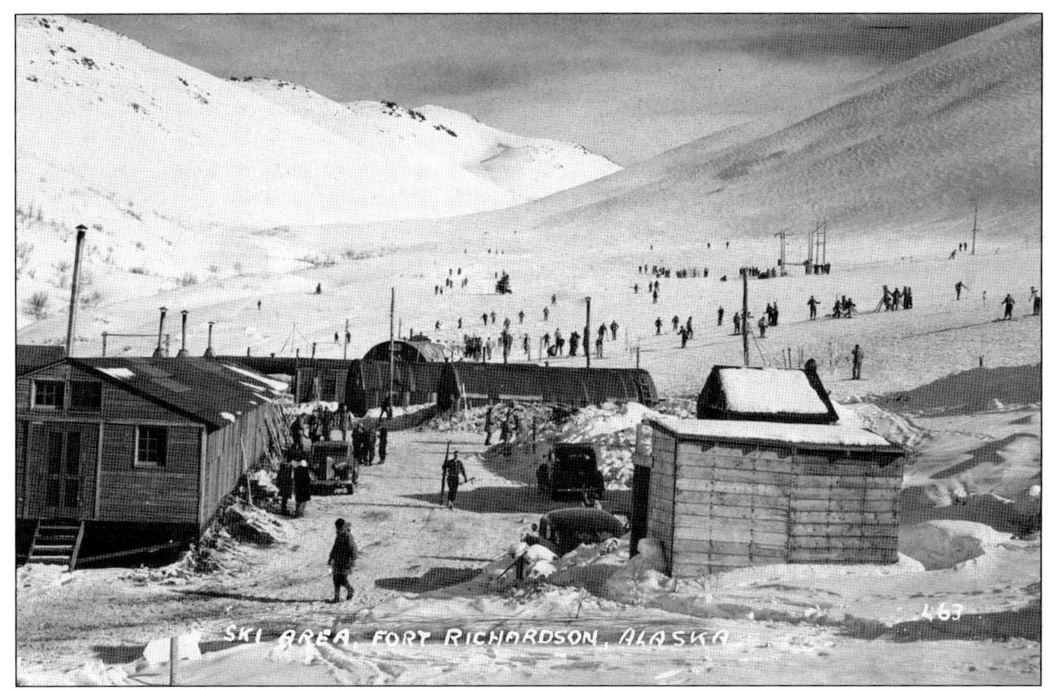

Soldiers stationed at Fort Richardson and Elmendorf Field maximized the short summer and fall with football and baseball games. As the cold of winter set in and snow piled up, the soldiers recreated by hitting the slopes and learning to ski. For many of the new recruits, Alaska's harsh winters were a culture shock. But many nonetheless made the most of it.

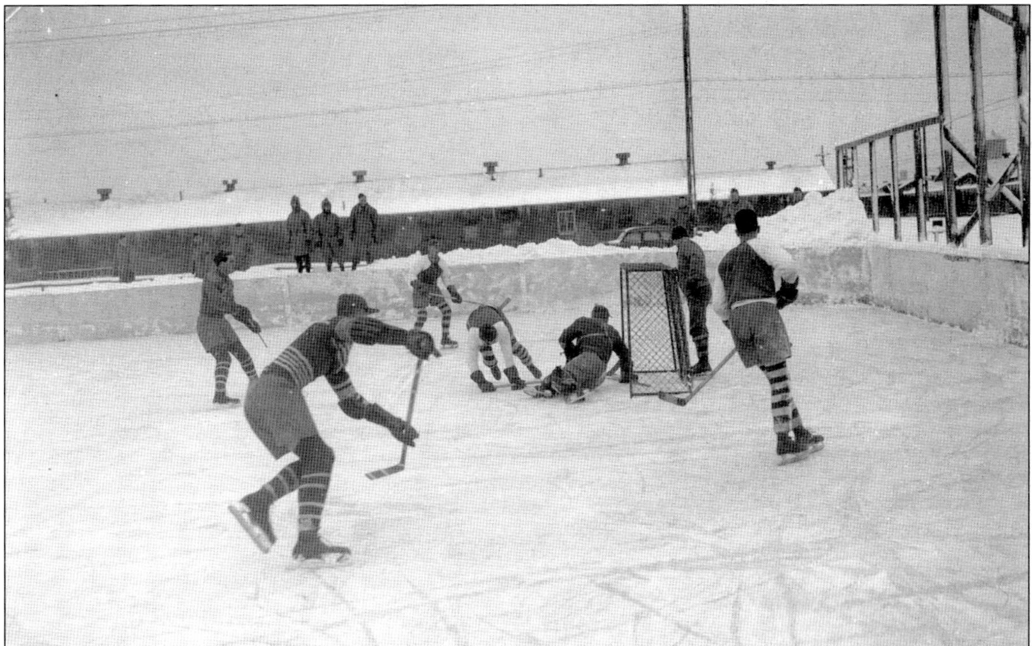

Soldiers with the 54th Troop Carrier Squadron battle the 39th Air Depot Group in a game of ice hockey in early 1944. The two military bases brought thousands of young men who creatively passed the time, even as they maintained their readiness for war.

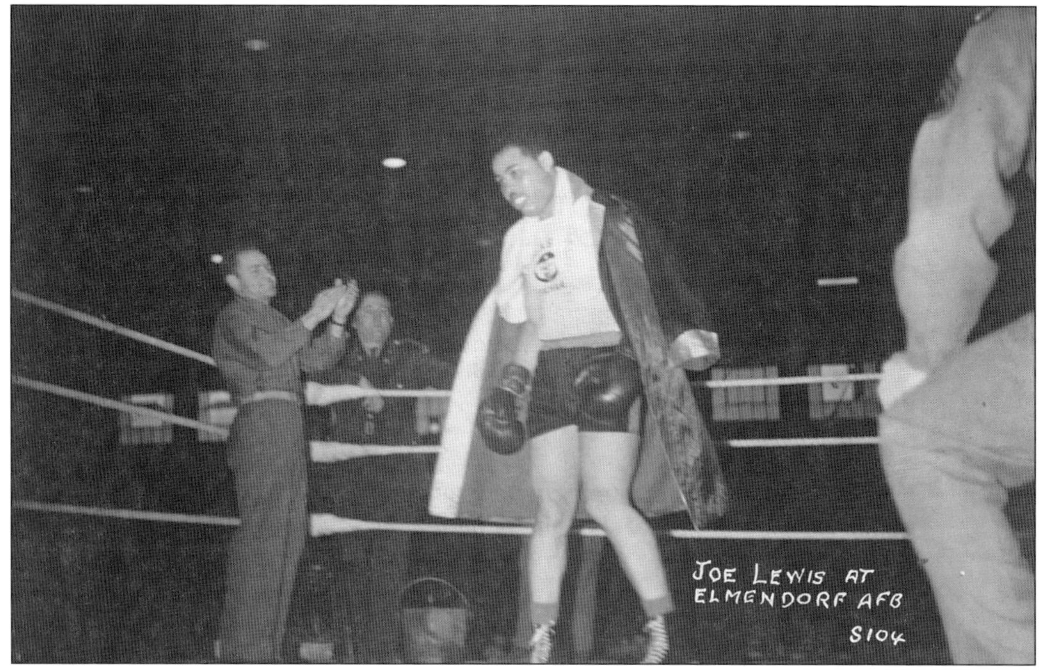

Joe Louis (note the incorrect spelling in the photograph caption) traveled to Alaska as part of the Special Services Division. While few disputed Louis's combat readiness, the Army decided that his talent and celebrity were best suited to raise the spirits of the GIs. Louis gave boxing demos and met with soldiers in over 100 locations around the world.

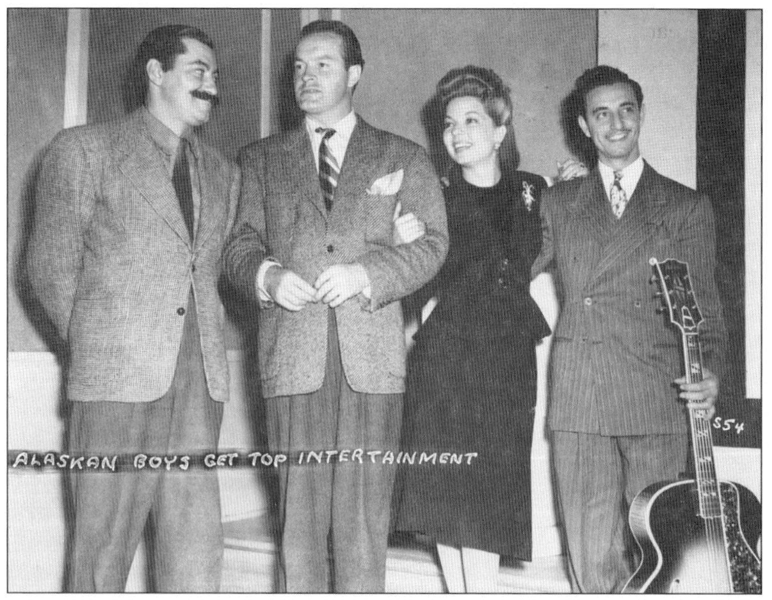

Bob Hope traveled to Fort Richardson in 1942 on one of his many United Service Organizations (USO) tours and found a receptive audience among the service members. In addition to Hope (center left), the photograph depicts musician and comedian Jerry Colonna (left), singer and actress Frances Langford (center right), and musician Tony Romano (right).

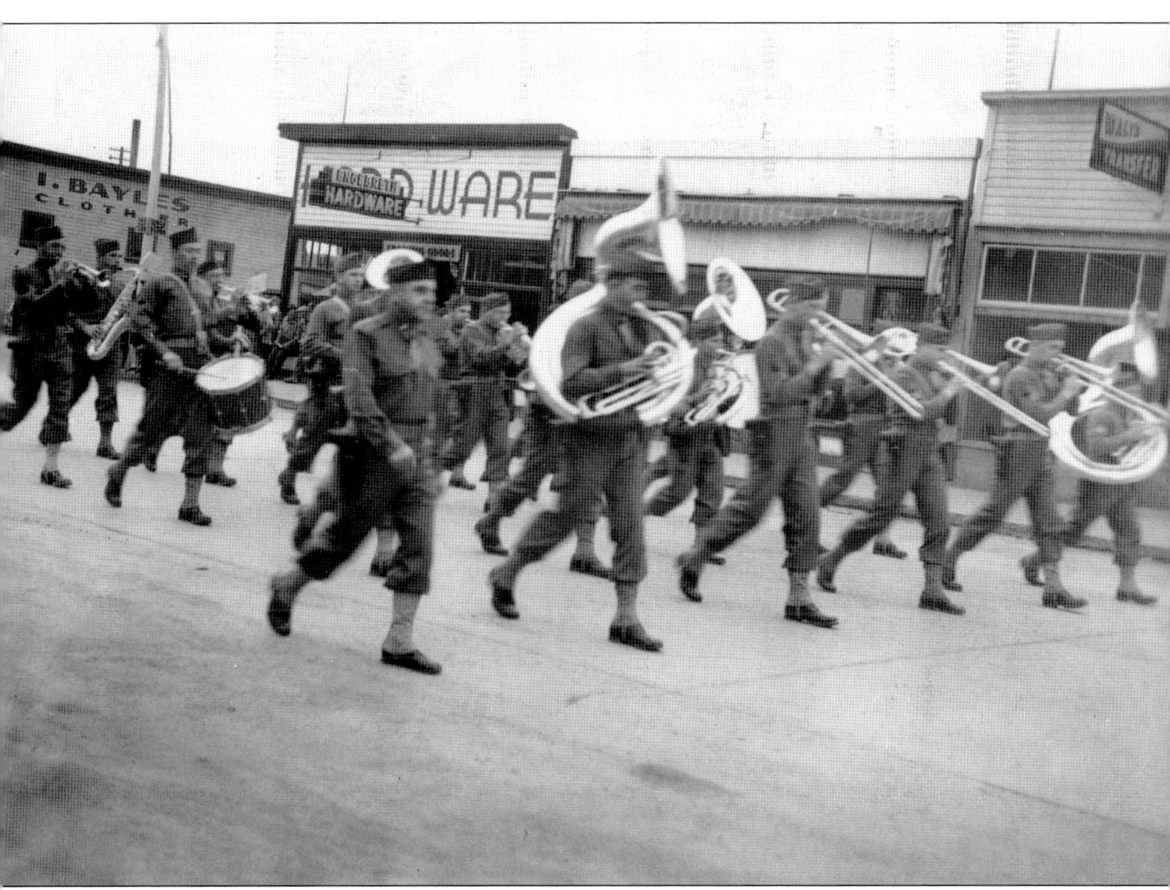

Alaskans have long embraced the military presence in the territory and then the state. In turn, military members have embraced life in Alaska. Here, a military marching band parades down Fourth Avenue downtown in the early 1940s, just as the United States had entered World War II and Alaska had taken on even greater strategic significance.

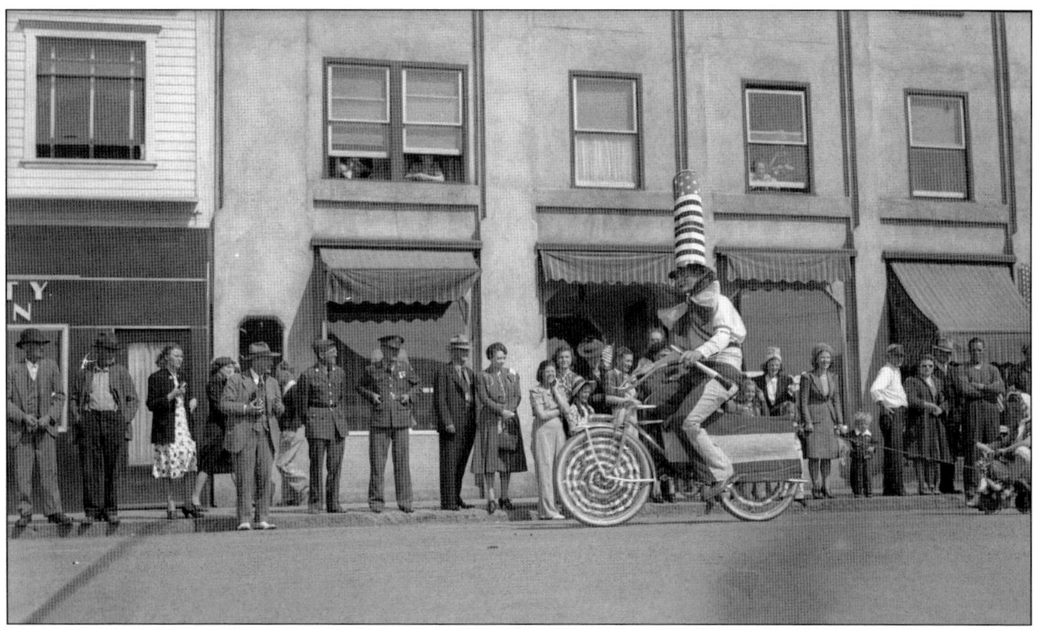

Meanwhile, service members take in the festivities of the 1940 Independence Day parade as a man in an oversized bow tie and top hat donned with the stars and stripes bicycles past. Several years later, amid the Cold War, the military rolled two tanks along Fourth Avenue during Fur Rendezvous festivities in 1958.

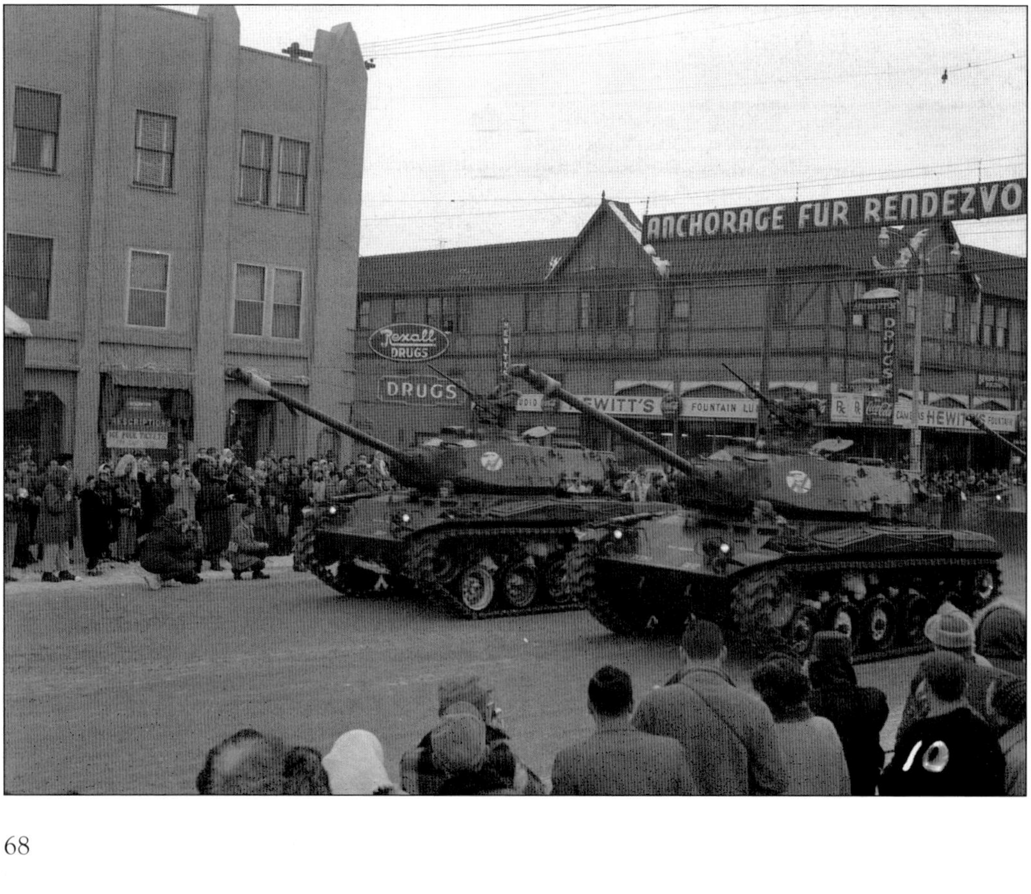

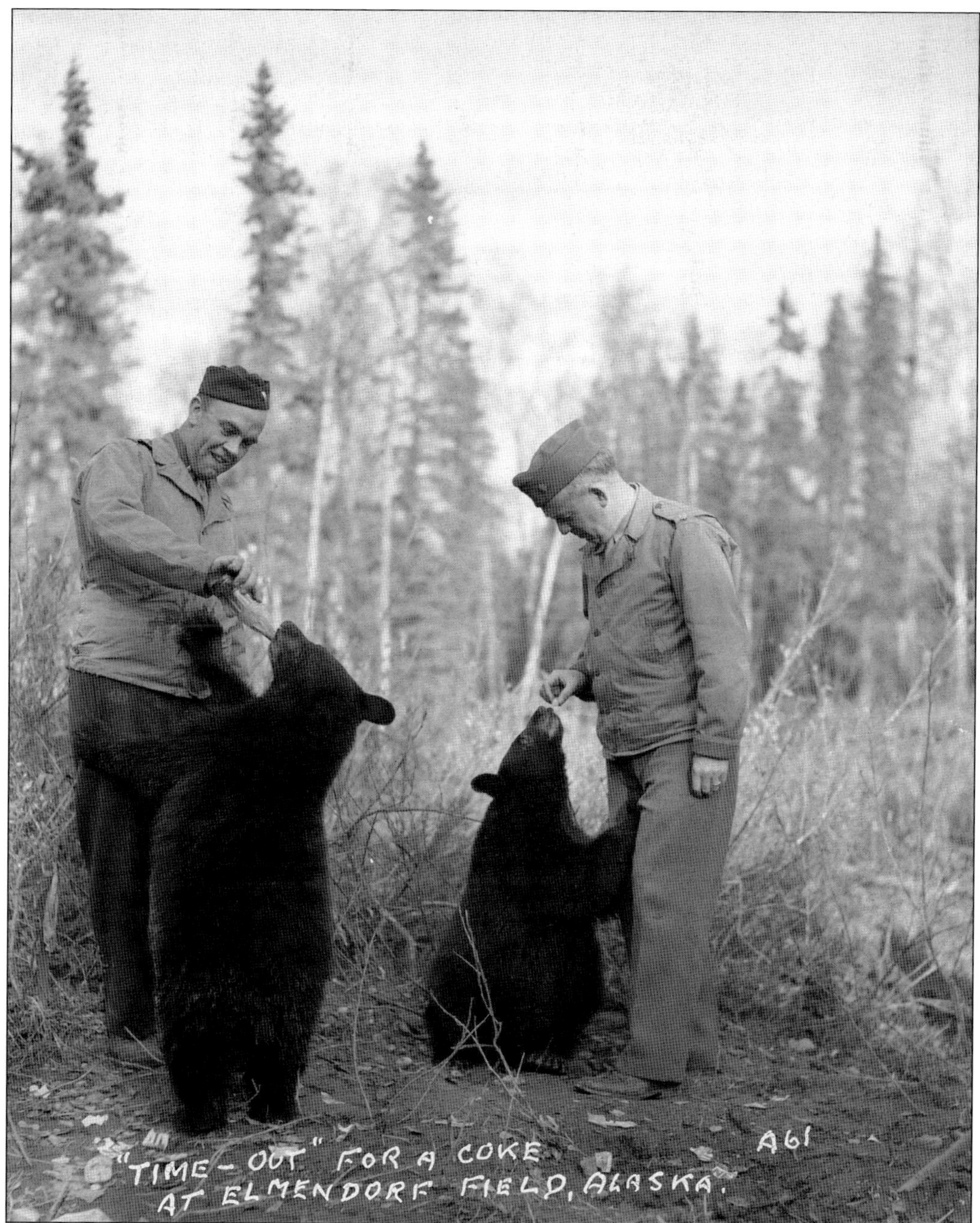

Soldiers at Fort Richardson take time out of their schedules to entertain two black bear cubs. Anchorage sits at the base of the Chugach Mountains, and residents regularly run into the surrounding wilderness. Not surprisingly, people and animals at times come face-to-face with one another. The soldier to the left shares his Coke with the bear, and the soldier on the right feeds the other cub what looks like a berry or possibly a grape. These kinds of interactions have long been barred, and for good reason. A bear who has come to rely on humans for food and has become acclimated to a human environment poses a risk to people as well as itself. Still, these kinds of interactions were common until wildlife experts advocated to put an end to such behavior.

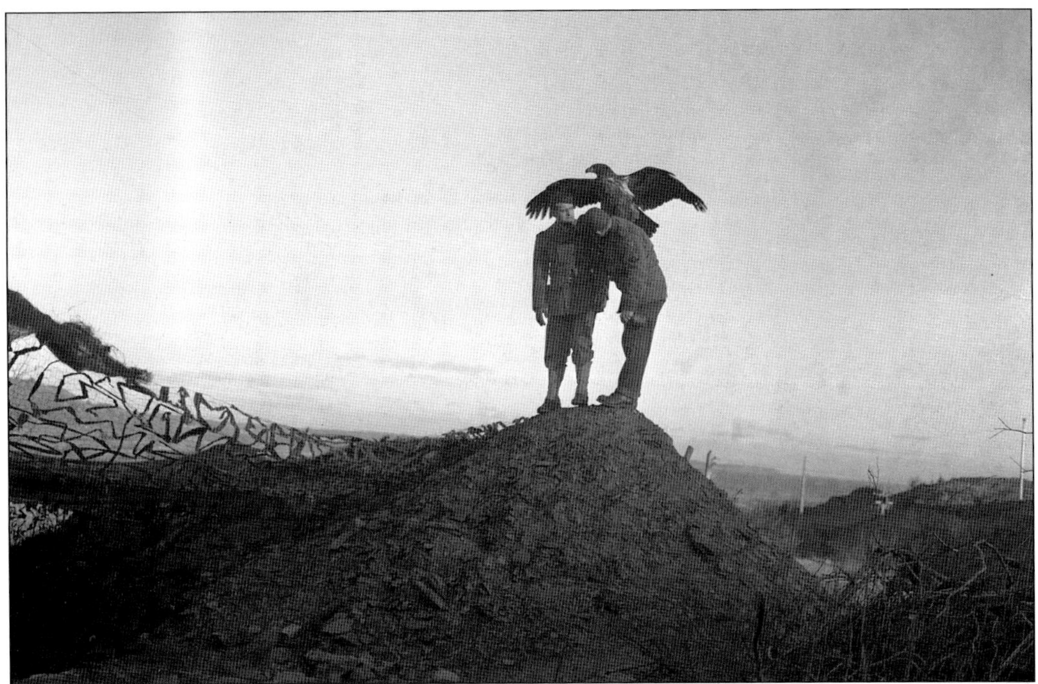

Two airmen take time to explore the grounds around Elmendorf Field in the 1940s (it is possible to identify the men as members of the Army Air Force by the insignia near the top of the left arm) and are confronted not by a precocious cub but an eagle.

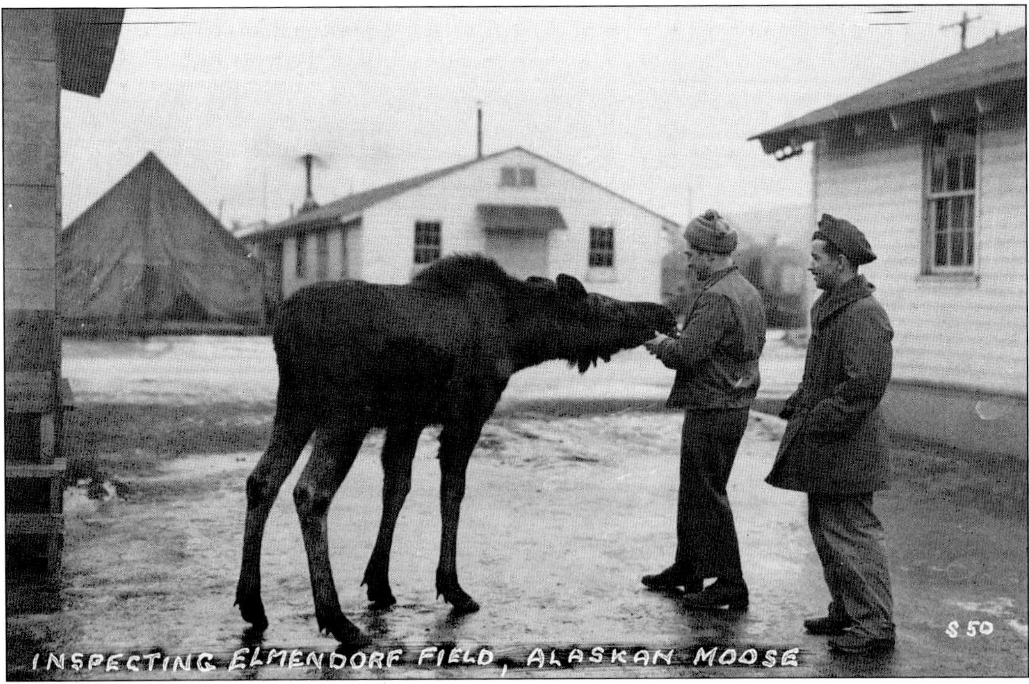

A moose roams freely among soldiers and airmen. Fort Richardson and Elmendorf Field may have restricted who was permitted on base, but that would not stop the array of animals who did not always obey orders.

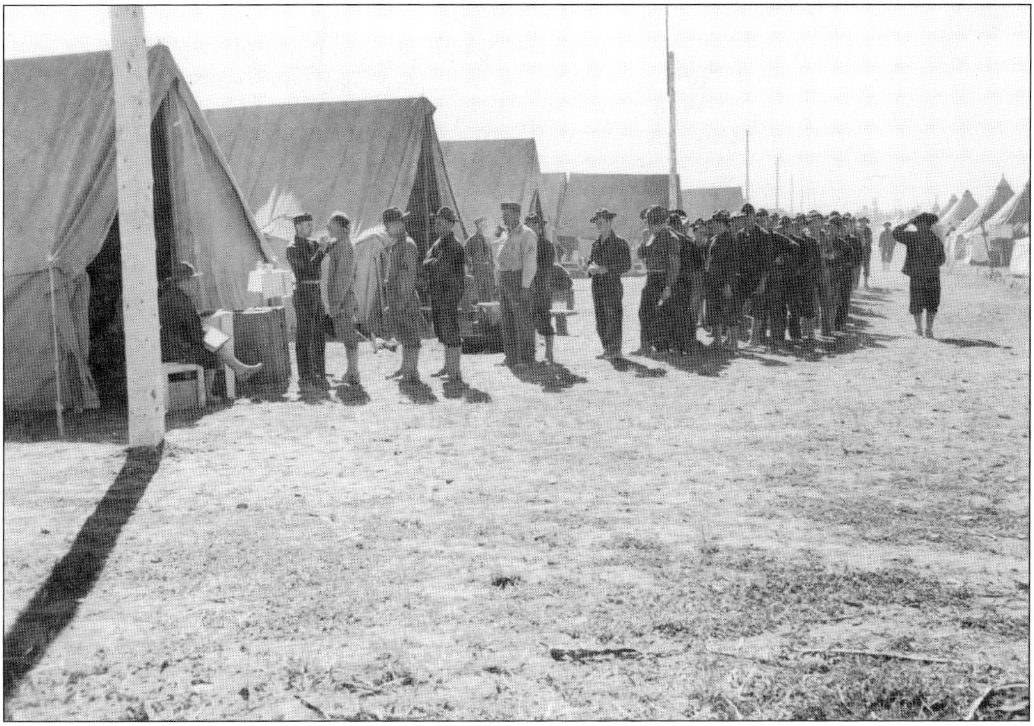

Soldiers lined up for a brief checkup before basic training commenced at Fort Richardson in 1940. Even before the Japanese bombing of Pearl Harbor in Hawai'i on December 7, 1941, the military had begun to ramp up its presence in Alaska. That effort would, of course, accelerate after the nation entered the war. Permanent barracks took the place of the tents within a few months.

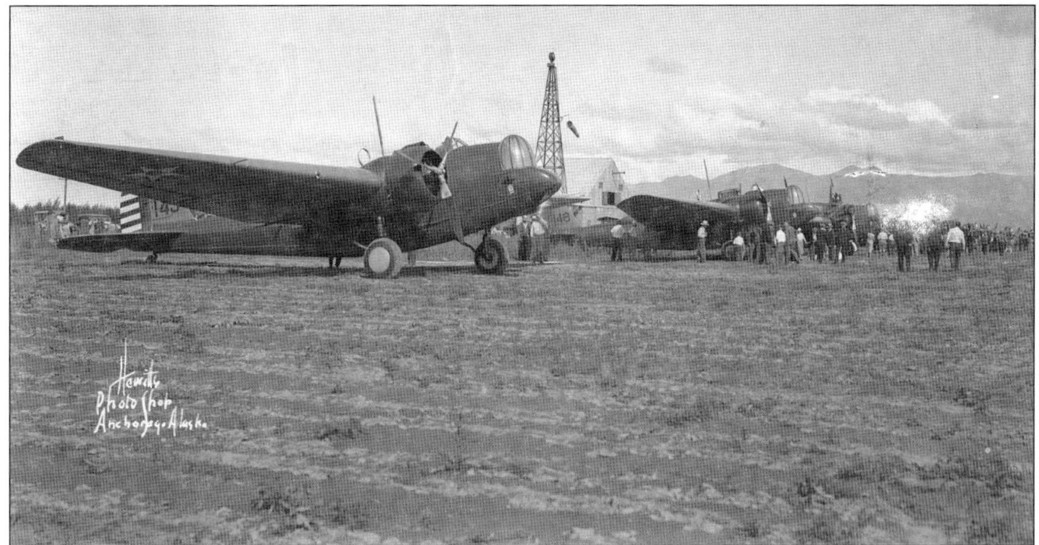

Anchorage residents and military members gathered to view a shipment of Martin B-10 bombers that arrived at Merrill Field during World War II. Alaska played an important role in the Lend-Lease program, which facilitated sending military goods to allies overseas. Alaska's position in the Far Northwest of the continent made for a relatively convenient trip over the North Pole to the Soviet Union.

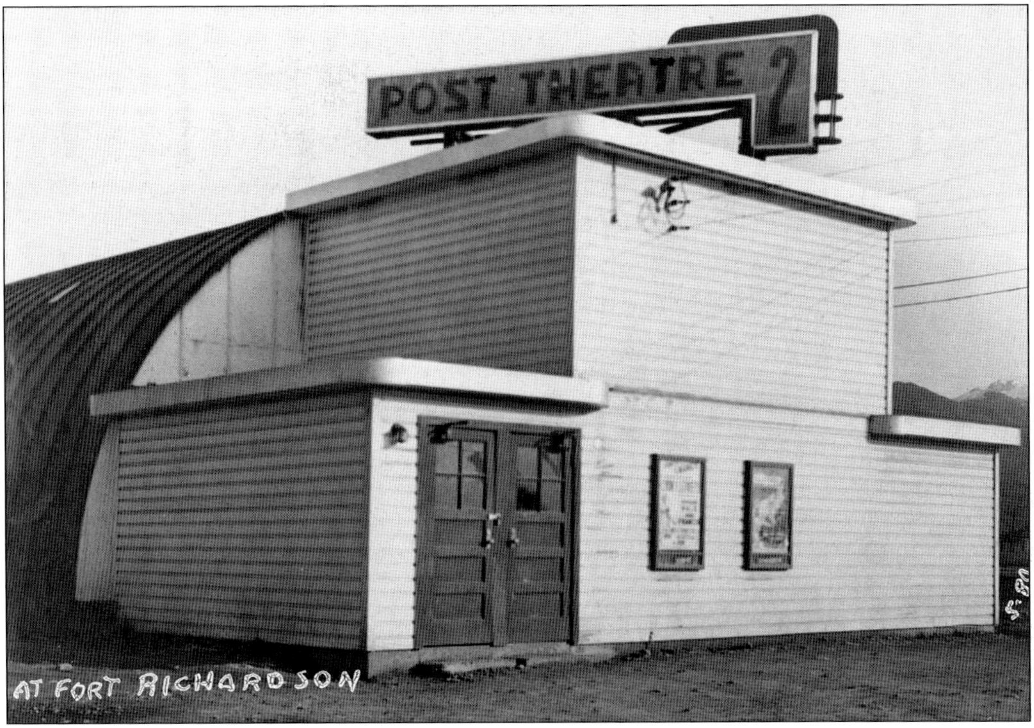

The impact of the military and World War II can be seen throughout Anchorage. One of the more subtle ways has been the proliferation of Quonset huts. These recognizable structures, made of corrugated steel, were initially used by the military as cheap and easily assembled structures to house soldiers and store materials for the war. Over the years, several Quonset huts have been repurposed. Some, in like this photograph, served as movie theaters and entertainment venues. Others have become iconic Anchorage restaurants like the Garden of Eatin', below.

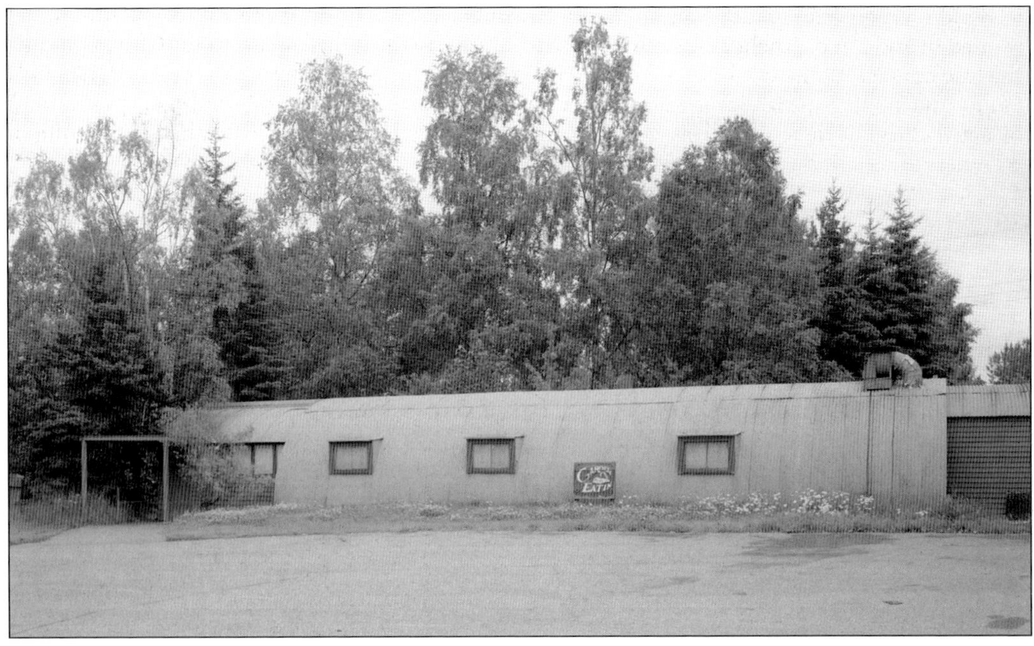

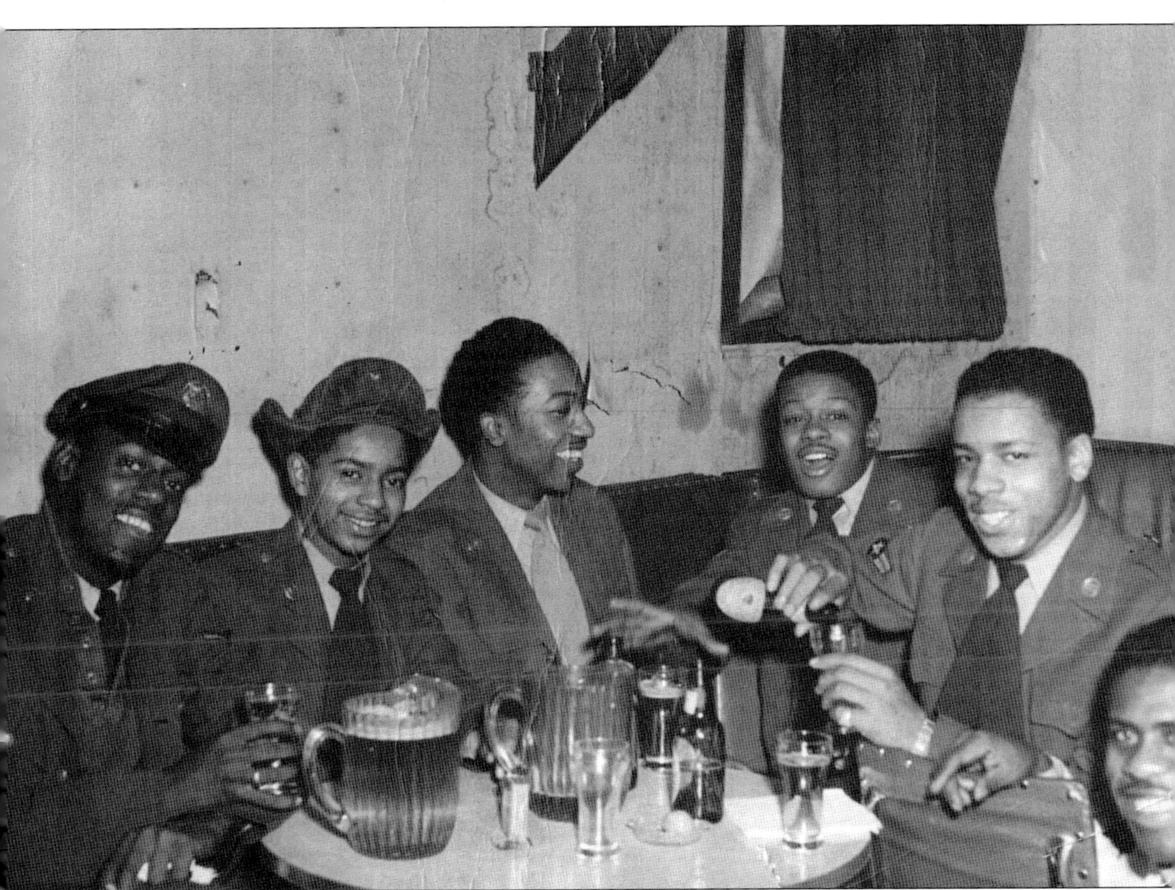

Six soldiers relax with a drink in the early 1950s outside of Fort Richardson. The military has long fostered a unique camaraderie among service members. As thousands of young men and women rotated in and out of Anchorage's military installations, many forged lifelong bonds and remained in close contact. Some even elected to remain in Alaska, drawn to the area's open spaces, public lands, and opportunities for outdoor adventure. Anchorage has among the highest percentage of active-duty soldiers as well as veterans, signaling the comfort and ease that many military members and their families feel with life in Alaska.

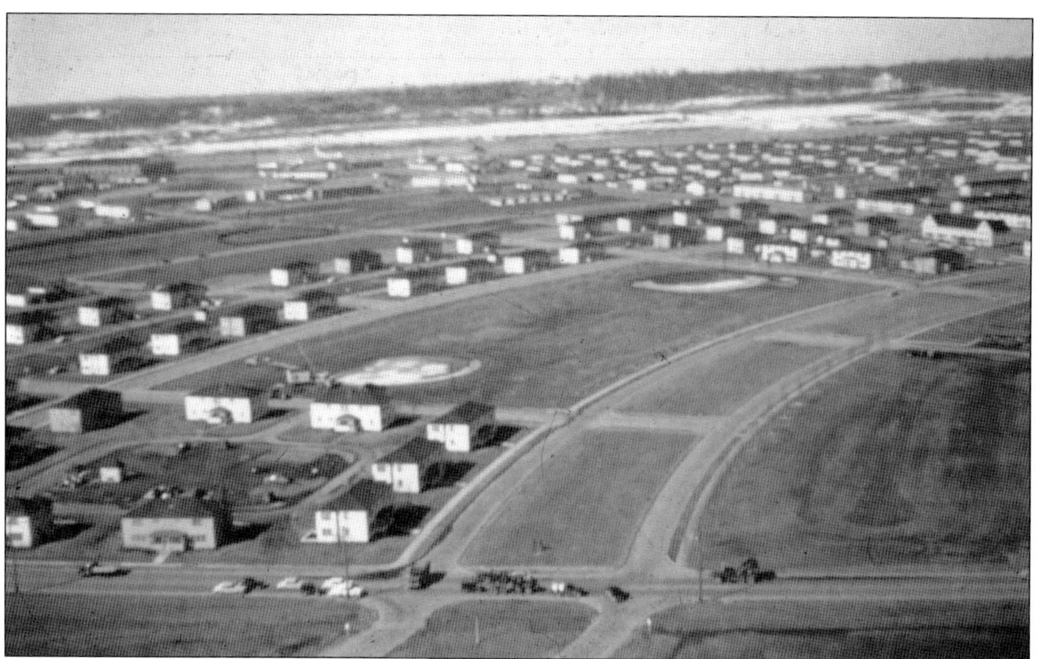

During the Cold War, both Fort Richardson and Elmendorf Air Force Base grew and became deeply woven into Anchorage's social, cultural, and economic fabric. The military built additional housing to accommodate the increasing numbers of servicemen and their families. This photograph shows an aerial view of Elmendorf Air Force Base housing in the summer of 1954.

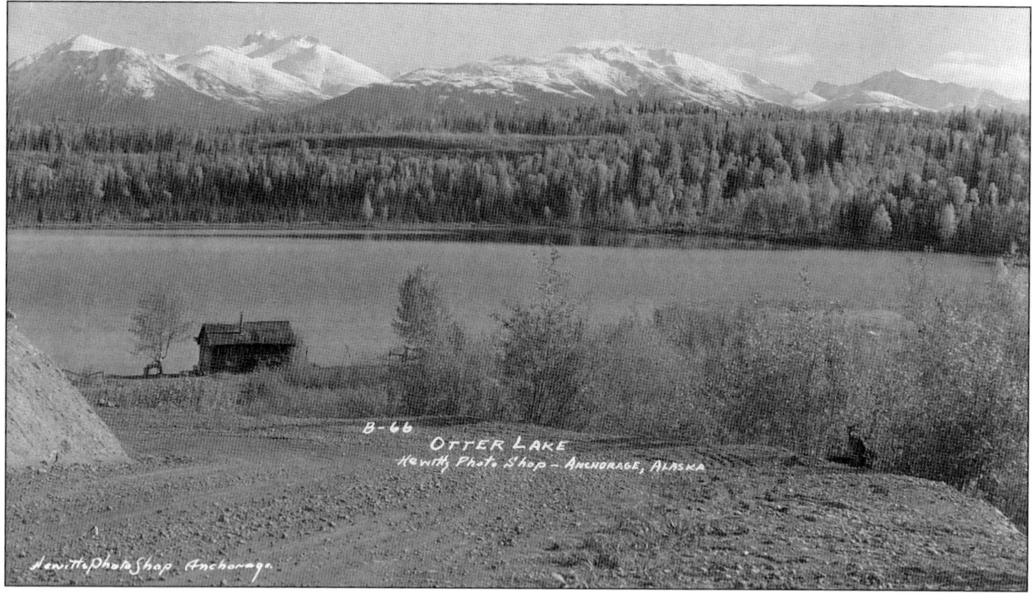

Otter Lake, which lies on the property of Fort Richardson, is no longer accessible to nonmilitary residents in Anchorage. However, it has long been a favored spot to recreate among military members. A boathouse sits alongside the shore and provides service members an opportunity to kayak, rowboat, or sail across the water. Cabins were also constructed a short hike from the lake and have proven popular camping spots. The lake is known as a hot spot for wildlife activity throughout the year.

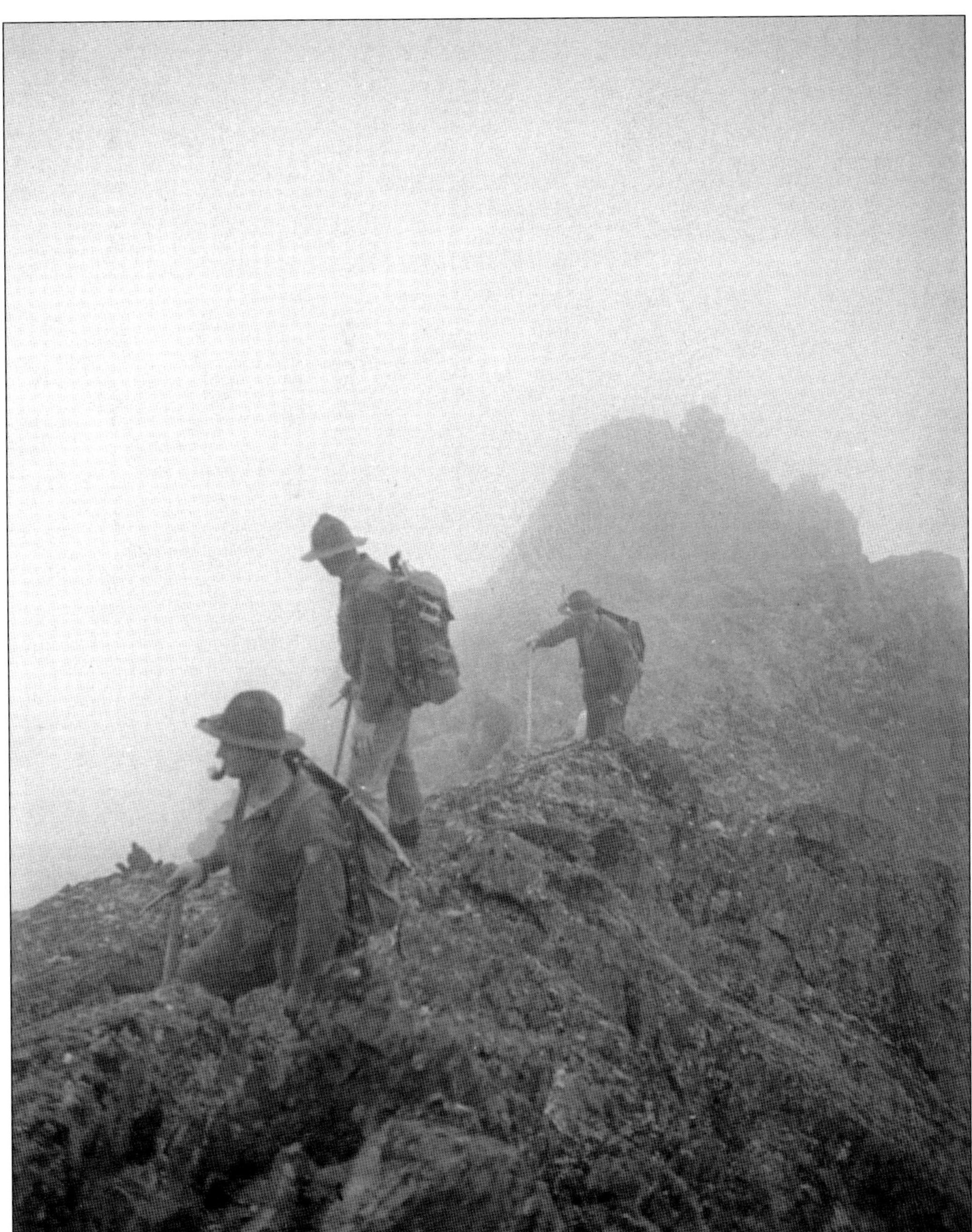

Four Army soldiers (one is barely visible through the fog) scale the Chugach Mountains outside of Anchorage and just beyond Fort Richardson in the 1940s. Anchorage abuts a vast wilderness and a daunting natural environment, which has provided an ideal setting for training in cold weather and otherwise challenging conditions. It is not unusual for military members to train in Alaska to obtain a unique skill set that equips them to deal with harsh environmental challenges that they may encounter elsewhere in the world. The scale of Alaska's landscapes, from the continent's highest mountains to swift-moving rivers and frozen lakes to the omnipresent wildlife, issues opportunities to challenge oneself and grow as a soldier.

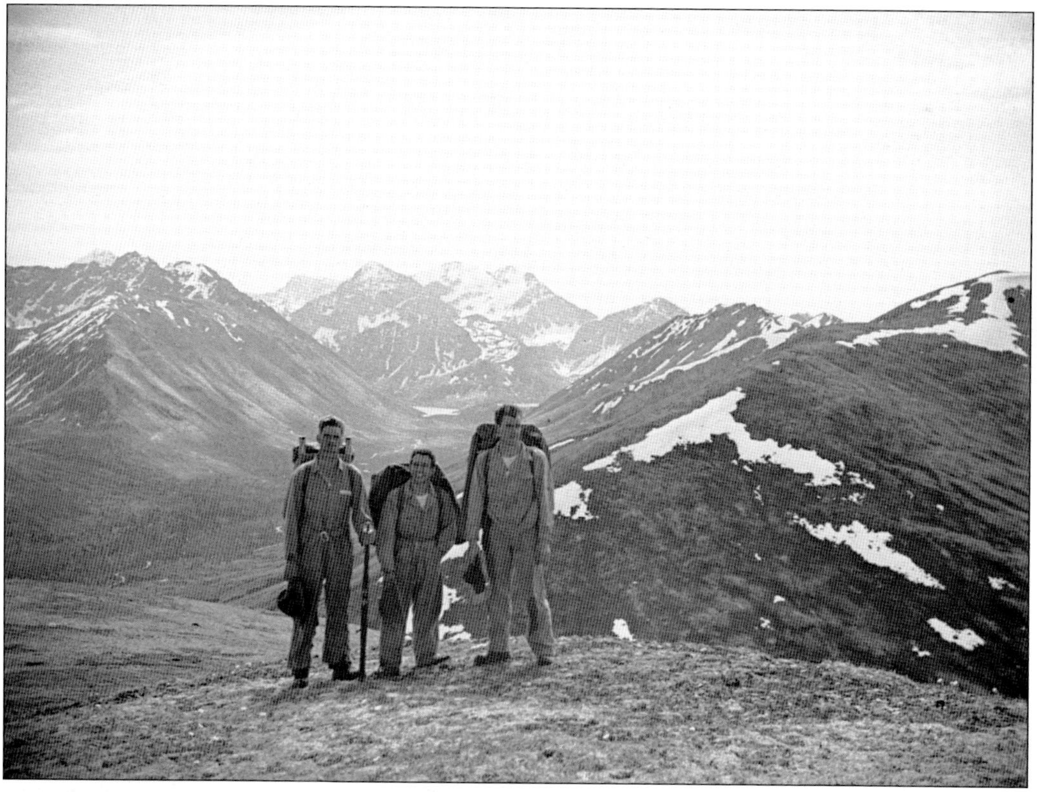

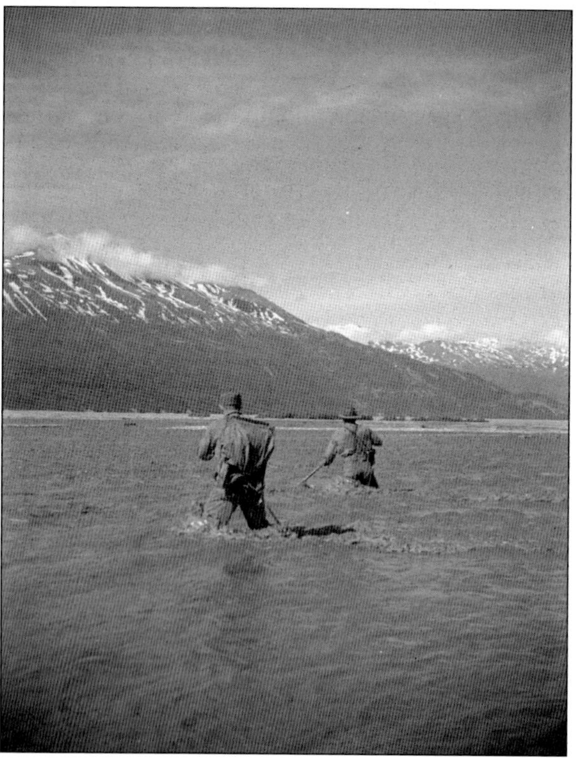

Soldiers scale a ridgeline in the Chugach Mountains and wade through the icy Knik Arm, known for its swift currents and mudflats. These undated photographs were likely taken in the 1940s, either during World War II or shortly after.

Five

Anchorage Comes Apart

On March 27, 1964, Good Friday, a megathrust earthquake with a magnitude of 9.2 shook Southcentral Alaska in what to date has been the largest quake recorded in North American history. Anchorage experienced extensive damage as businesses, homes, roads, and bridges buckled and collapsed. The soil liquefaction and subsequent landslides led to further devastation throughout the region. In addition to the immediate physical damage, the earthquake triggered deadly tsunamis along Alaska's southern and eastern coasts. Nine individuals from Anchorage died because of the earthquake, a surprisingly low number given the level of destruction in the municipality. However, the tsunami-induced floods along Prince William Sound's coastal communities led to most of the deaths attributed to the earthquake, a figure that eventually exceeded 100.

In the aftermath of the quake and its tragic consequences, Anchorage leaders upgraded building codes and fortified new infrastructure. The disaster prompted the community to reevaluate its seismic preparedness and develop tighter construction standards. Today, Anchorage is better equipped to withstand earthquakes, with considerably stronger building designs, reinforced infrastructure, and improved emergency response systems. The 1964 earthquake also served as a catalyst for seismic awareness and preparedness nationwide, ultimately making Anchorage and the broader Alaskan region more resilient to future seismic events.

Indeed, Anchorage and its surroundings are among the most seismically active population centers in the United States. Yet, within days of the quake, Alaskans pulled together and began to rebuild. While the earthquake may have devastated entire parts of town, the residents of Anchorage were determined to make their community stronger than before. And within a few years, they had largely done so. Earthquakes remain an ever-present threat to daily life. On November 30, 2018, a 7.1-magnitude earthquake struck Anchorage with an epicenter just 10 miles from downtown. The quake damaged several commercial buildings, homes, and roads, but there were miraculously no reported fatalities, a testament to the preparedness of Anchorage residents. Still, Alaskans know that it is never a matter of if but when the next big one will strike.

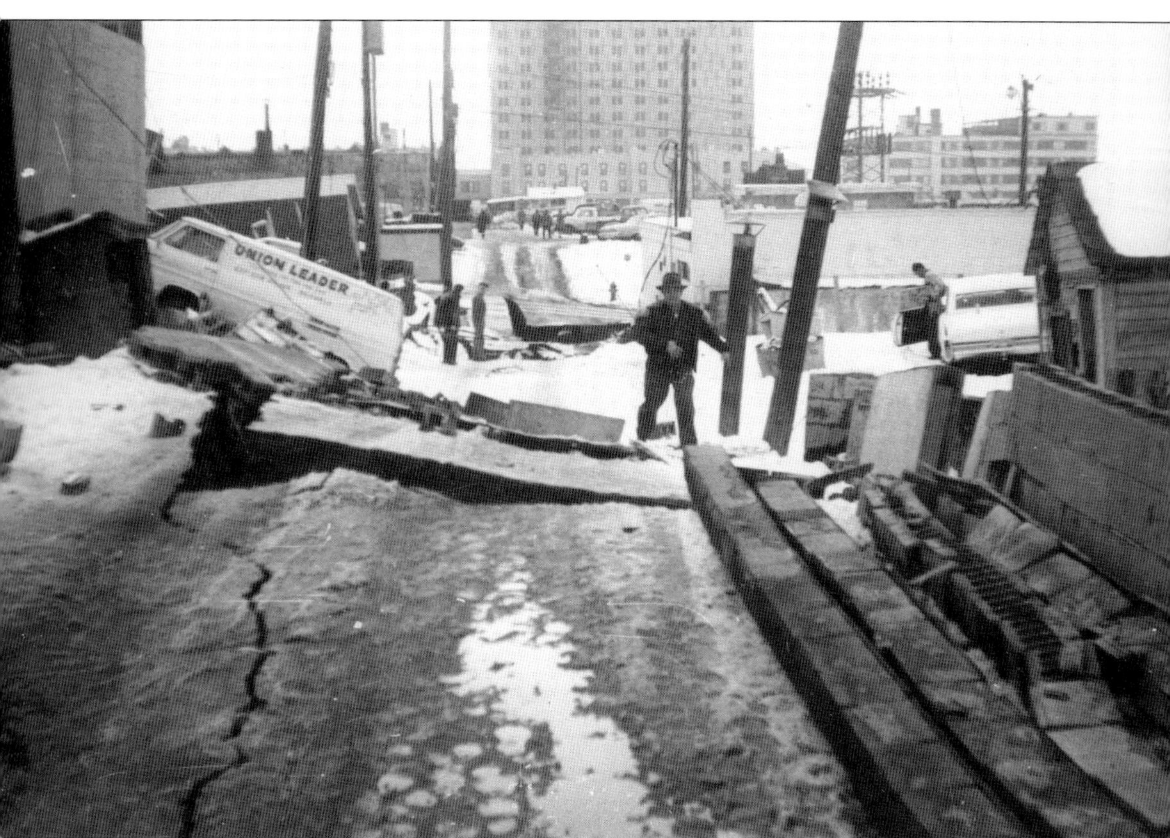

A man surveys the damage across an alley north of Fourth Avenue in downtown Anchorage. C Street is visible to the west. Anchorage residents endured a terrifying five minutes of shaking, only to come to grips with a city that had neighborhoods mostly or even entirely destroyed. A section of downtown Anchorage experienced a landslide that resulted in a segment of Fourth Avenue dropping over 10 feet. A portion of the Turnagain neighborhood collapsed from atop a bluff into the Knik Arm. Much of the northern and western parts of Anchorage were built on what was known as Bootlegger's Cove Clay, a marine silt that liquefied amid the shaking.

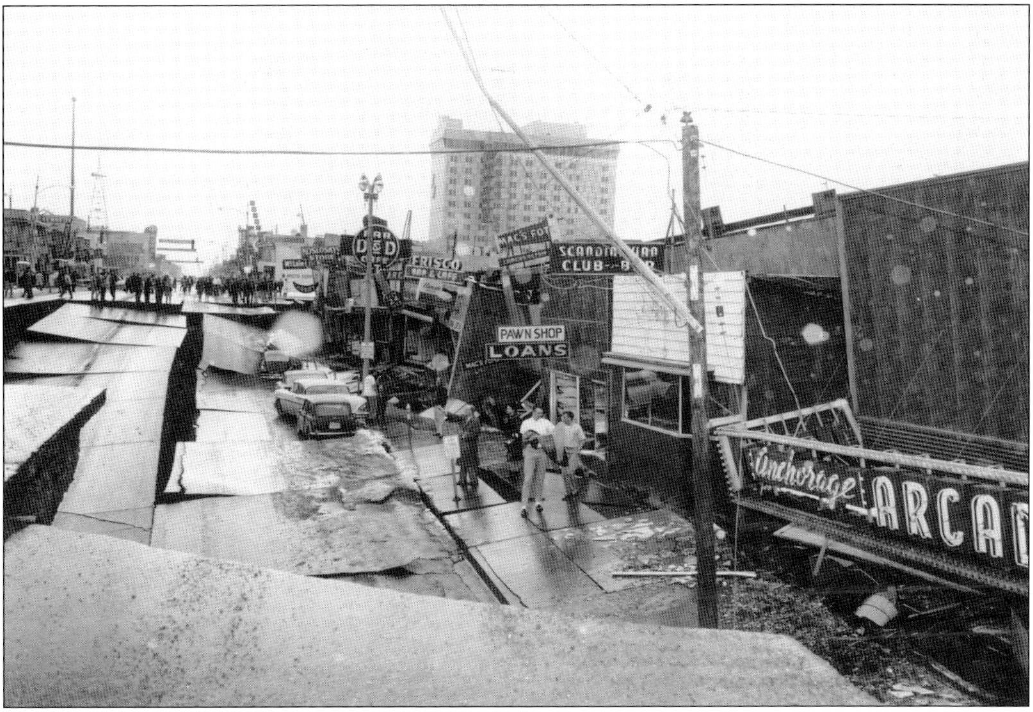

These two views of Fourth Avenue are from the same vantage point but taken several hours apart. Note the collapse of the street and storefronts from one photograph to the next. Within minutes, the street sank roughly seven feet below grade. But over the next several hours and days, the street and businesses collapsed deeper into the earth by as much as 14 feet. The Anchorage Arcade was nearly swallowed whole. While many of the iconic photographs of the earthquake capture the damage done downtown (such as these photographs), other parts of town and beyond experienced equal or greater damage.

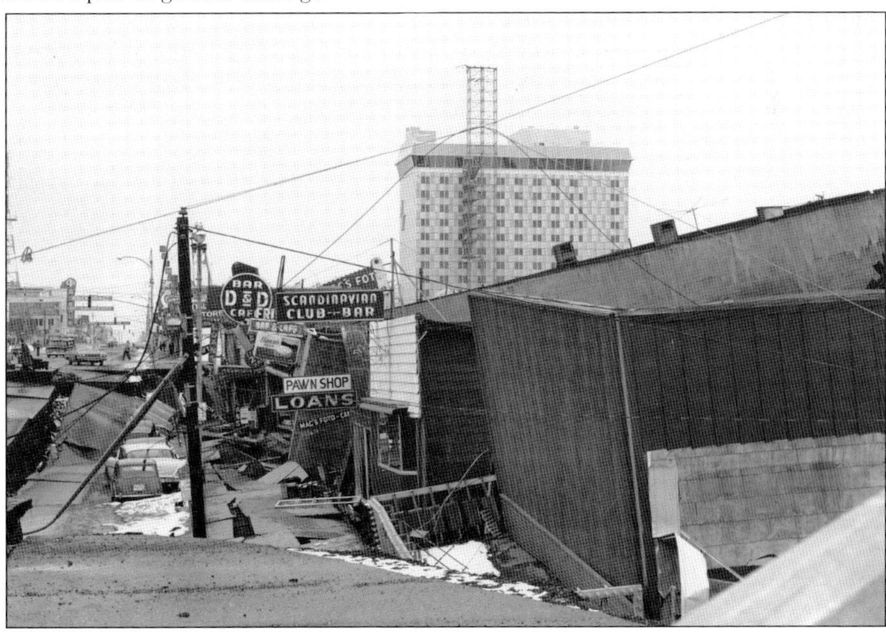

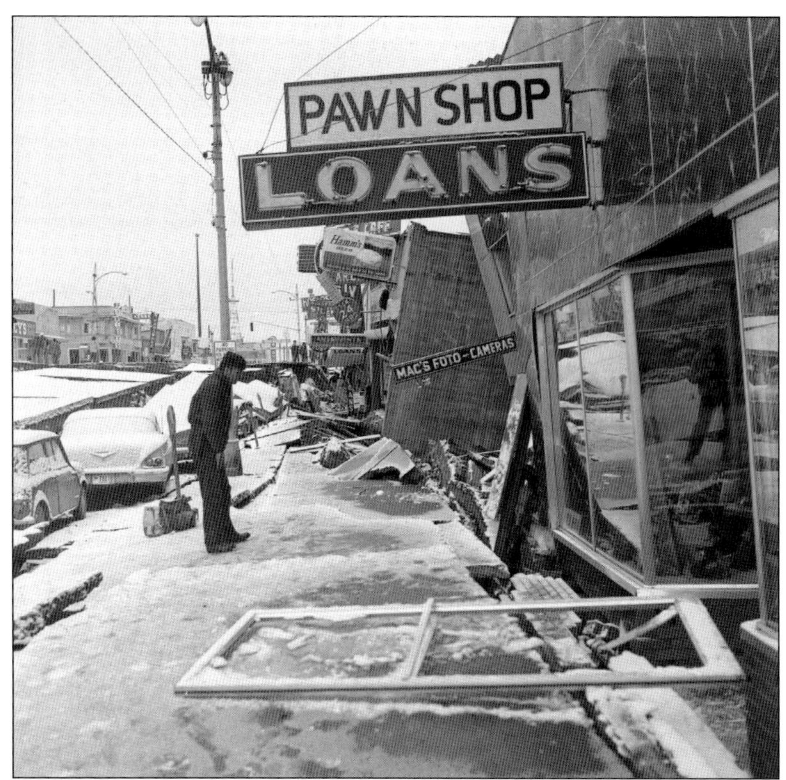

Downtown along Fourth Avenue was among the areas most devastated as the road collapsed and destroyed area businesses such as Bagoy's flower shop, the Green Dragon cocktail lounge, and the Bowling Emporium, among other establishments.

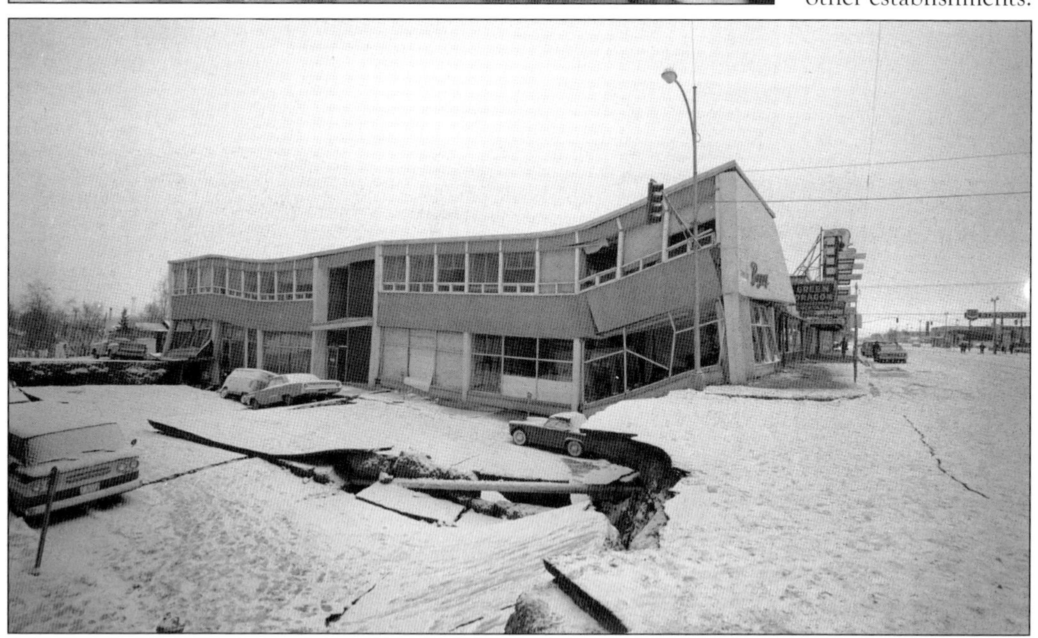

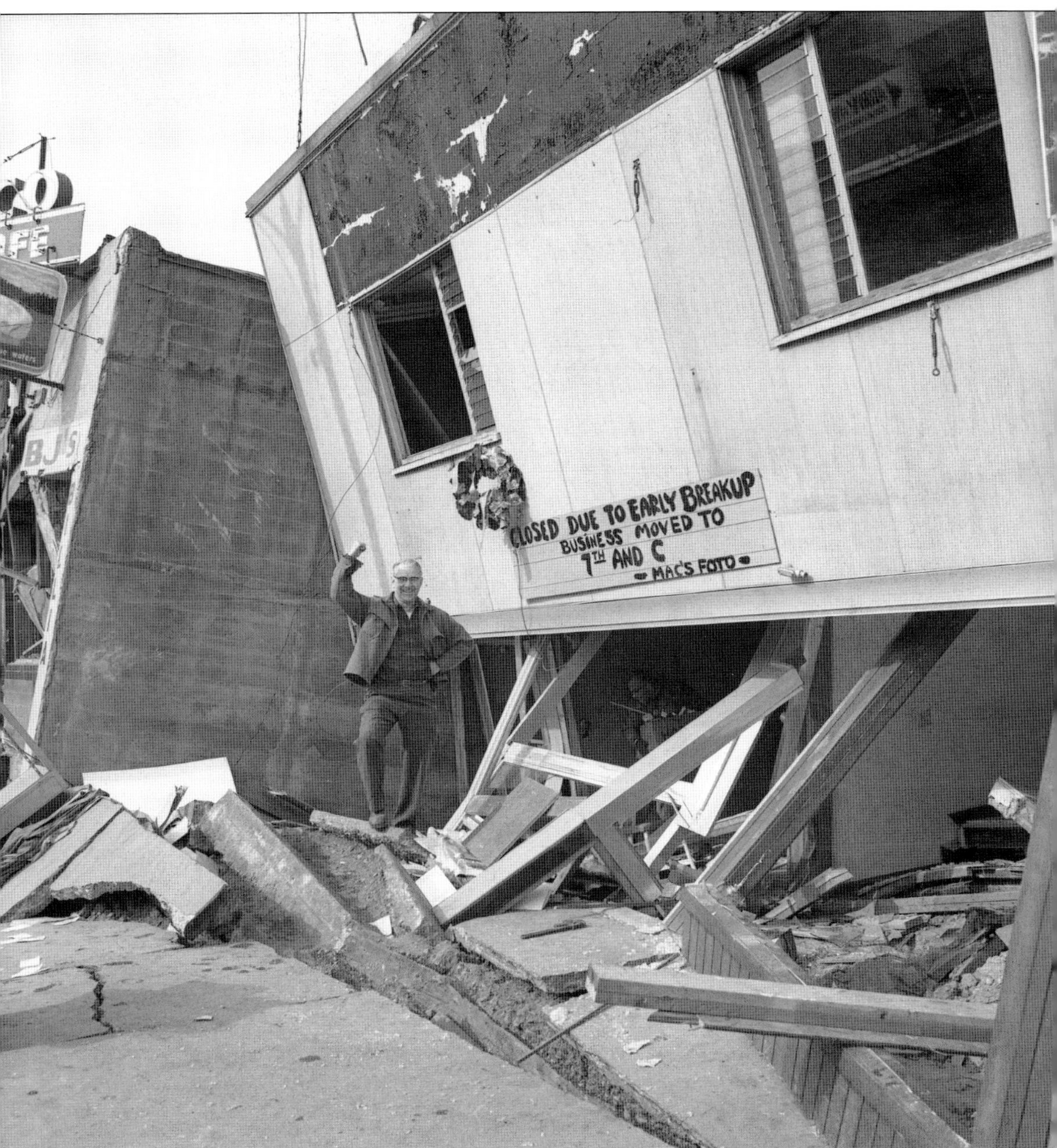

Keeping a sense of humor amid the destruction, the owner of Mac's Fotos grins and pumps his fist. The improvised signage, which proclaims "closed due to early breakup" references springtime in Alaska, known as "breakup" as the snow and ice melts, as well as the obvious physical state of the business in the quake's aftermath.

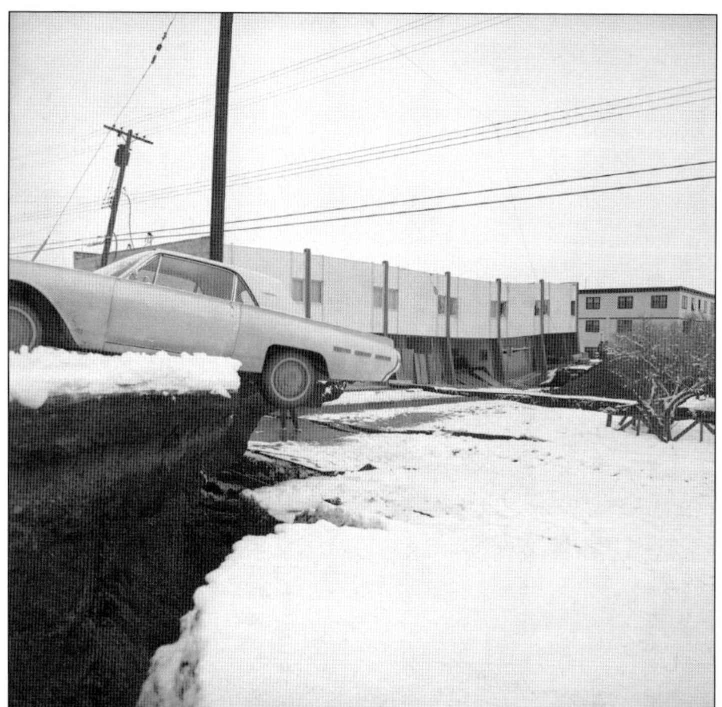

A vehicle is separated from its parking spot just outside of an area school. Miraculously, no motorists were killed as a result of the shaking or in its immediate aftermath.

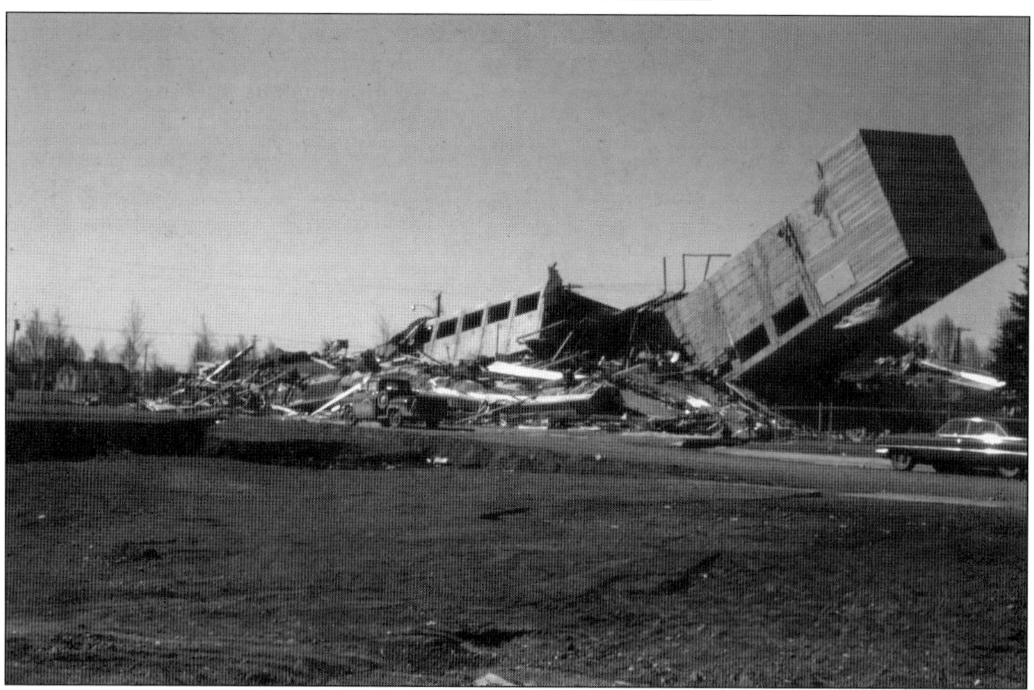

An overturned apartment complex highlights the force of the shaking that occurred. It was one of hundreds of homes, apartments, and businesses that were destroyed within minutes. This photograph was taken later in the spring of 1964, at least a month or so after the quake. Anchorage residents began rebuilding nearly immediately, but evidence of the earthquake's damage could be seen around town for years after the seismic event.

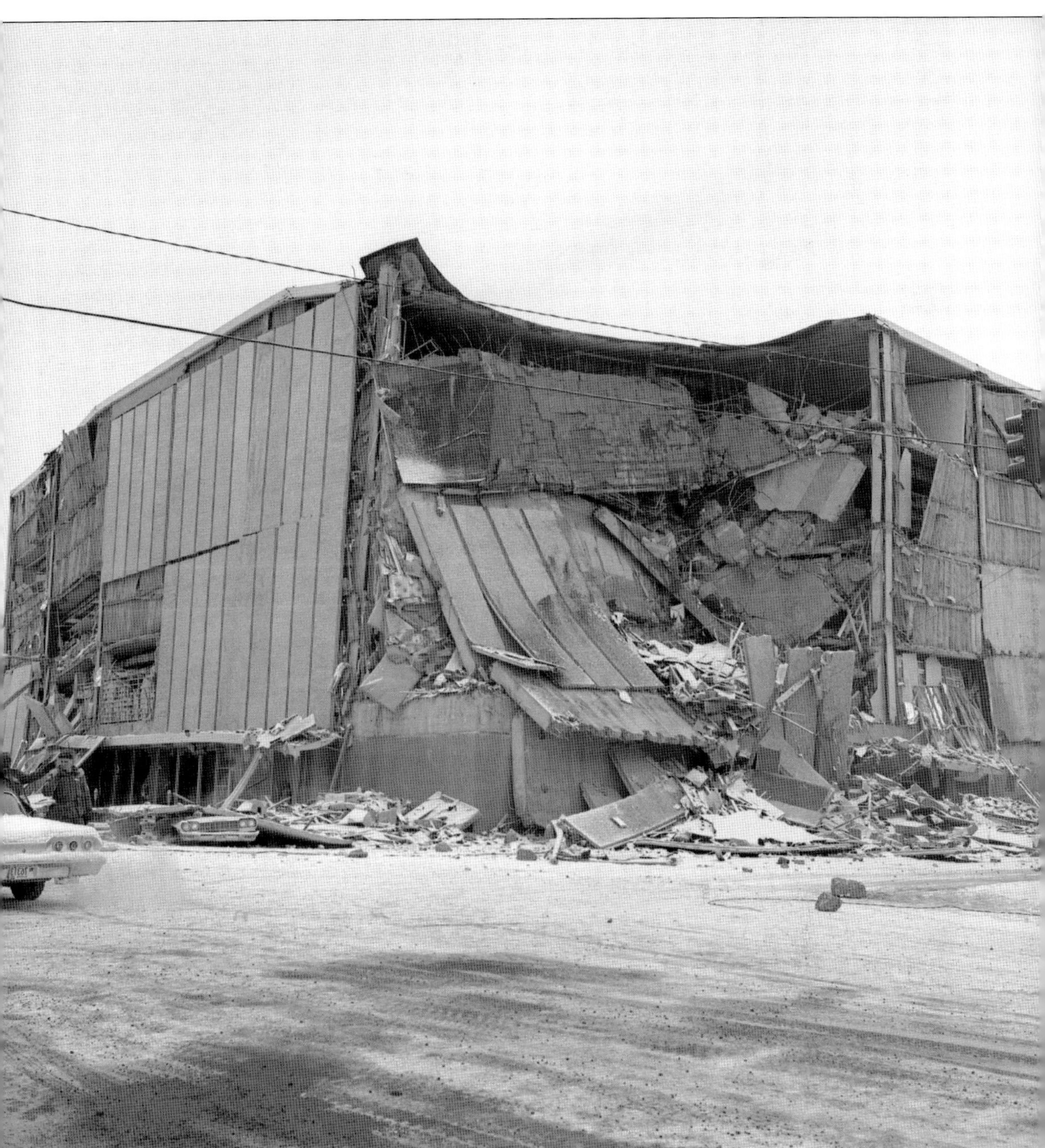

JCPenney's department store, one of the flagship businesses anchoring the downtown retail area, was destroyed in the quake. But like much else in town, JCPenney would eventually return to downtown Anchorage in a renovated space that was rebuilt and up to a stronger building code. Today, JCPenney anchors the Fifth Avenue Mall.

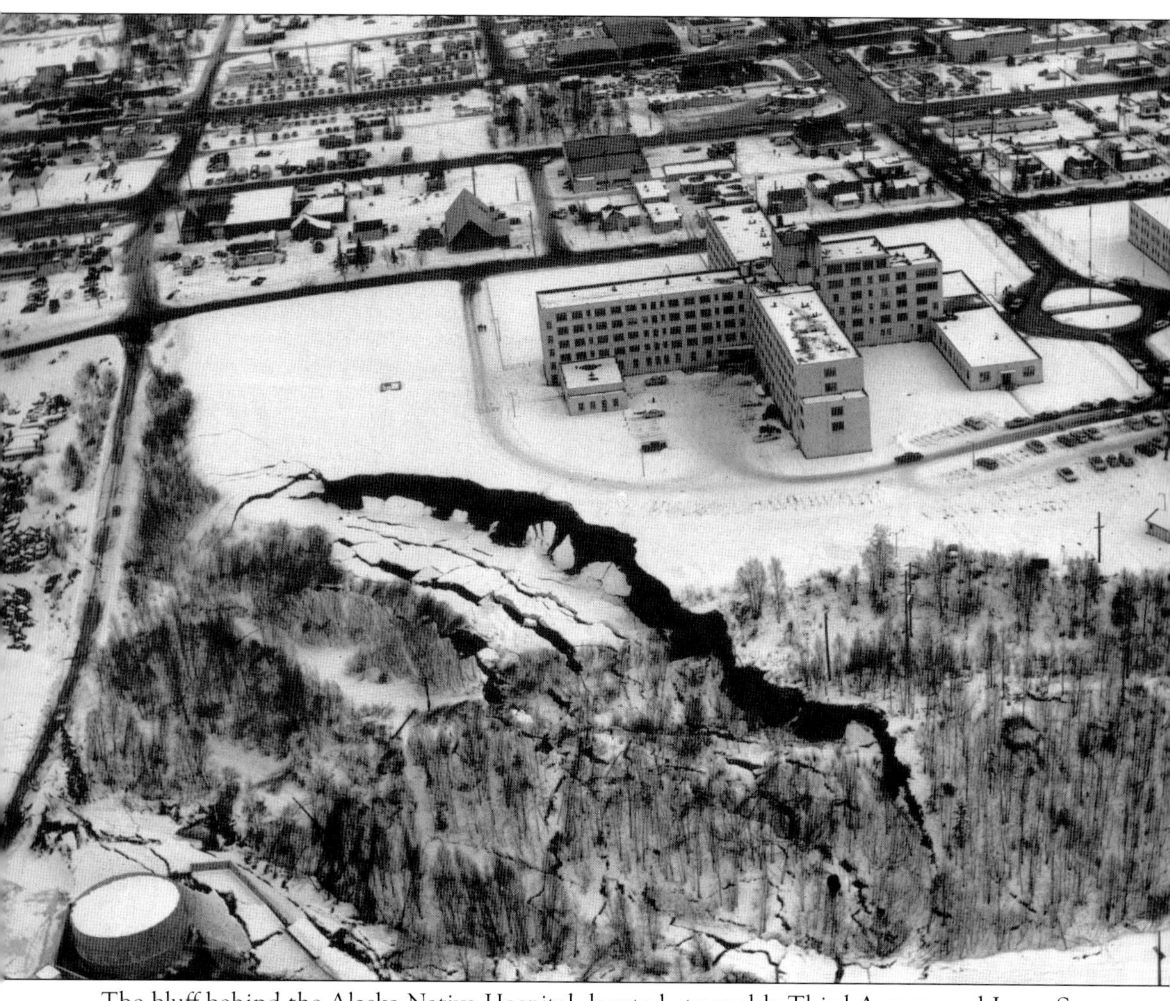

The bluff behind the Alaska Native Hospital, located at roughly Third Avenue and Ingra Street, buckled and failed. The hospital, located on East Third Avenue, suffered damage but not irreparably so. In fact, the hospital continued to serve patients until the Alaska Native Medical Center opened in 1997 about five miles southeast of downtown in Anchorage's University-Medical (U-Med) District.

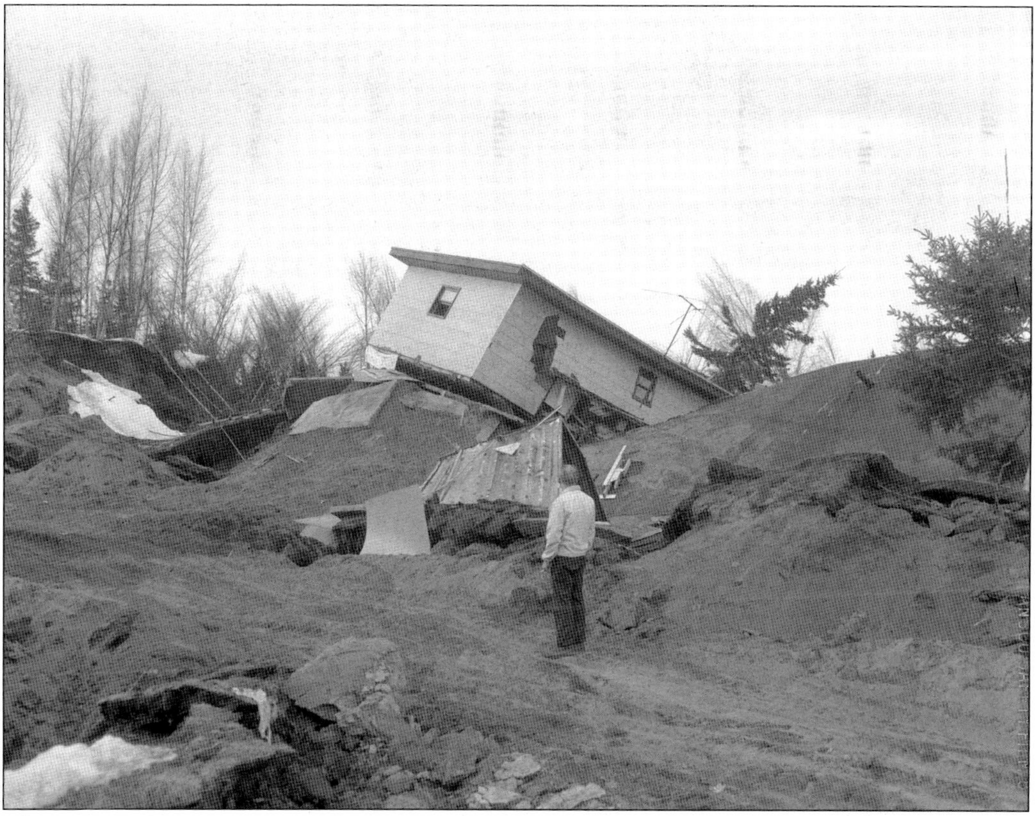

The west Anchorage neighborhood of Turnagain was among the most heavily damaged during the earthquake. The violent shaking produced a geologic phenomenon known as liquefaction. When this occurs, the soil loses its ability to support the built environment and effectively behaves as if it were a liquid rather than a solid. Seismologists have compared the liquefaction of soil in a particularly strong earthquake to a bowl of jelly shaking violently.

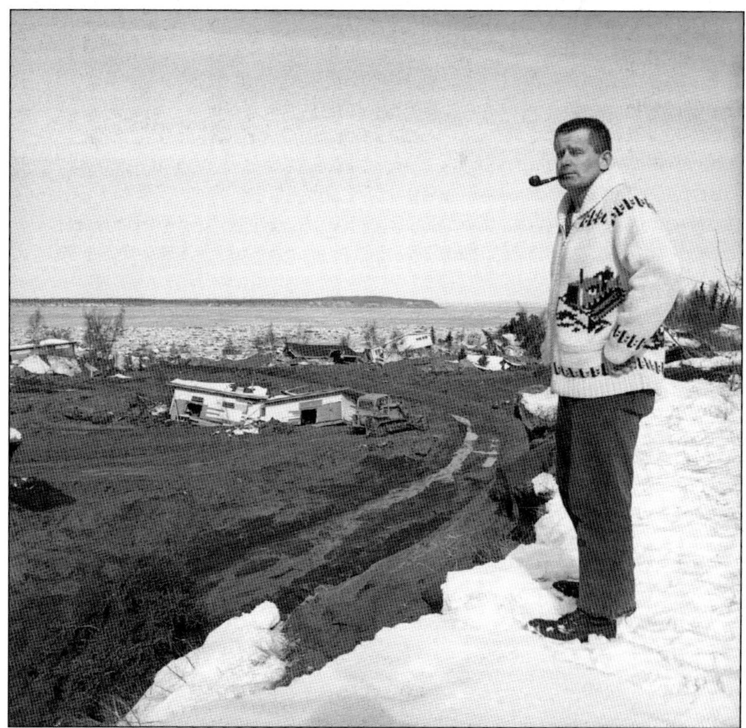

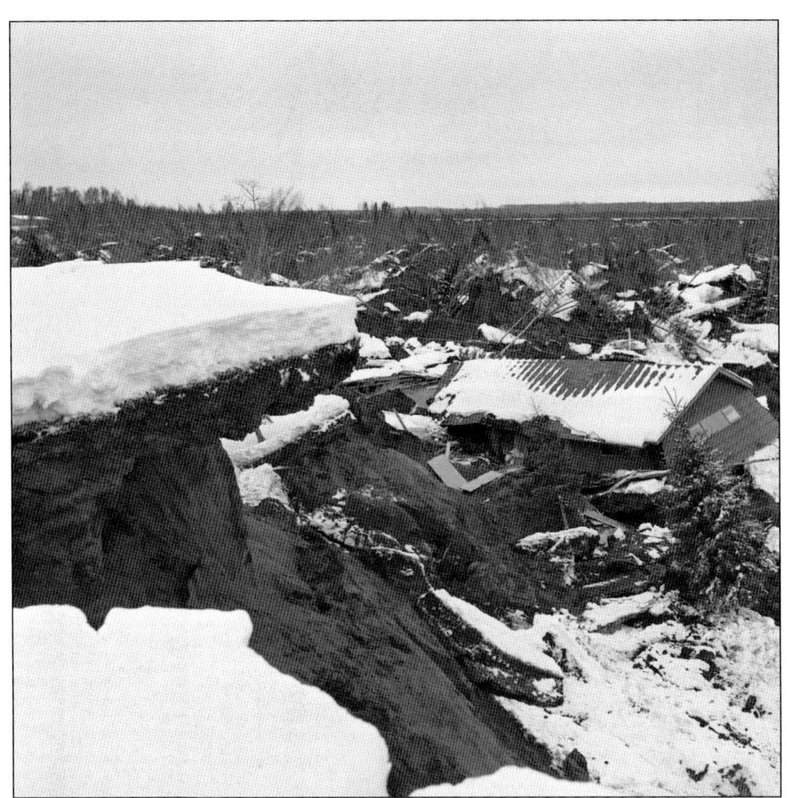

Several homes in the Turnagain neighborhood collapsed, and the sections of the surrounding bluffs fell into the Turnagain Arm, creating a new landscape. Landslides destroyed other properties. Today, residents and visitors can walk along the Tony Knowles Coastal Trail and see first-hand where the landslides occurred and witness how entire portions of the coast fell into the mudflats and water below.

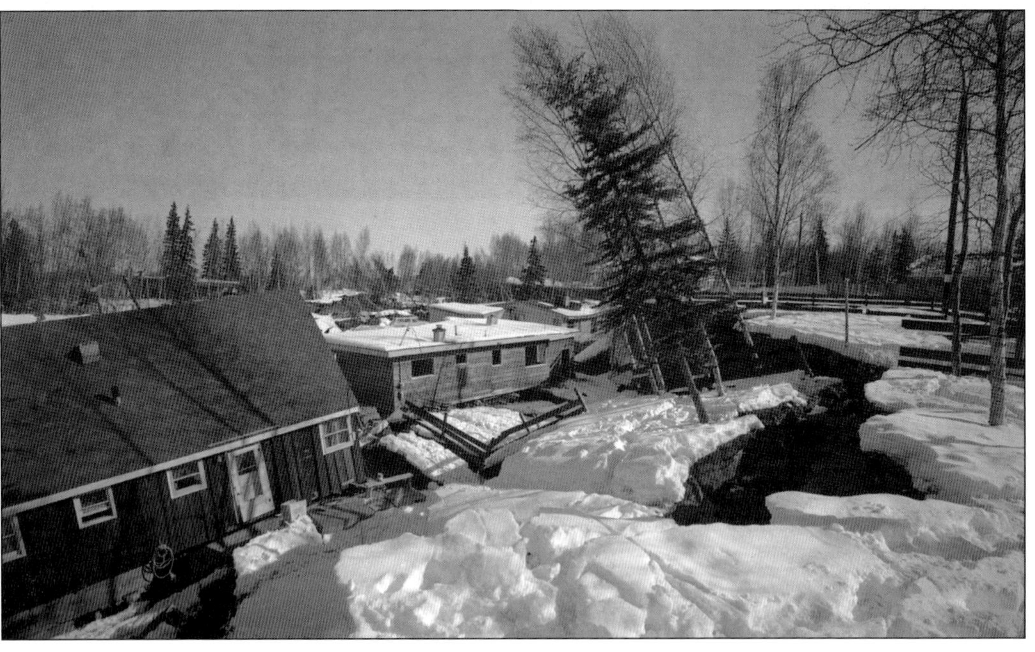

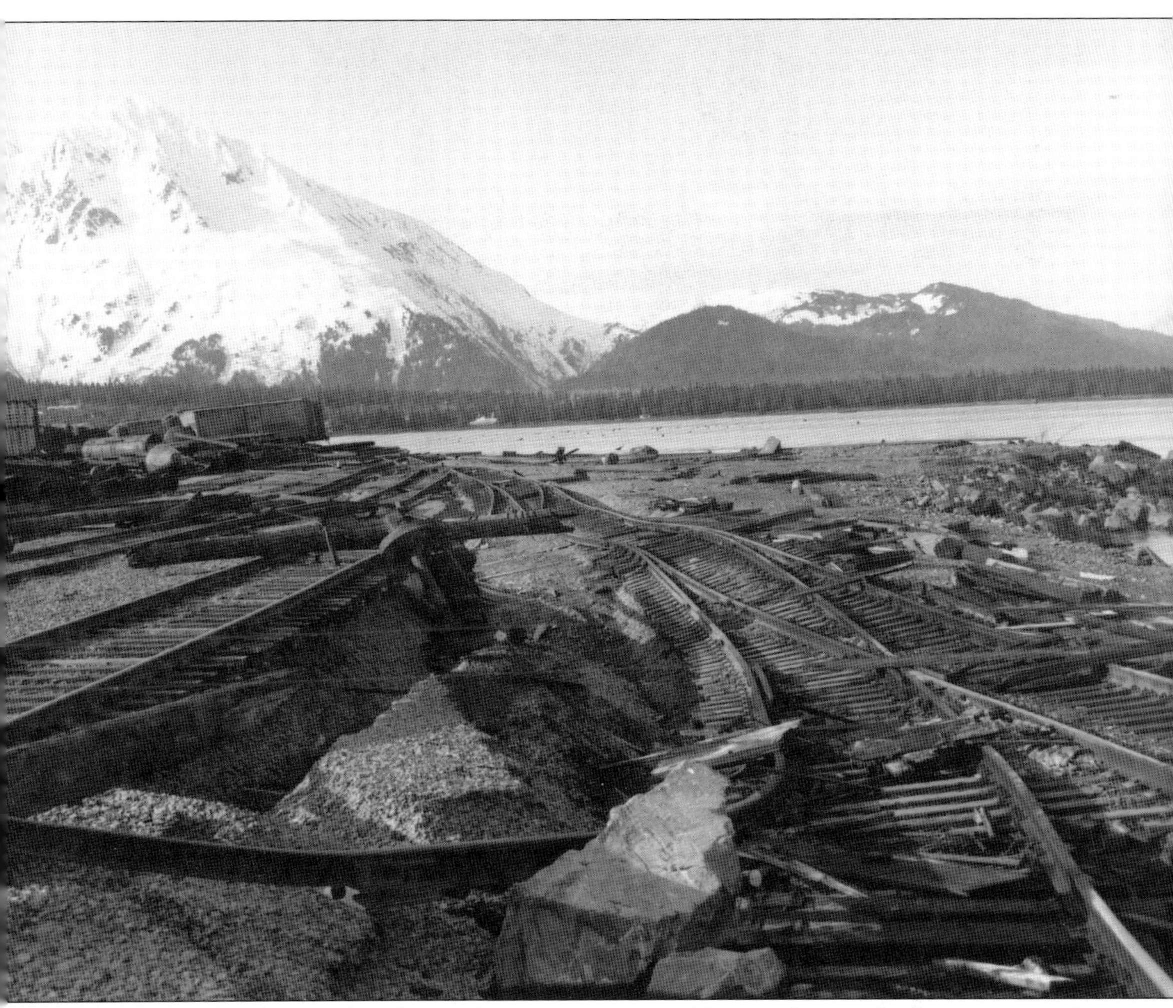

The Alaska Railroad, central to the state's transportation and logistical network, also experienced considerable damage due to the earthquake. Entire sections of steel rail were twisted and laid to waste. The quake sent railroad ties and ballast into the Turnagain Arm and buried sections of the line under the coastal mudflats. Remarkably, on April 6, not even two weeks after the earthquake, the first freight train left Anchorage on restored track to resume coal service to the power plants at Fort Richardson and Elmendorf Air Force Base. The first train out of Whittier brought 125 cars loaded with freight into Anchorage on April 20, not even a month from the time the quake hit. Seward received its first freight train from Anchorage on September 13, just shy of the six-month mark. The brisk pace with which the workers repaired and even strengthened the track stands as a testament to the resiliency of Alaskans during the time of crisis.

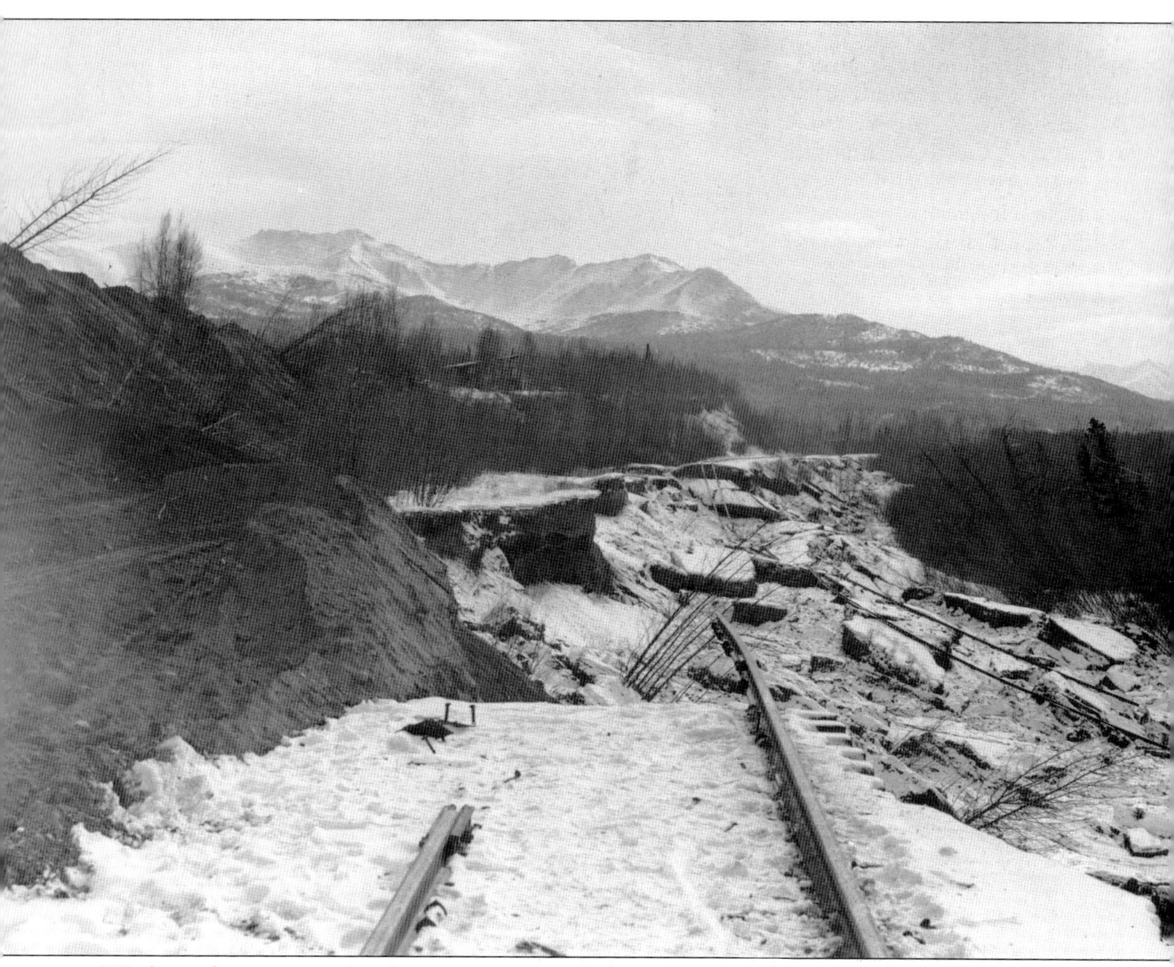

Workers almost immediately set out to assess the railroad and concluded that it would require nearly roughly $35 million in repairs. Thousands of Alaskans relied on the railroad, and each day it was out of commission brought compounding problems. Teams worked around the clock for weeks on end to restore the Alaska Railroad's core services in and around Anchorage. Other stretches of the railroad would take considerably longer to repair. Aside from the track, over 500 spans of wood trestles were badly damaged or destroyed. Fortunately, the steel bridges withstood the shaking, but 34 required repairs before the railroad could fully resume service along the entirety of its routes.

An Alaska Railroad worker operates a ditcher to rehabilitate the track in the aftermath of the earthquake. These men and women took the opportunity to not only repair the track but also strengthen it under the correct assumption that the region would experience additional earthquakes in the future.

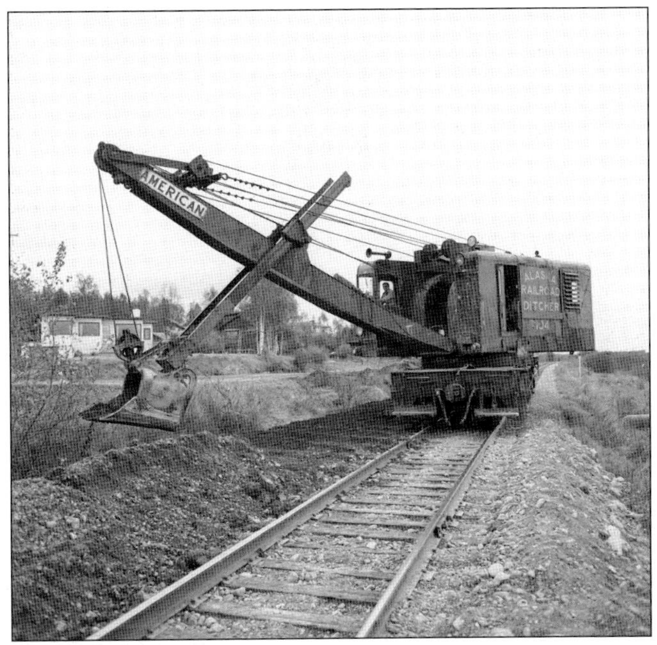

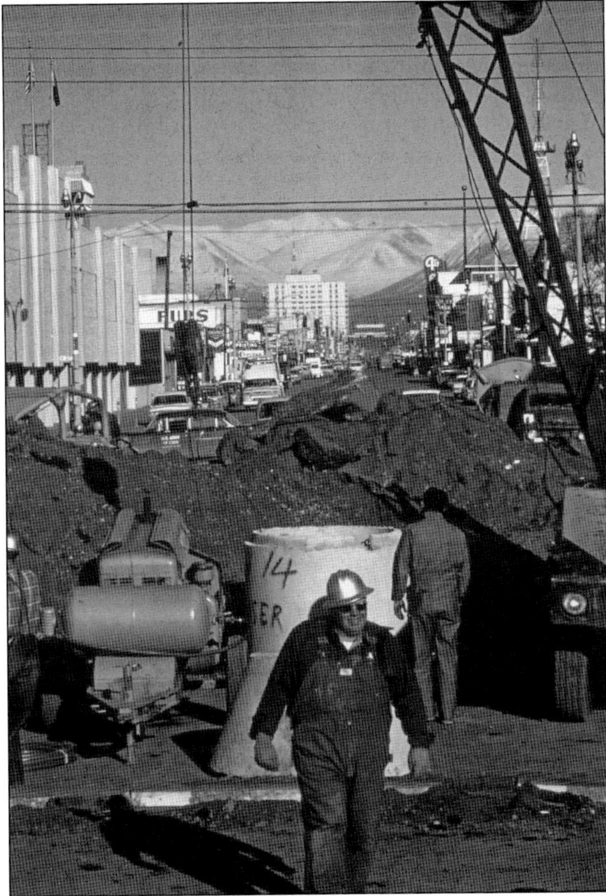

Even as Anchorage residents surveyed the damage, men and women throughout town pitched in and began to rebuild. The most visible destruction included buildings, homes, and roads. But water and sewage lines, power stations, and other critical infrastructure and utilities also required costly repairs. Workers here lay a new water line along downtown's Fourth Avenue just days after the quake.

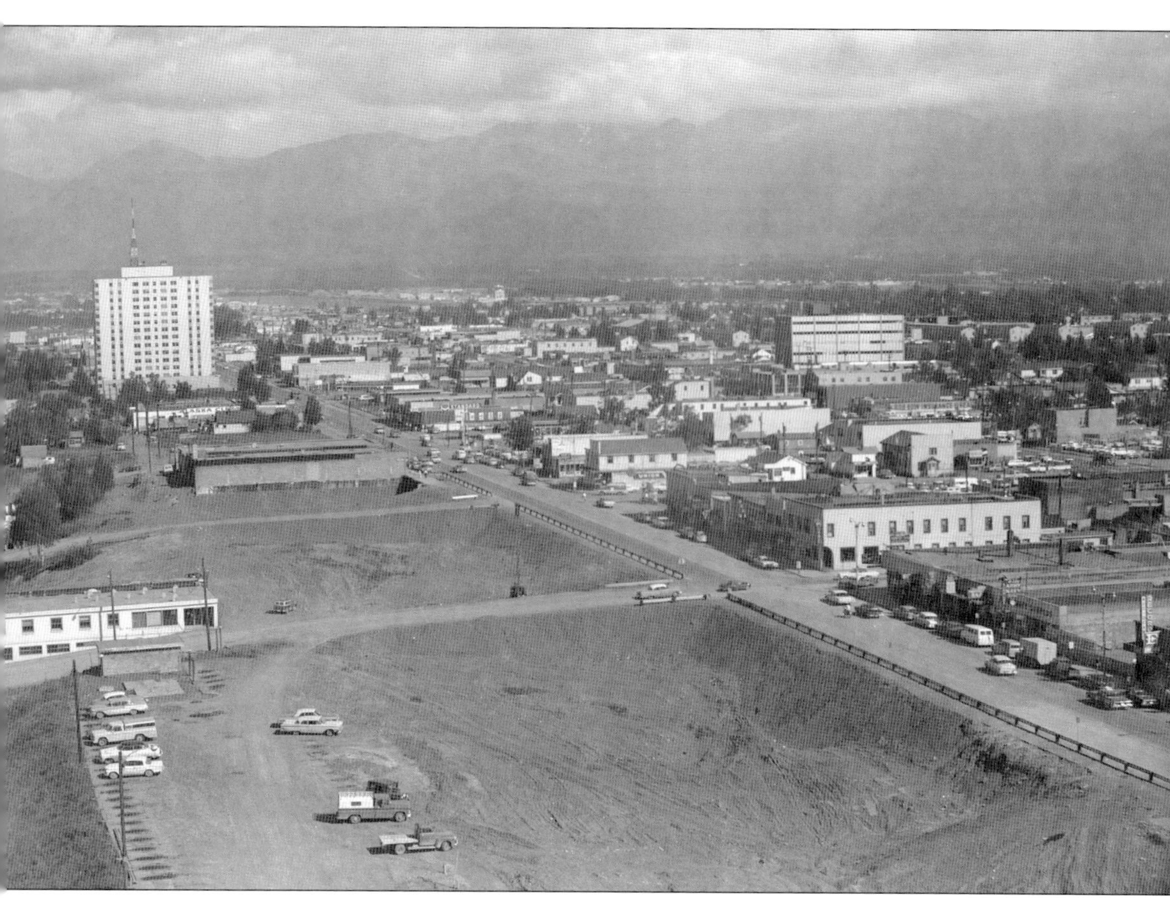

By the summer of 1967, just three years after the Good Friday earthquake, a largely rebuilt downtown had begun to take shape. Over three blocks of Fourth Avenue's north side were leveled, regraded, and prepared for redevelopment. Over the next decade, new shops, restaurants, and hotels opened. Alaskans had shown resilience and dedication to rebuilding their state's largest city.

Six

A Municipality Comes Together

Four years after the earthquake, geologists for Atlantic Richfield Company and Humble Oil and Refining Company struck oil around Prudhoe Bay on the state's North Slope. The deposit contained the most extensive source of crude oil ever discovered in the nation's history. It also resulted in a powerful new revenue source for the young state. But to recover and transport the oil required the state to settle land claims with those who called Alaska home for thousands of years. The Alaska Native Claims Settlement Act (ANCSA) of 1971 thus allocated 44 million acres of land and nearly $1 billion to Alaska Native peoples. The legislation created 12 regional and over 200 village corporations. Anchorage then played a role as the financial hub of Alaska's oil industry and an urban gathering place for many Native corporations, their leaders, and Alaska's diverse Native peoples.

Furthermore, ANCSA facilitated the construction of the Trans-Alaska Pipeline System (TAPS). Stretching approximately 800 miles from Prudhoe Bay in the north to Valdez in the south, the pipeline ensured that oil reached global markets. Although the pipeline itself does not traverse Anchorage, the construction effort created boomtown conditions as thousands moved north for well-paid construction jobs. Flush with cash, many laborers stayed or temporarily settled in Anchorage and parted with their money in bars, restaurants, clubs, and various other venues.

The 1970s were also a decade of political transition for Anchorage, as the city merged with the outlying borough to form a single municipality. With the confidence of a unified municipal government and abundant financial resources, Anchorage's mayor, George Sullivan, turned the page on the 1970s and welcomed the 1980s by dedicating a portion of the oil revenues to improving the community's civic and cultural infrastructure. But the oil boom did not last. By the middle of the 1980s, global oil prices cratered, and revenue dried up. Those who weathered the economic downturn were joined by an increasing population of residents from East Asia, the South Pacific, the Middle East, Latin America, and elsewhere in the lower 48 states. As the 20th century concluded, Anchorage touted a cosmopolitan culture that one would expect to find in cities far larger.

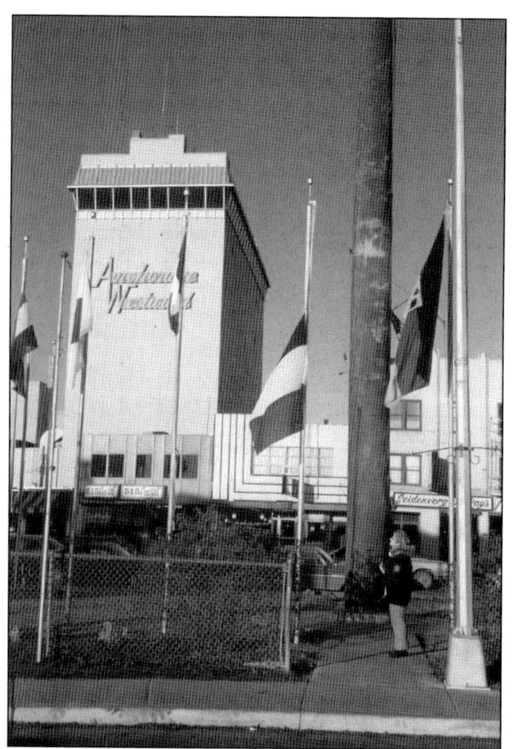

The Anchorage Westward Hotel, photographed in November 1970, reflected Anchorage's aspirations to become a global destination. International flags greeted visitors as Alaskans placed an increasing emphasis on tourism during the latter decades of the 20th century.

The Barratt Inn is pictured in May 1976. Anchorage's economy in the 1970s and early 1980s boomed largely due to the oil from Alaska's North Slope but also as a result of the construction of the Trans-Alaska Pipeline. Thousands of pipeline workers took up residency at inns, motels, and hotels along Spenard Road. The Barratt Inn may not have been luxurious, but it did the job for those in need of a bed and shower.

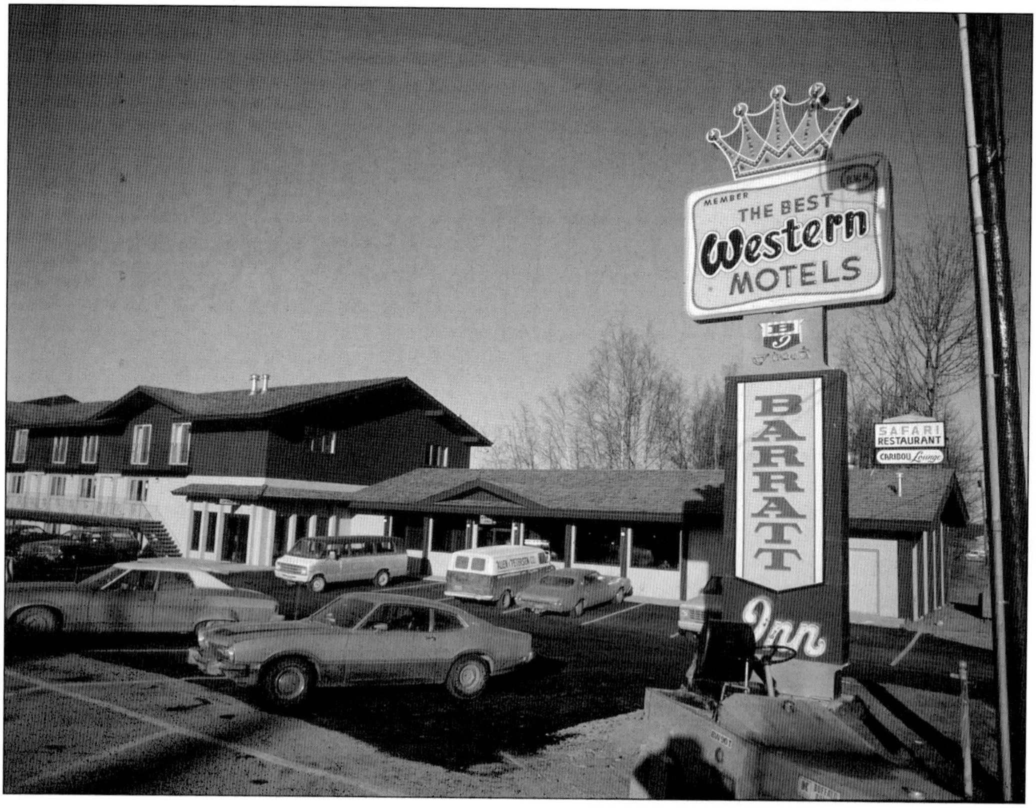

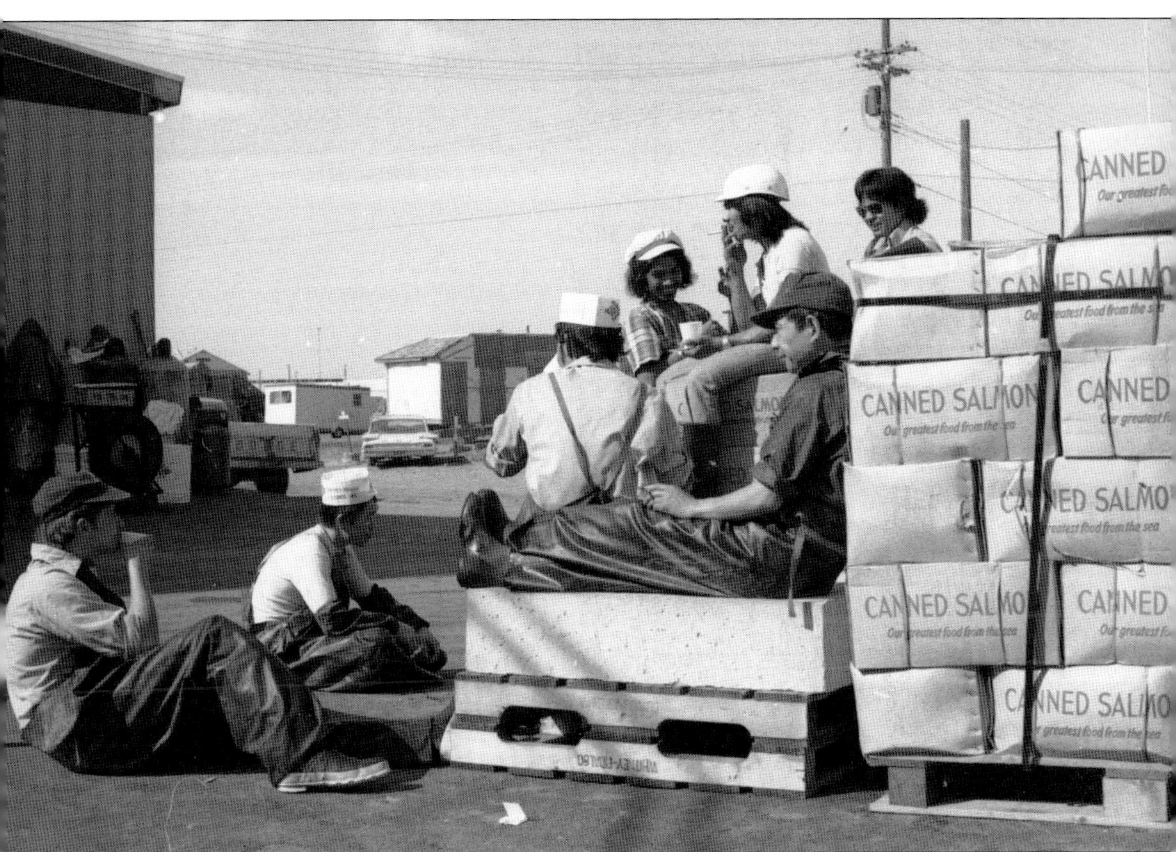

Alaska's economy became more dependent on oil through the 1970s, but other sectors remained important. Commercial fishing and canning had been features of Alaska's economic history from before Anchorage was incorporated. The Whitney-Fidalgo Cannery (operated by Whitney-Fidalgo Seafood Inc.), located along the banks of Ship Creek not far from downtown Anchorage, was the community's last operating cannery. Seen in this photograph in the early 1970s, the cannery employed a seasonal workforce, including many Filipinos who had long been central to Alaska's canning industry. Most of Alaska's canneries have historically been located well outside of Anchorage, usually in Southeast Alaska or elsewhere along the southern coast and Bristol Bay. But during the peak of the salmon runs in the summer, the Whitney-Fidalgo Cannery could receive more than 20,000 fish at a time in its hold, all of which would need to be canned in short order.

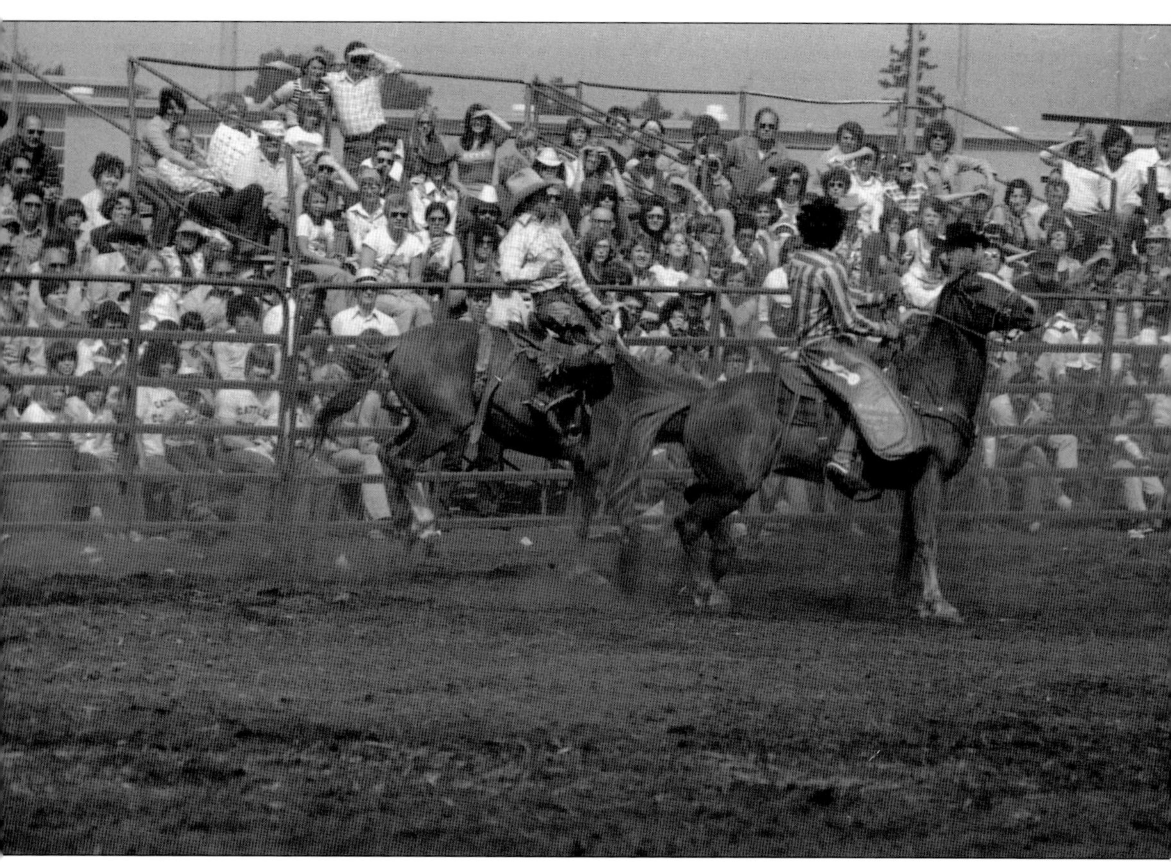

Anchorage High School (now known as West Anchorage High School) hosted a rodeo in the summer of 1977. While Alaska has never been known for its rodeo, the oil industry and pipeline construction brought thousands of Texans and Oklahomans to the state, and they, in turn, brought with them their culture and pastimes. The oil boom thus not only changed the economics of the young state, but it also changed the demographics and culture. To this day, many Alaska families trace their heritage to the American South and have roots in the oil industry.

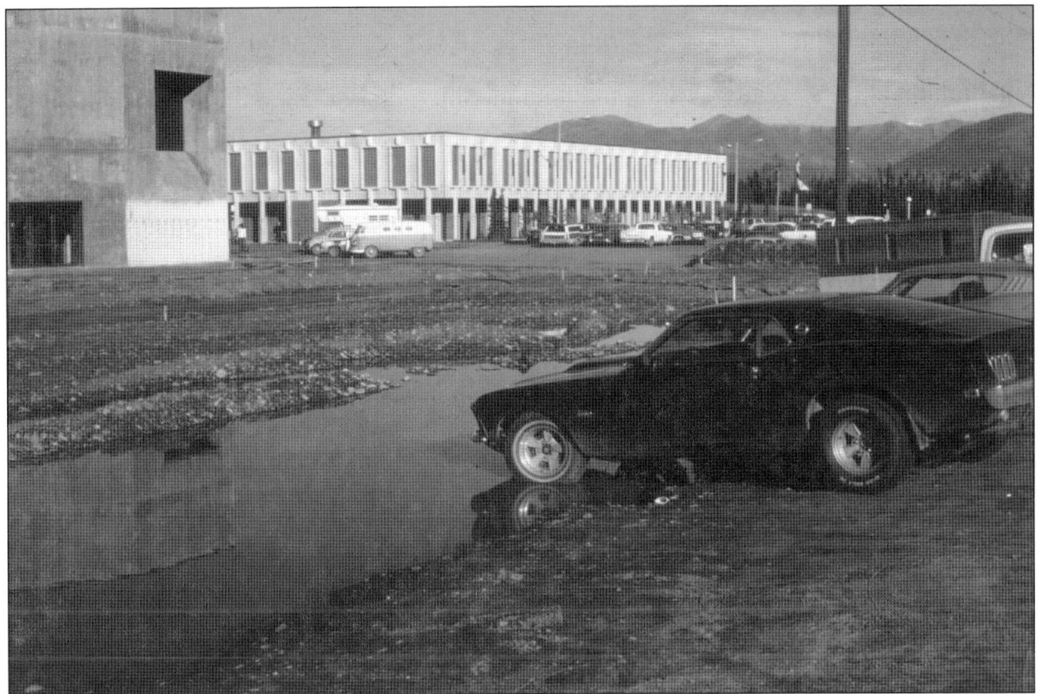

As Anchorage grew, residents demanded access to higher education. The Anchorage Community College (now the University of Alaska Anchorage) satisfied the demand. This photograph, taken in the early 1970s, shows an unpaved parking lot in the foreground, the construction of West Campus (left), and what is now Eugene Short Hall (right).

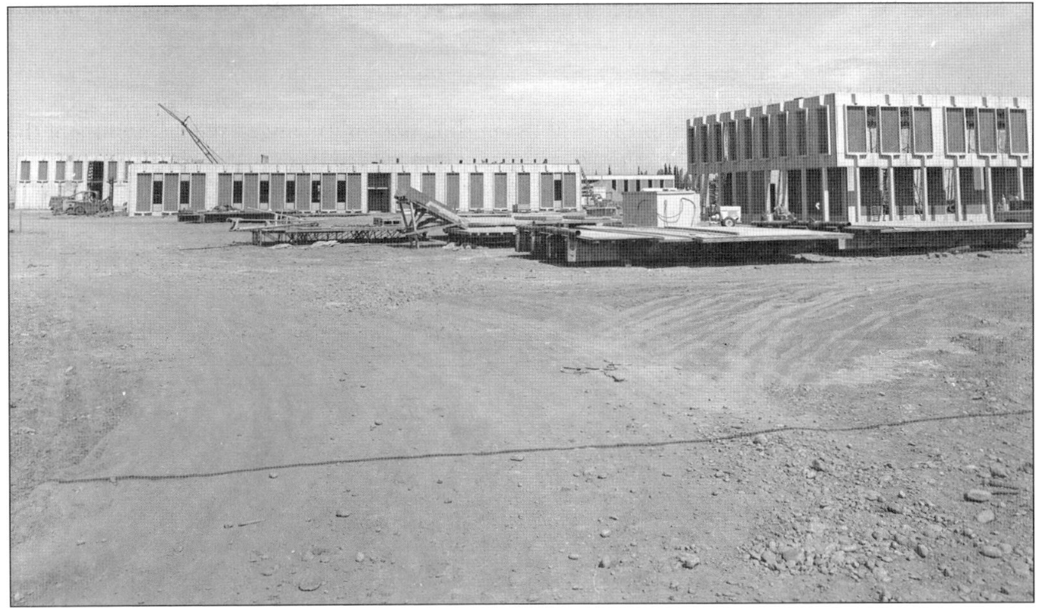

The community college added Eugene Short Hall, Sally Monserud Hall, Beatrice McDonald Hall, and Gordon Hartleib Hall to compose the quadrangle that is now the West Campus of the University of Alaska Anchorage. In 1971, these buildings were under construction, and the modern university had yet to take shape.

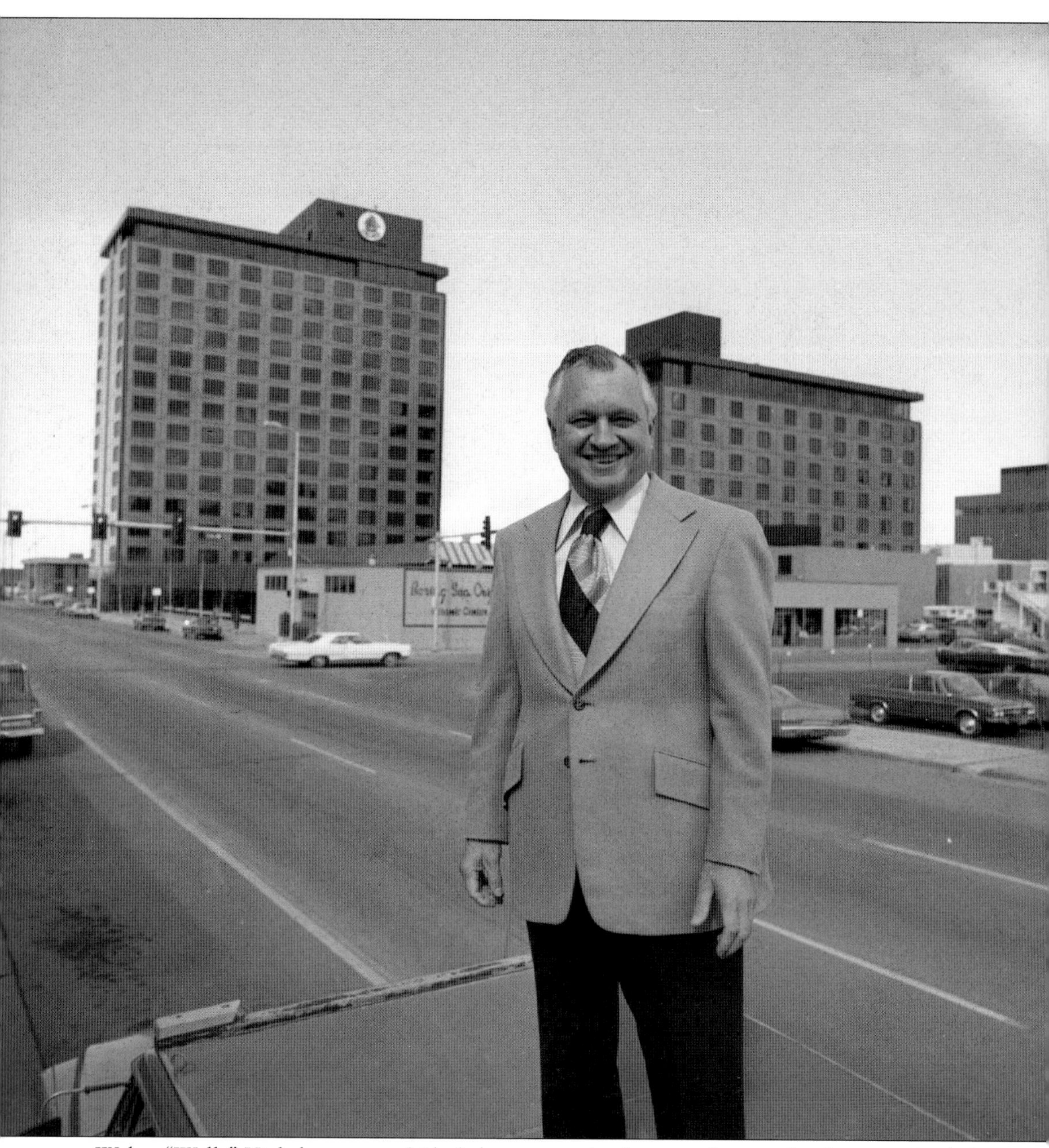

Walter "Wally" Hickel was one of Alaska's most outsized personalities and politicians. Hickel was born in Kansas and endured the Dust Bowl and Great Depression before he made his way north to Alaska. He found early work with the Alaska Railroad and eventually made a successful career in construction and real estate development before entering politics. He would go on to serve as governor and secretary of the interior under Richard M. Nixon. He is depicted here standing in front of the Hotel Captain Cook, a crown jewel of downtown Anchorage's hospitality sector. This photograph was likely taken in the mid-1970s between the construction of the second and third hotel towers. Hickel, the developer and real estate investor, was determined to rebuild after the 1964 earthquake, and the "Cook," as Alaskans refer to it, was the center of his vision for a city that rose like a phoenix from the destruction of the preceding decade.

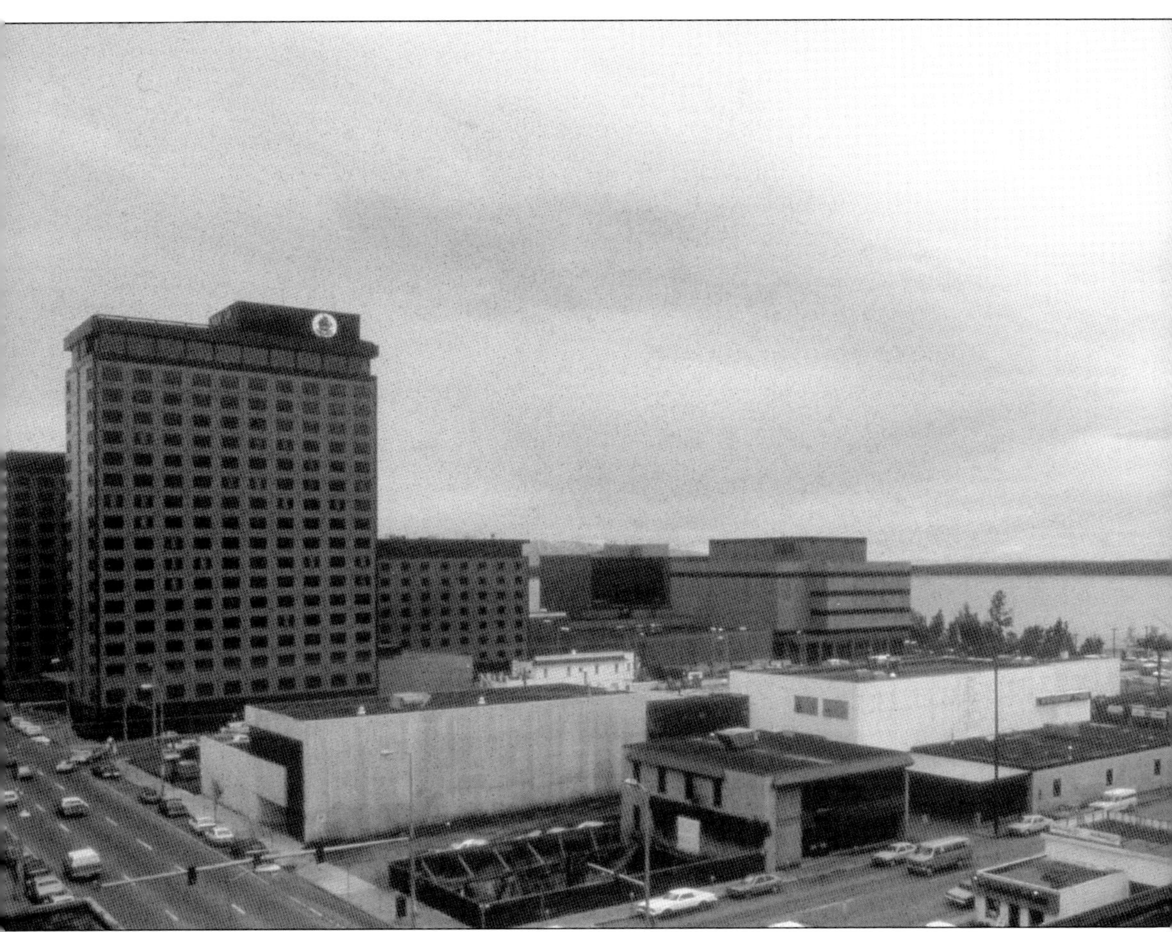

By the early 1980s, the Hotel Captain Cook was complete. With 546 rooms, the hotel hosts thousands of visitors at any given time. The hotel is a series of buildings that dominates the western edge of Anchorage's skyline. The Crow's Nest, one of Alaska's premier restaurants, resides on the top floor of Tower III and provides impressive views of Anchorage, the Cook Inlet, and the Chugach Mountains. The hotel also hosts a downstairs restaurant, a wine bar, and several retail shops. The art and décor in the hotel reflect the Pacific explorations of Capt. James Cook, taking on a late-18th-century British Empire maritime motif.

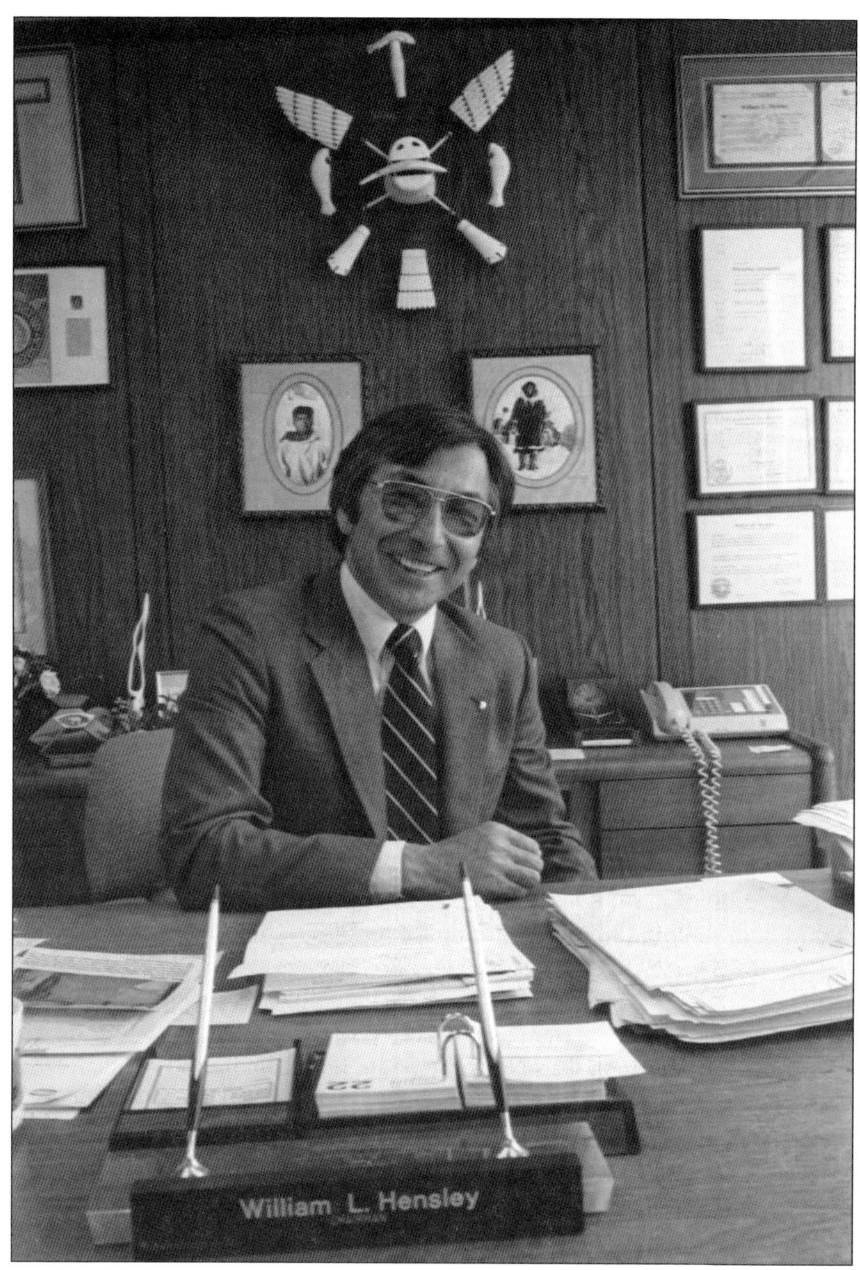

In the late 1960s and 1970s, Alaska Native leaders organized a social movement that demanded state and federal authorities recognize their rightful claims to the land. Willie Iġġiaġruk Hensley, an Iñupiaq man who grew up in rural northwest Alaska, emerged as one of the leaders of the land claims movement. Before the state could develop its resource-rich North Slope, Alaska Native people were determined to receive fair compensation and recognition for the land they had stewarded for thousands of years. The result, the Alaska Native Claims Settlement Act, was signed into law in 1971 by Pres. Richard M. Nixon. Hensley, photographed here in Anchorage, also served in the Alaska legislature and several other leadership roles in the generation to follow. ANCSA also led to the creation of Alaska Native corporations, many of which have their headquarters in Anchorage.

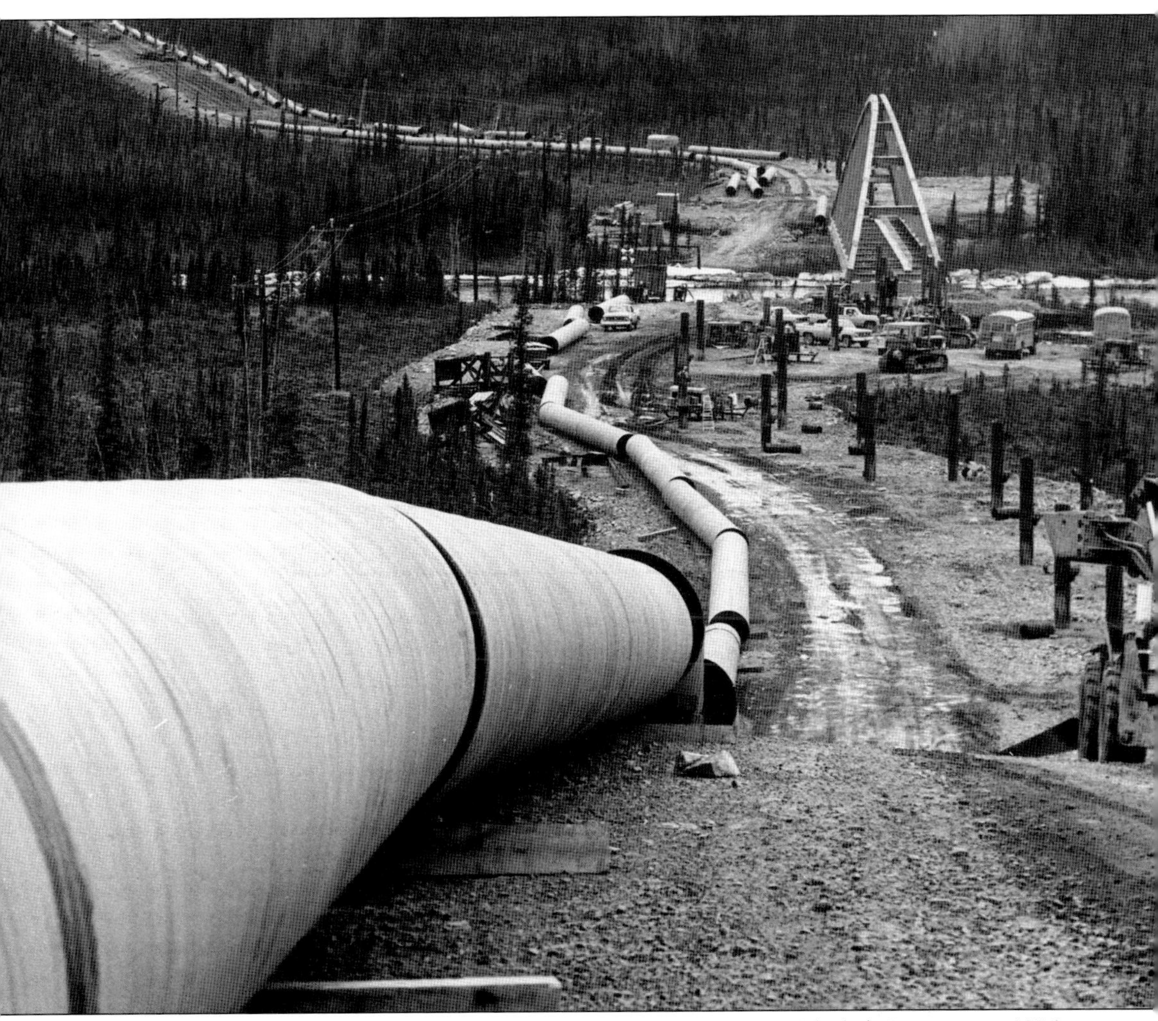

This photograph was taken along the pipeline construction route in Alaska's Interior in 1976. After the discovery of oil on Alaska's North Slope in 1968, the industry had to transport the oil roughly 800 miles to the state's southern coast to ship to markets and refineries along the West Coast and beyond. After much debate about how best to transport the oil, Alaskan and oil industry leaders proposed that the most feasible solution would be a pipeline that would start at Prudhoe Bay on the North Slope, cross the rugged Alaskan wilderness, and terminate near the ice-free port of Valdez. While TAPS does not go through Anchorage, the municipality was nonetheless central to the construction effort, as thousands of workers came through en route to the more remote construction camps. While most of these workers eventually left the state once the pipeline began transporting oil in 1977 and the construction project concluded, many others elected to stay, start families, and put down roots.

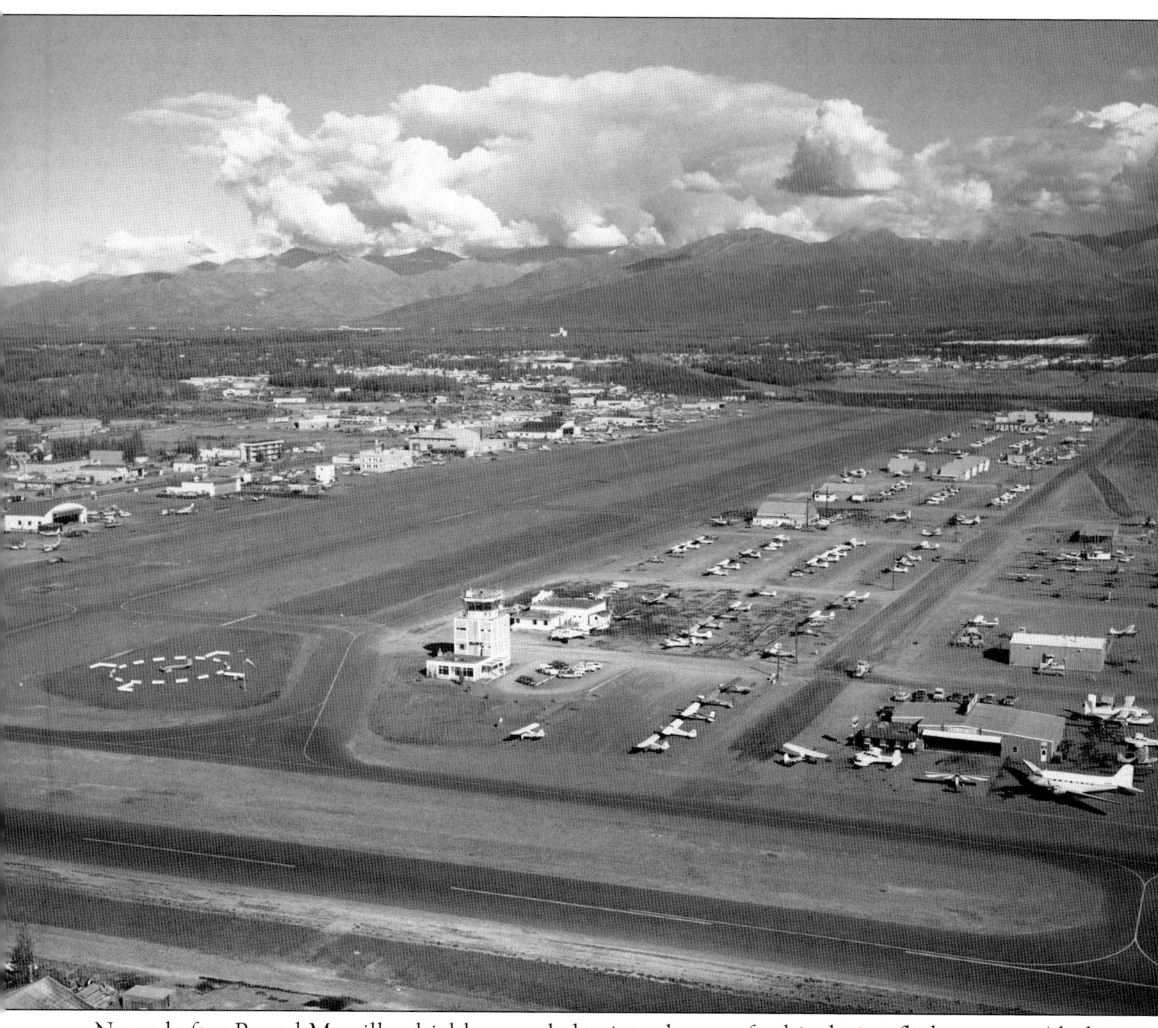

Named after Russel Merrill, a highly regarded aviator known for his daring flights across Alaska and the North Pacific, Merrill Field first opened in 1930 and served as Anchorage's only public-use airport until 1950. The control tower is visible at the center of the photograph, taken in the 1970s. Located less than two miles from downtown Anchorage, Merrill Field no longer receives jets, but it still accommodates single-engine planes and smaller aircraft such as helicopters; it also hosts a flight school. The field is owned by the Municipality of Anchorage and remains a pillar of the state's extensive aviation infrastructure.

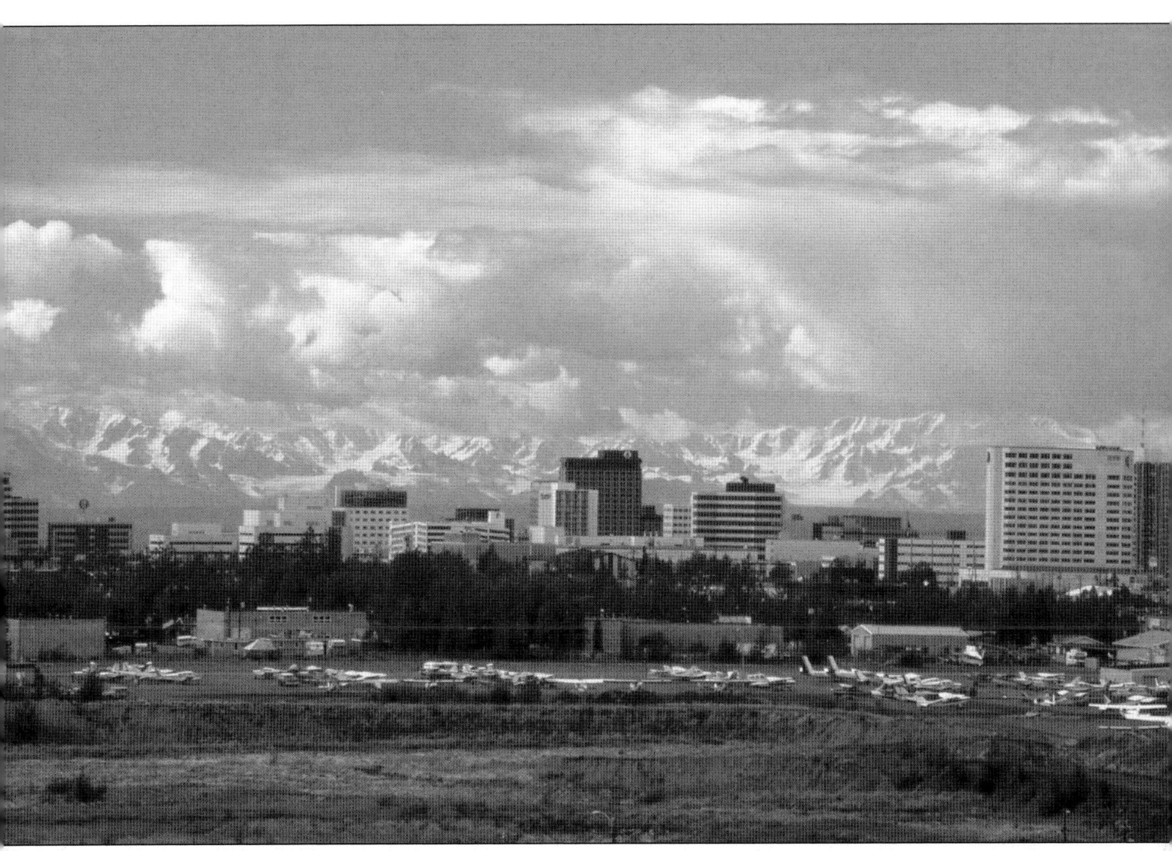

This impressive view of the Anchorage skyline was taken in 1979 from Merrill Field. The snow-capped Alaska Range is prominent in the background. By the late 1970s, Alaska had become a considerably wealthier state due to the influx of oil revenue. However, the real transformation of Anchorage's skyline and its cultural amenities would take place in the 1980s with an initiative known as Project 80s. That, too, would rely on revenue from oil.

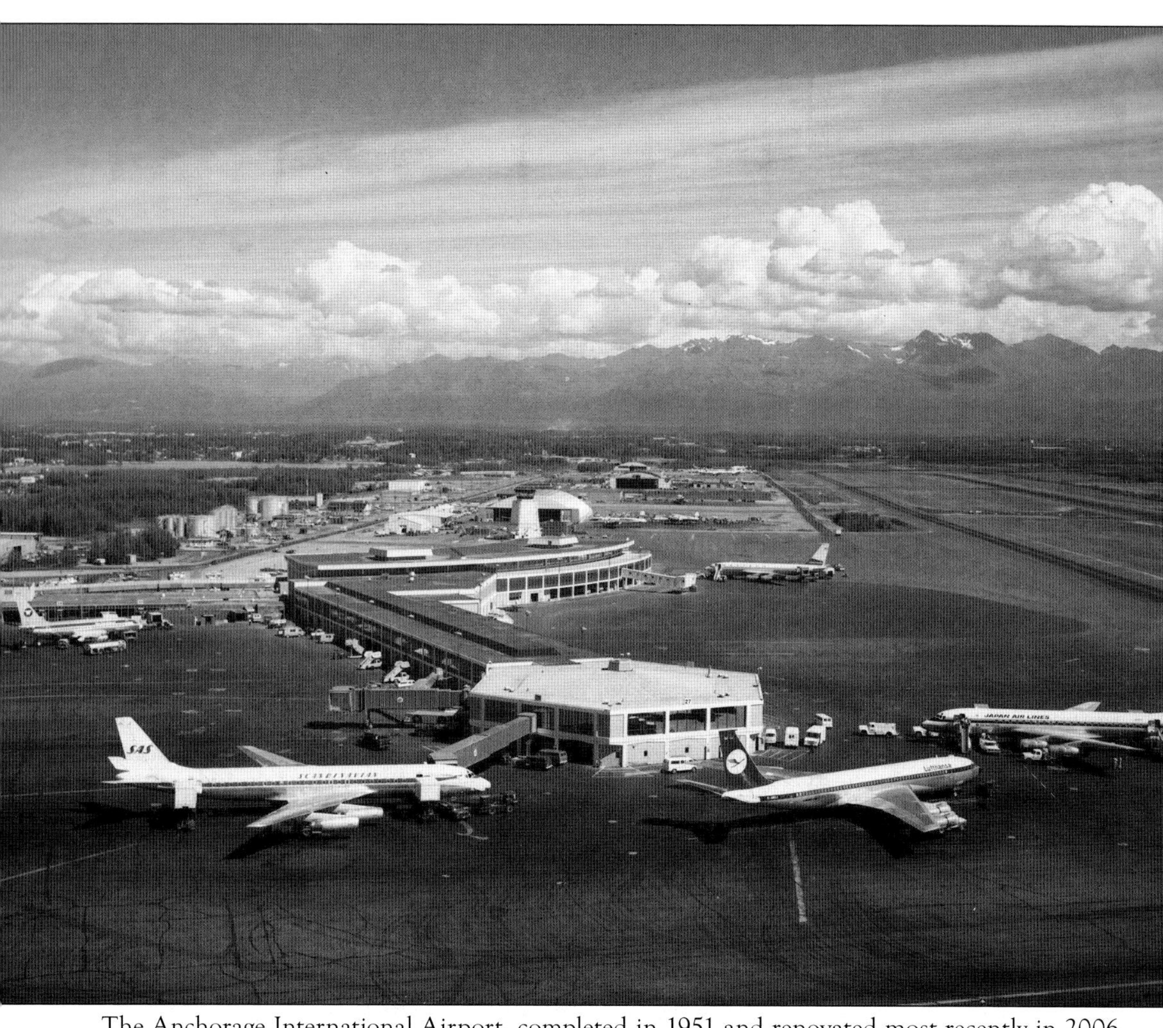

The Anchorage International Airport, completed in 1951 and renovated most recently in 2006, assumed its current name, the Ted Stevens International Airport, in 2000 by an act of the Alaska State Legislature to honor Alaska's longest-serving senator. Depicted here in 1970, the airport has become one of the busiest in the world for cargo. Anchorage is located within nine hours by air of major population centers in North America and East Asia, and it is roughly equidistant from New York City and Tokyo, Japan (around 3,500 air miles to each destination). It is possible to reach most European destinations in nine hours or less by flying over the pole. Today, the airport is central to Anchorage's economy and serves as Alaska's gateway to the world.

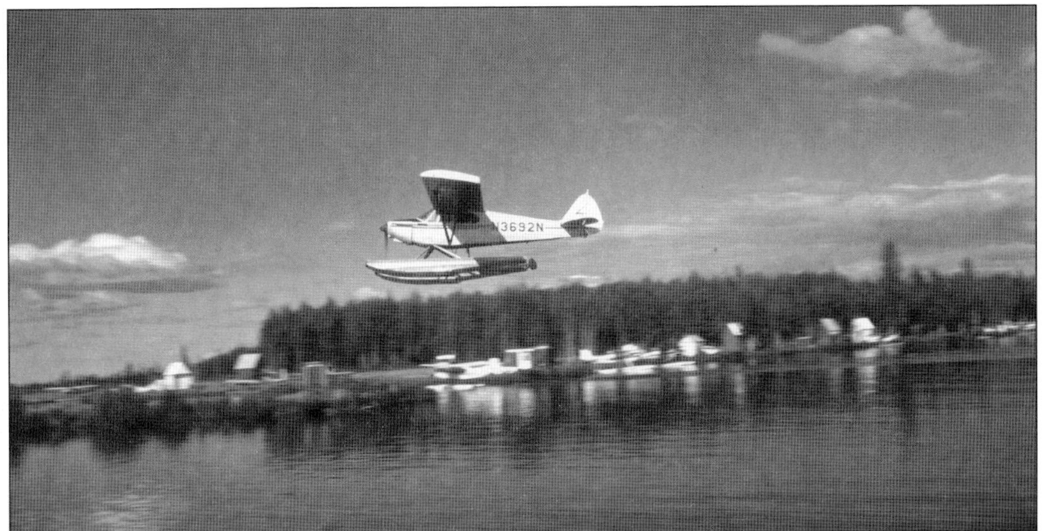

Lakes play a prominent role in the lifestyle of many Anchorage residents. Lake Spenard was once a place of retreat and recreation, but by the 1950s and 1960s, it had become the primary access point for floatplanes and off-limits to sunbathers, swimmers, boaters, and fishers. This image, taken in 1973, depicts a still common scene. The sound of floatplanes buzzing overhead and taking off from and arriving on Lake Spenard is a regular part of life in Alaska's hub city.

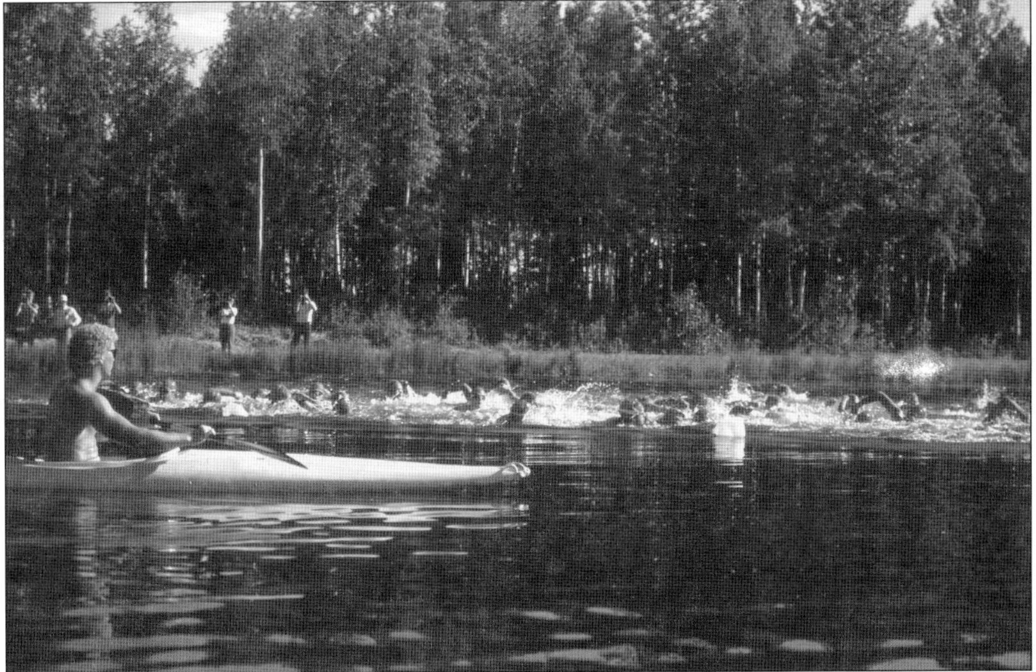

Goose Lake is adjacent to the campus of the University of Alaska Anchorage in Anchorage's U-Med District. It is among the most popular recreational lakes in Anchorage. Located along the Chester Creek trail, the lake is also convenient to reach via bicycle. The lake hosted a triathlon in the summer of 1984, as photographed here. Warm and sunny days are precious in Anchorage. Not surprisingly, sunbathers, grillers, and swimmers break for the beach when temperatures rise during Anchorage's abbreviated summer.

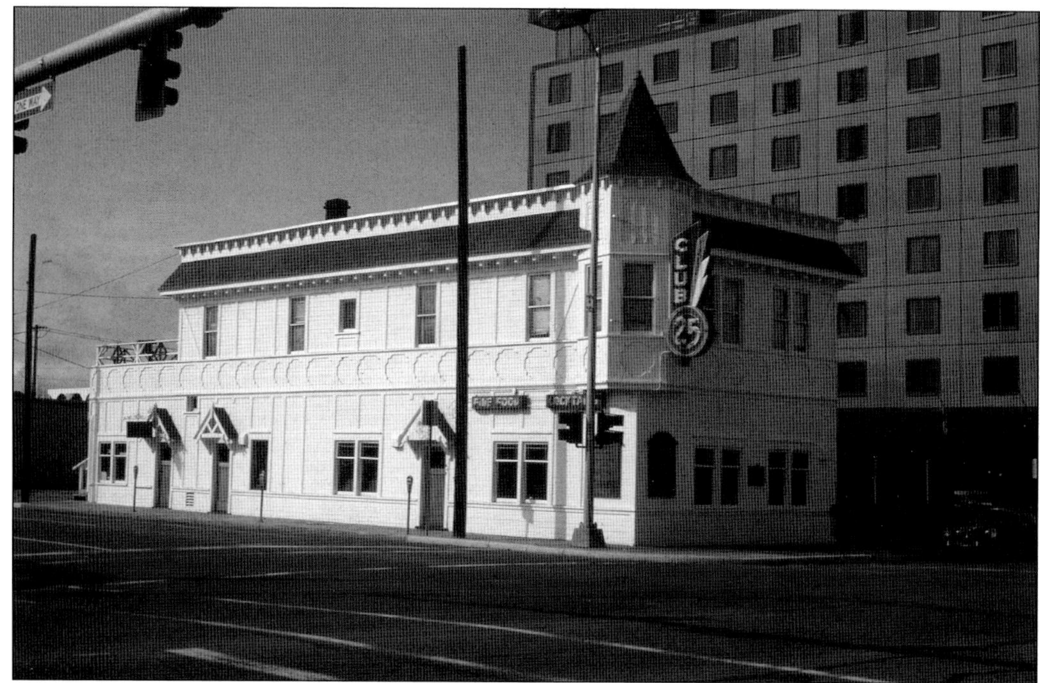

Old meets new. Upon completion of the Hotel Captain Cook, Anchorage's skyline had taken on a modern appearance. However, a few older buildings survived. Club 25 (formerly known as the Larson and Wendler Building, constructed in 1915) sat in the shadow of the newly constructed hotel. This photograph was taken in 1984, just before the building was relocated to avoid demolition to its current location at 400 D Street. It remains the oldest commercial building in Anchorage.

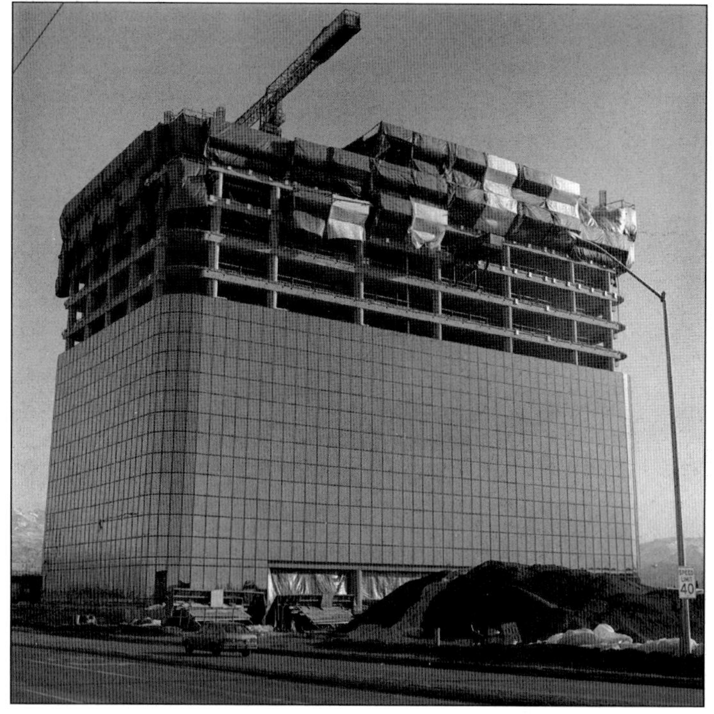

The Frontier Building, one of the most recognizable buildings in Anchorage's Midtown, was constructed in 1982. Like the downtown Atwood Building, the Frontier Building is defined by its glass exterior and modern design. Today, the building houses the Japanese Consulate, among other tenants.

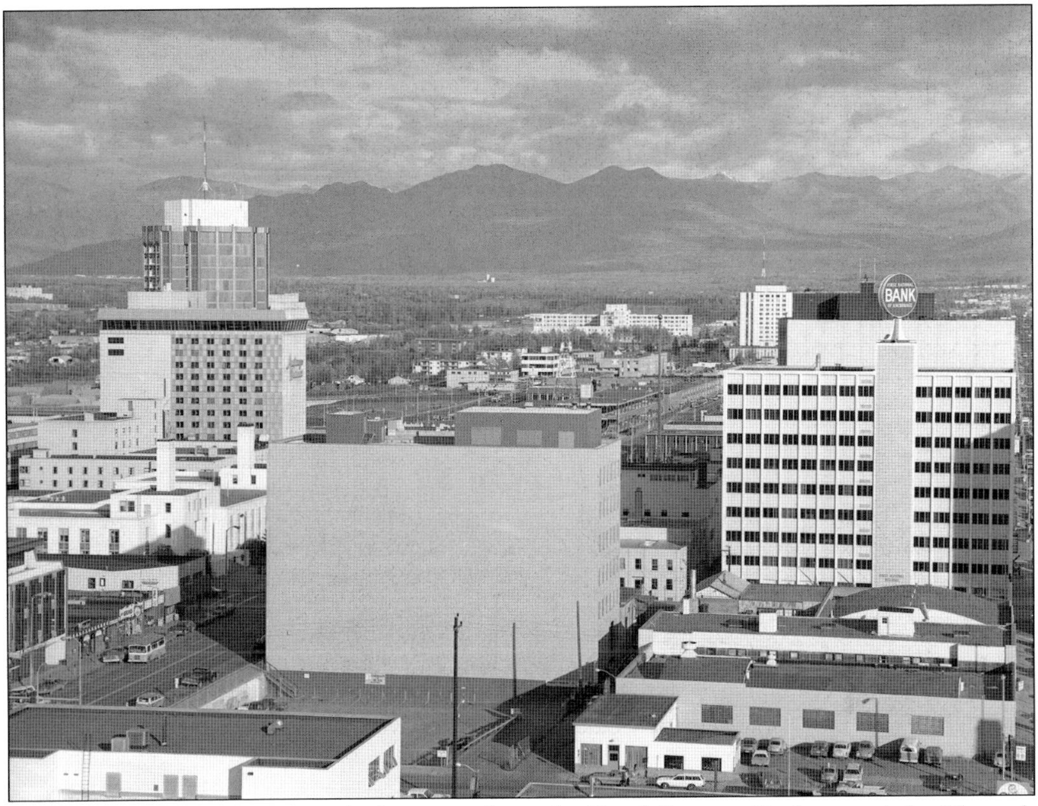

The Anchorage skyline is seen looking east from the Hotel Captain Cook toward the Chugach Mountains in the early 1980s at a time when the city was experiencing a building boom.

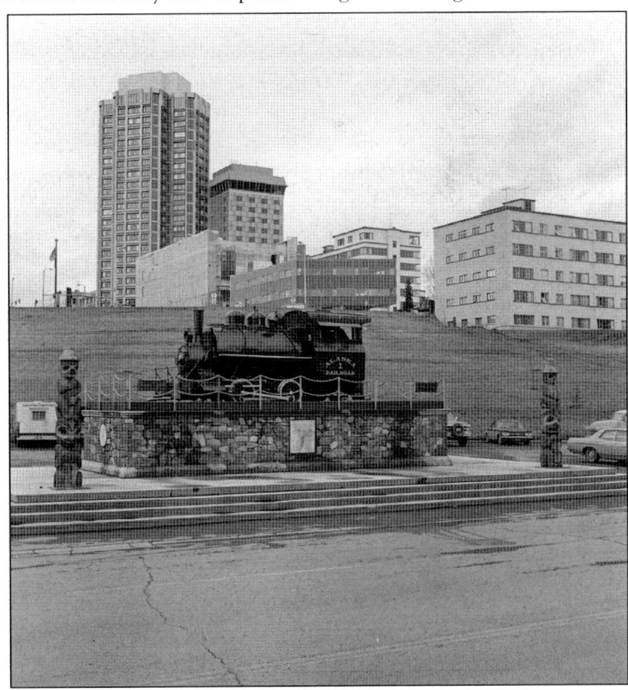

A view from the parking lot of the Alaska Railroad depot looks south toward downtown in the late 1980s. The No. 1 Alaska Railroad locomotive dominates the foreground, but a few other details are notable. Two totem poles frame the locomotive, a curious choice since totem poles are not part of the local traditional Dena'ina culture. These are more representative of Tlingit, Haida, and Tsimshian culture found in the state's Southeast. A fixture of the Anchorage skyline since the 1960s, the downtown Hilton looms in the background. At over 200 feet, it was the tallest building in Alaska until the completion of the Atwood and ConocoPhillips Buildings in the 1980s. The American flag waving to the left of the Hilton marks the Eisenhower Statehood Monument.

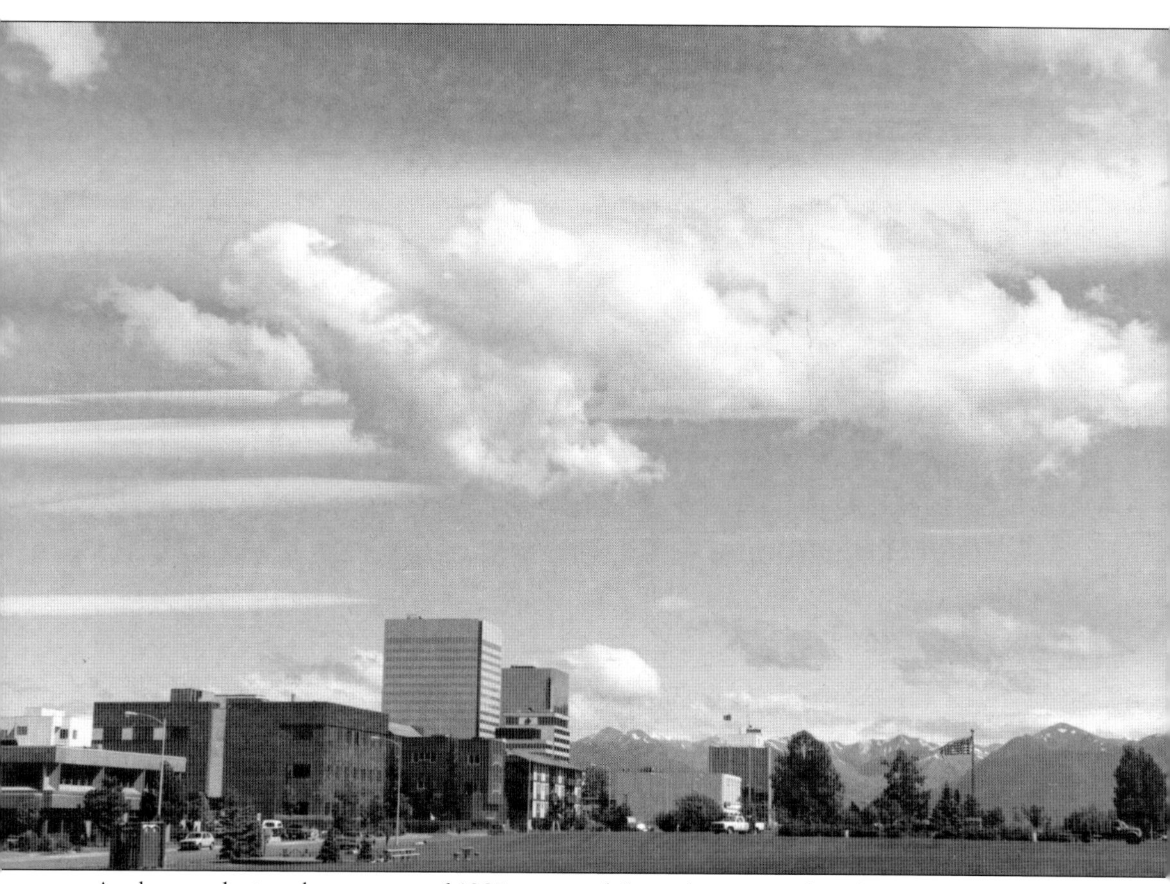

Anchorage during the summer of 1987 is viewed from the west end of the Delaney Park Strip in this view looking east toward the Chugach Mountains. The newly constructed ConocoPhillips and Robert B. Atwood Buildings are the two most prominent buildings north of the park strip. Both were completed in the 1980s and are still the two tallest office buildings in Alaska. The ConocoPhillips Building (296 feet) houses the Alaska business operations for the Houston-based energy corporation. ConocoPhillips has long been a primary player in the development of Alaska's oil and gas. The Atwood Building (265 feet), meanwhile, hosts various government offices and public workers for the State of Alaska. While Juneau is Alaska's capital city, more state employees call Anchorage home; many of them report to work each day in the Atwood Building.

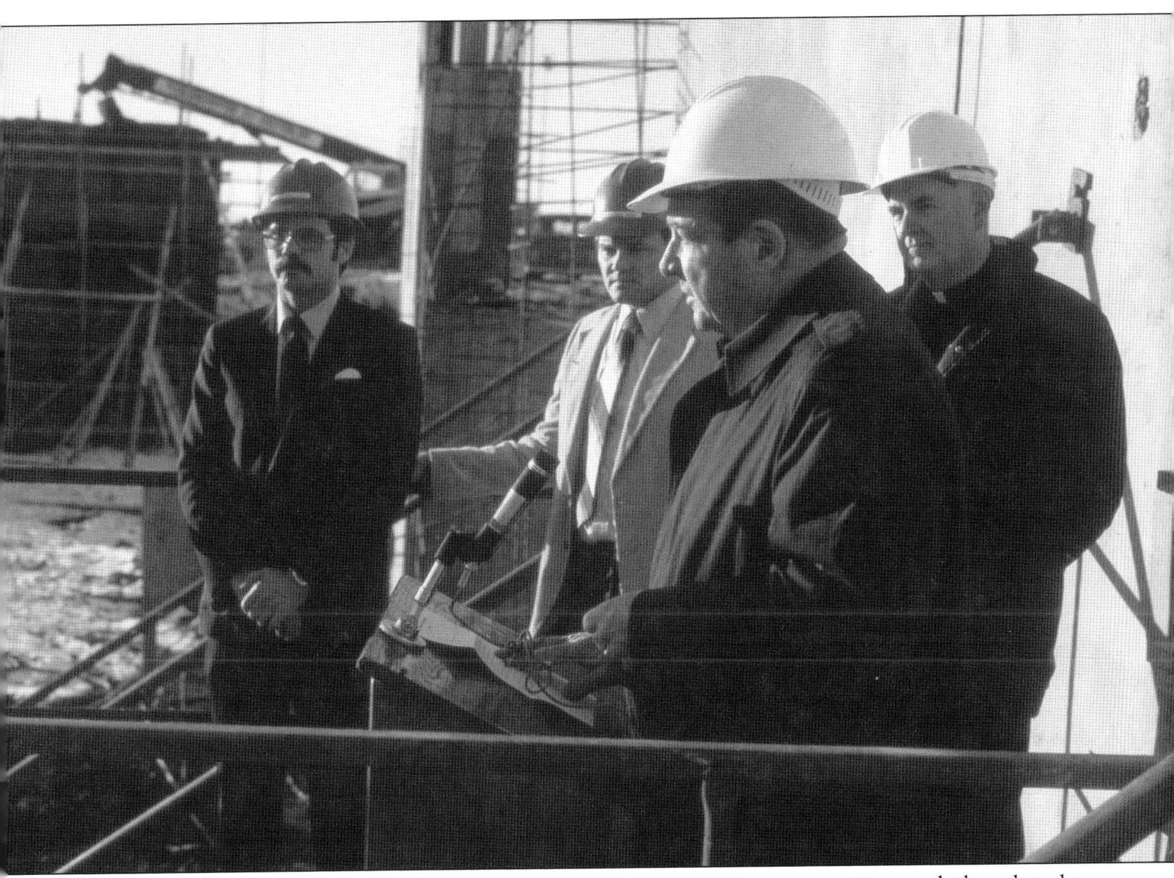

Anchorage mayor George Sullivan, in the foreground, initiates construction and then breaks ground for what would become the Sullivan Arena as municipal leaders gather in the spring of 1981. Flush with money from the development of North America's largest oil field on the state's North Slope, Anchorage and other Alaskan communities endeavored to improve their infrastructure, modernize their amenities, and build public works that would be the envy of most any other American city or town. Anchorage's population had increased from about 50,000 in 1970 to nearly 200,000 at the beginning of the 1980s. The staggering population growth required that the municipality invest to ensure a high standard of living and satisfy the demand of new residents who may have arrived from places with more entertainment and cultural offerings.

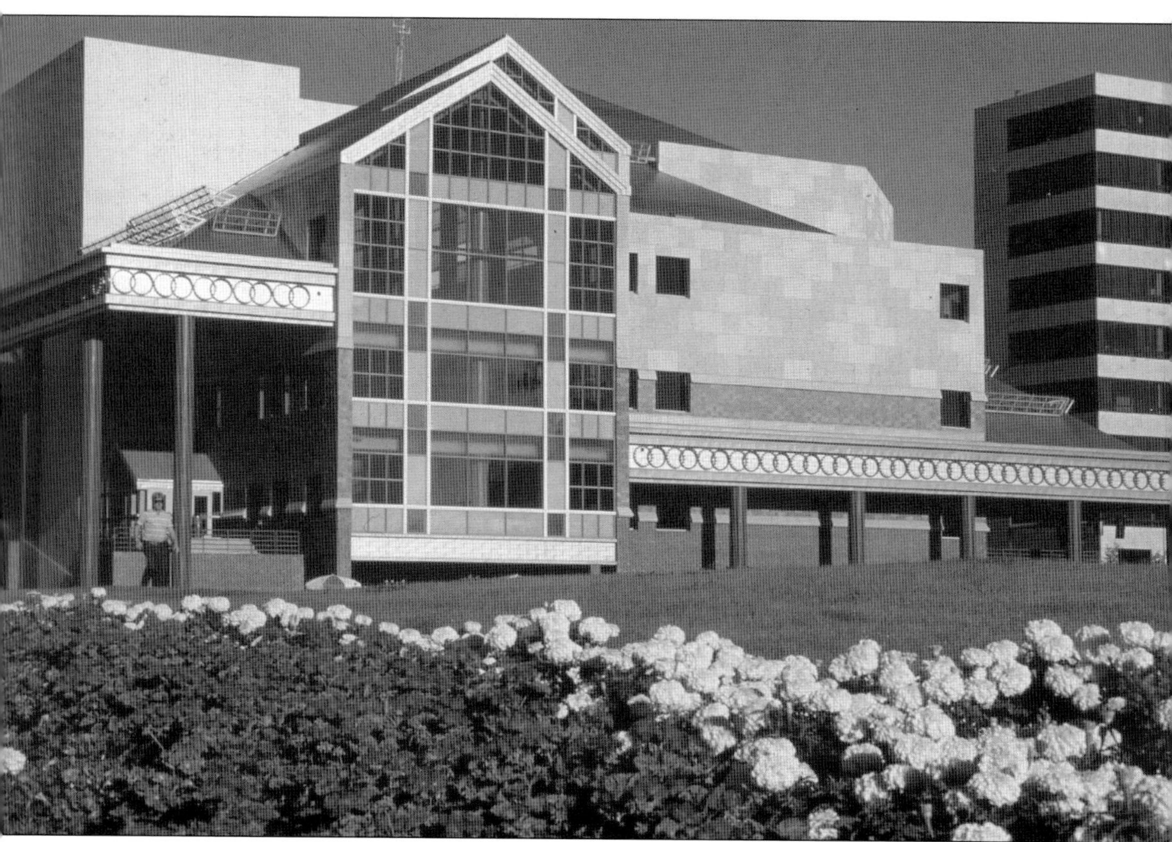

This photograph depicts the just-completed Alaska Performing Arts Center (PAC) in the summer of 1988. The construction of the PAC began as Alaska's economic fortunes had dwindled. The falling price of oil led to a significant economic decline throughout the state in the mid-1980s, thus ending an impressive cycle of economic growth that began with the discovery of oil on Alaska's North Slope in the late 1960s and continued broadly through the early 1980s. Still, the PAC opened in 1988 as Alaskans celebrated their new world-class facility for the arts. The PAC contains two separate theaters, one with 340 seats and the other with 700. The crown jewel of the facility, however, is the Evangeline Atwood Concert Hall, with 2,100 seats.

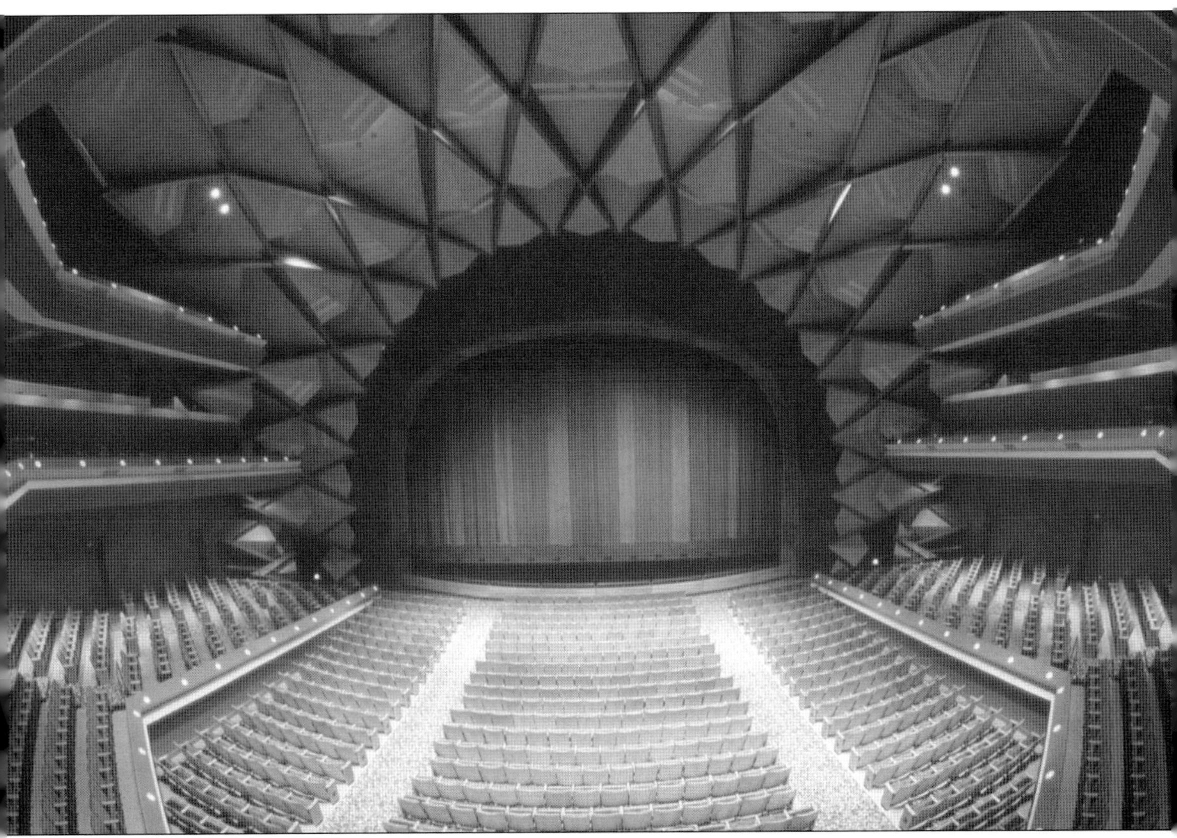

This is an inside view of the Atwood Concert Hall around the time the PAC opened in the late 1980s. With over 2,000 seats, the concert hall remains a premier venue for the performing arts in Alaska and regularly hosts national and international acts. Anchorage residents are grateful for well-known acts that make the trip north and regularly reward them with sold-out shows.

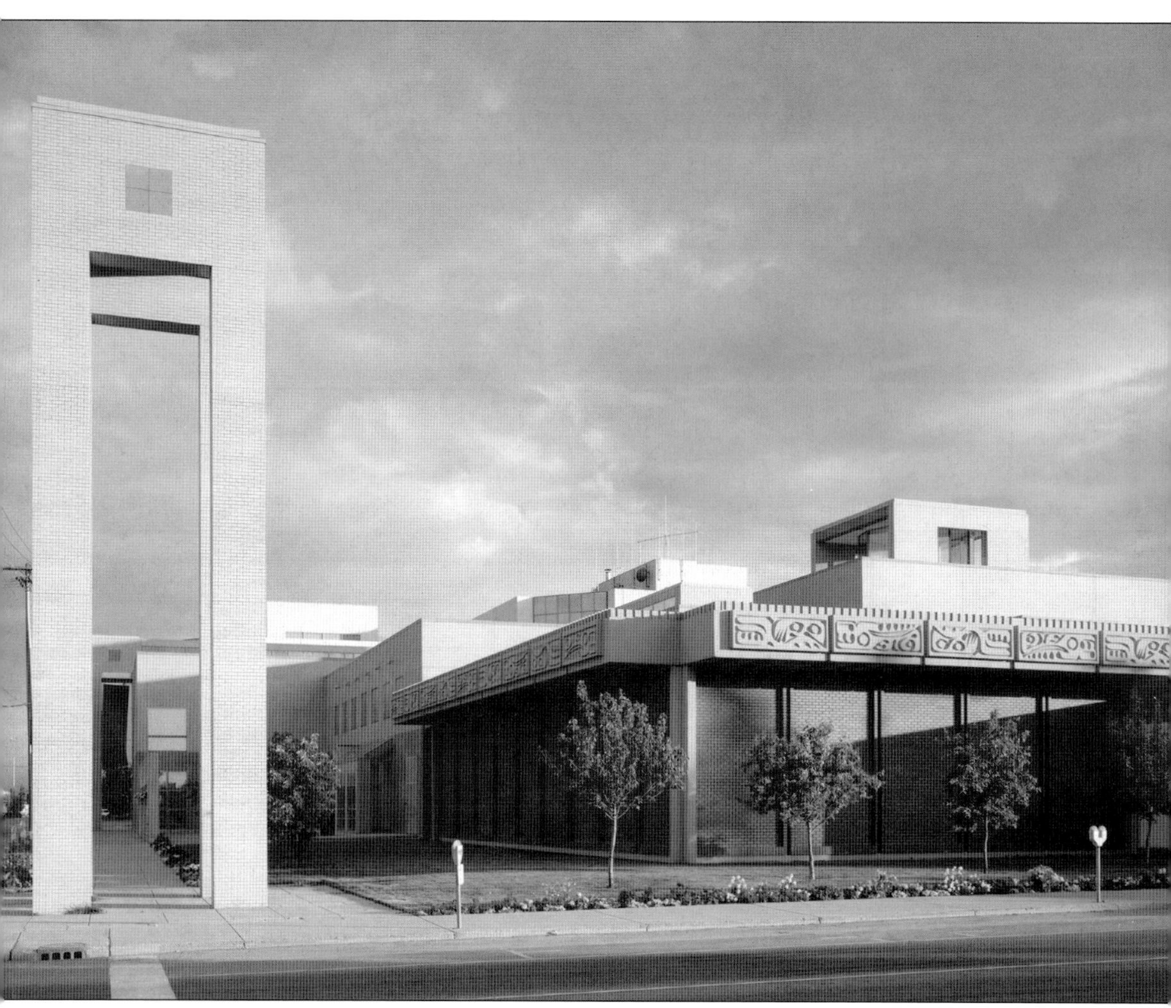

The Anchorage Museum opened in 1968 in partnership with the Cook Inlet Historical Society. The museum has gone through several renovations, including an extensive one completed in 2009 that added over 80,000 square feet to the building. It has served as a cornerstone of the community's arts and cultural scene with over 27,000 objects ranging from historical artifacts to rare books and prints to a world-class collection of art that emphasizes the unique culture and environment of Alaska and the Circumpolar North. The museum has, since 1992, also served as the home for the Smithsonian Institution's Arctic Studies Center, an affiliate of the National Museum of Natural History.

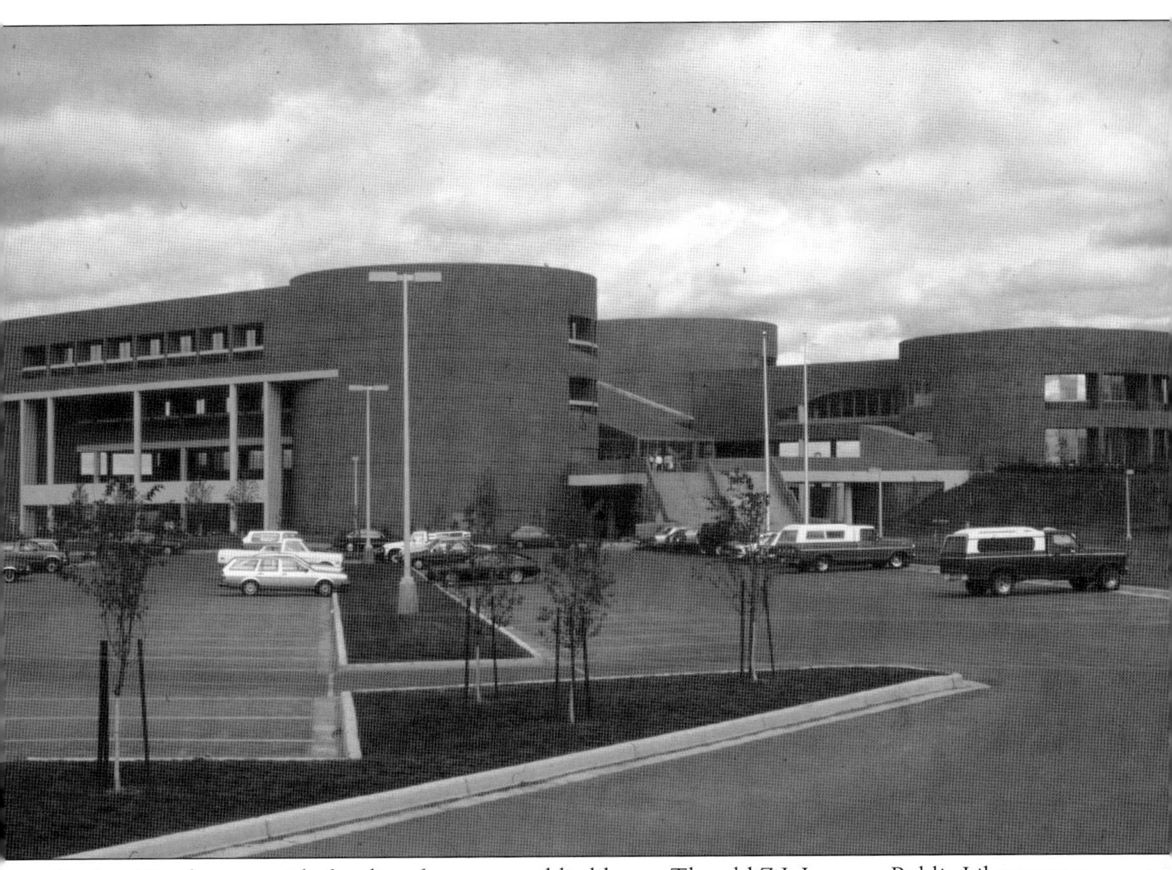

Project 80s also put aside funding for a new public library. The old Z.J. Loussac Public Library was downtown on the northeast corner of Fifth Avenue and F Street, across from where the William A. Egan Convention Center is located today. The updated library, photographed here in 1987, is also known as the Loussac Library. The new Loussac Library was completed in 1986 and hosts four levels covering roughly 140,000 square feet. Supreme Court justice Sandra Day O'Connor visited the library in 1987 to celebrate its first year of operations. The public library is central to Anchorage's civic life, even serving as the official chamber for the Municipal Assembly meetings. The library is named after Zachariah Joshua Loussac, a Russian-born Jewish émigré who served as the mayor of Anchorage between 1948 and 1951. Loussac was also an early philanthropist in the community who financially backed several projects in the 1940s and 1950s, including the construction of the first library.

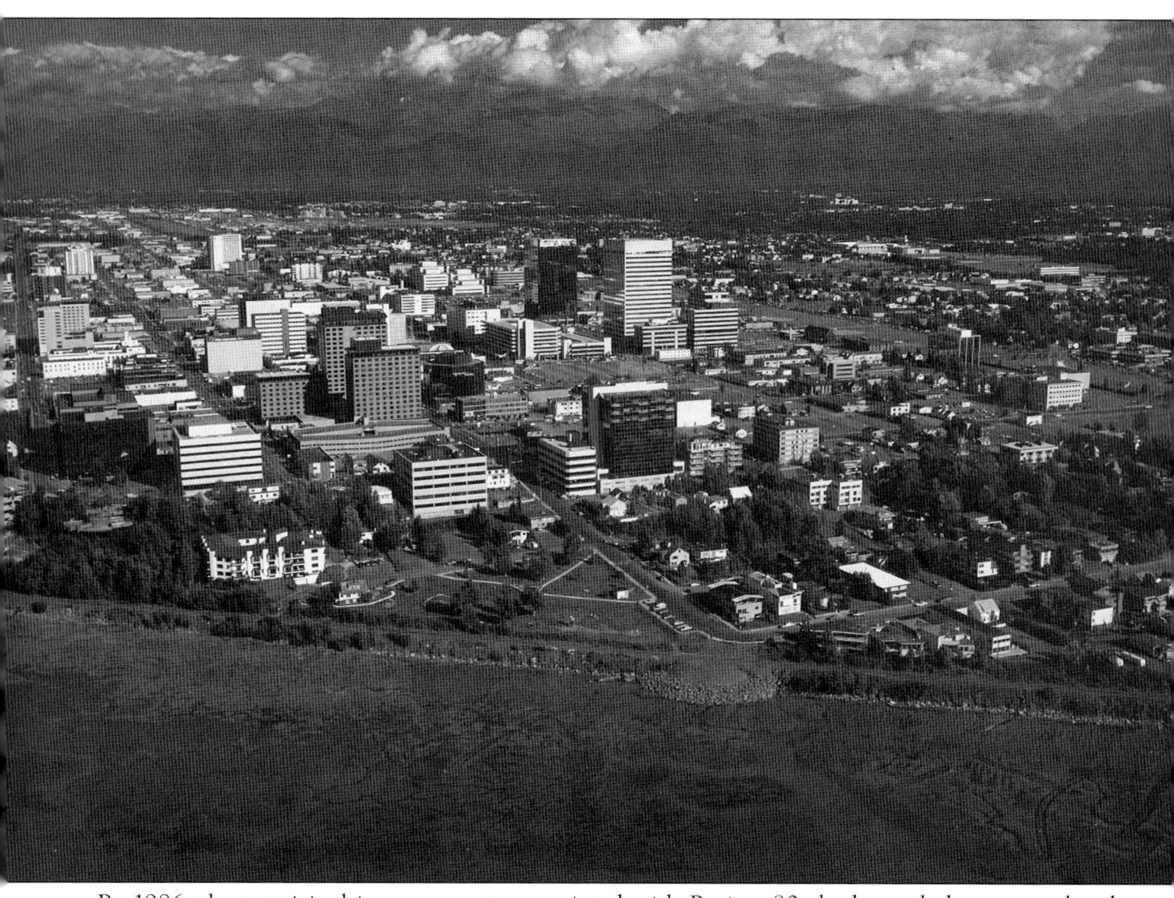

By 1986, the municipal improvements associated with Project 80s had mostly been completed, and the two tallest buildings in Alaska, the Atwood and ConocoPhillips Buildings, dominated the southern end of downtown, abutting the Delaney Park Strip. The two buildings, with their hundreds of white-collar and professional workers, have fortified Anchorage's downtown economy for over 40 years. Tourism, as exemplified by the three towers of Hotel Captain Cook, are on view at the center of the photograph. Elderberry Park, with its access to the Tony Knowles Coastal Trail, is visible in the lower foreground, and the neighborhood of Bootlegger's Cove, characterized by its precarious location on the mudflats of Knik Arm and array of low-rise condos and apartments, is seen to the park's lower right.

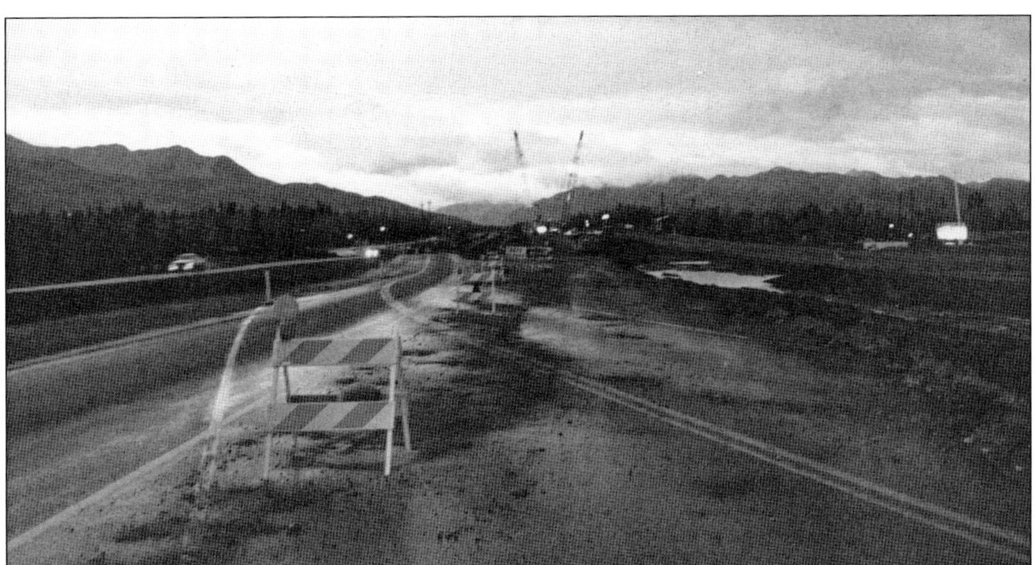

Downtown improvements and Project 80s were not the only major upgrades that Anchorage experienced in the 1980s. As the community continued to sprawl southward, the Huffman business corridor and an increasing number of subdivisions gave South Anchorage a suburban look and feel. Workers took pride in their accomplishments during the construction season of 1984 and had a little fun on the job, too.

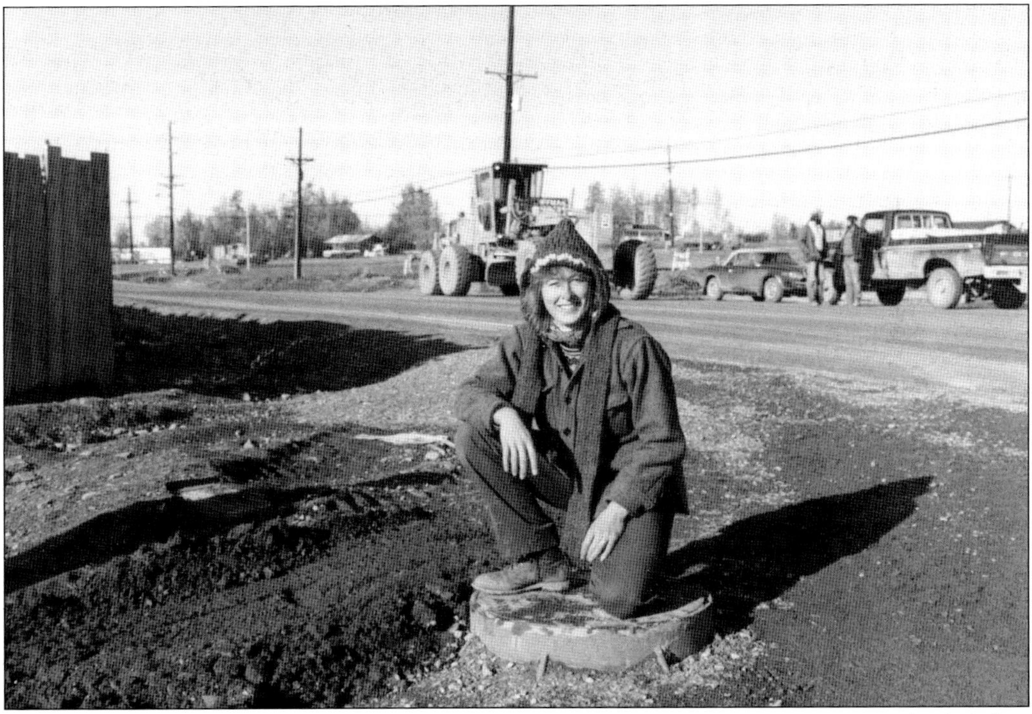

Ingrid Anderson, a grade checker, kneels over a manhole as the sewage system is built below Huffman Road in South Anchorage. The construction season is short and intense in Alaska. This crew was still busy at work in the late summer or early fall of 1984, racing to complete the improvements before the ice set and the snow fell.

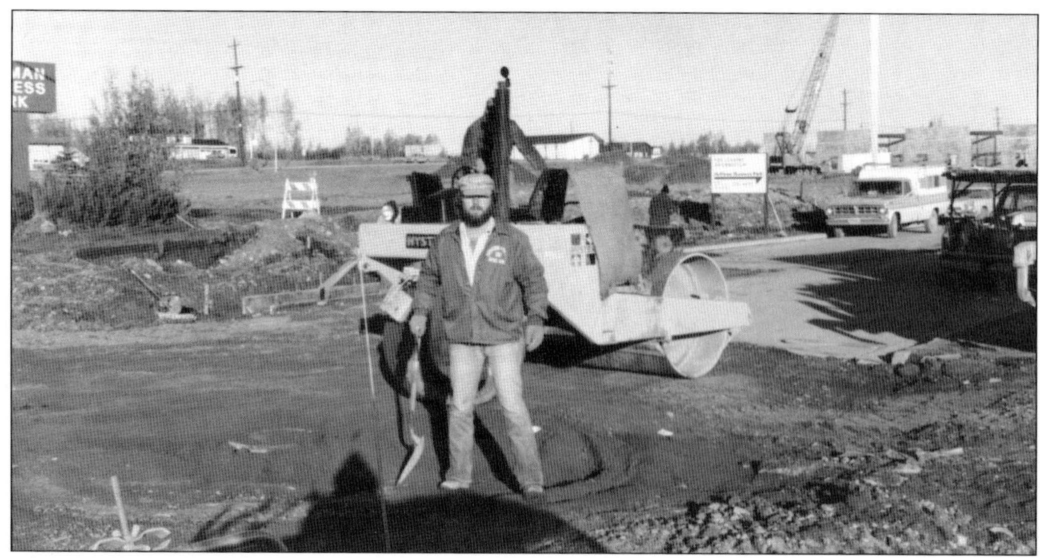

Chuck Pubanz (top) works with a shovel on the interchange at the Huffman business district while Tim Bull (below) steers a Hyster vehicle to even out Huffman Road before it is paved, anticipating a heavily trafficked area. Most of Anchorage's commercial activity occurs along discrete corridors moving from the north (downtown) to the south (Huffman business district). These business and commercial districts, except downtown and perhaps Spenard to some extent, are built for automotive travel and are not very pedestrian friendly. Residents of Anchorage sometimes joke that the fanciest restaurants and most upscale retail outlets are unassumingly tucked away in one of the many nondescript strip malls. In this regard, Anchorage resembles other cities and towns with populations that boomed in the post–World War II decades. These communities are usually more dependent on car travel and tend to have low population densities and few walkable neighborhoods.

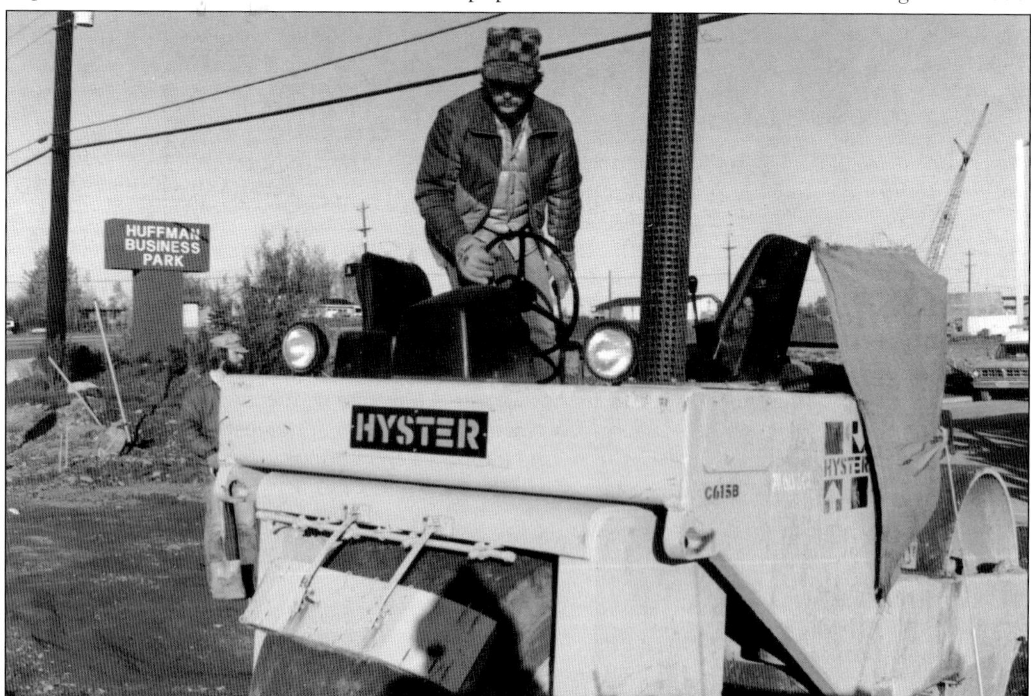

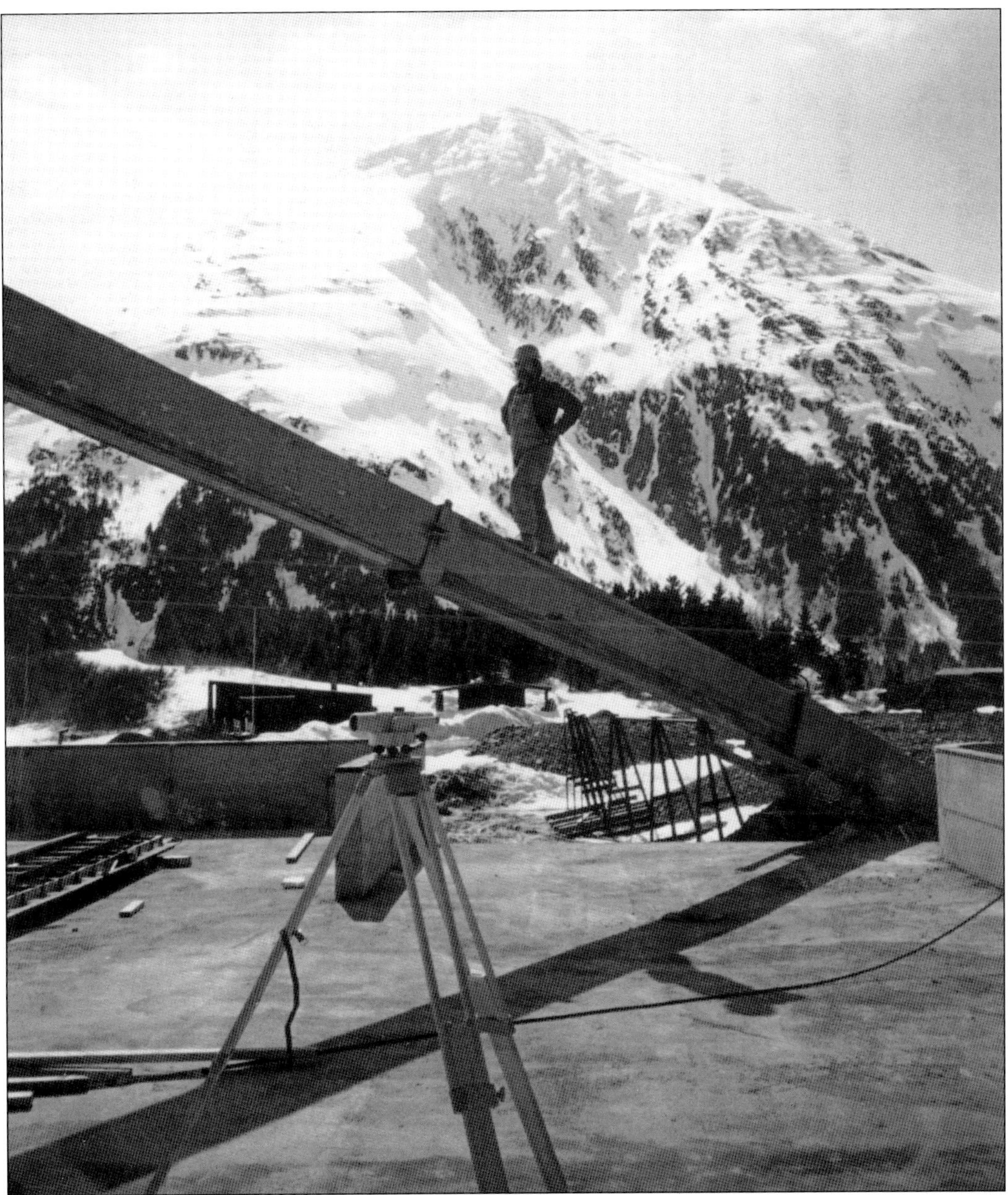

This photograph, from the Johnny Irons Collection, depicts a crane operator who fearlessly strolls up the crane boom with the snowy Chugach Mountains looming just to the south. Unlike the previous four photographs, this one is undated, and the precise location is not identified. However, it was likely taken during the spring in the mid-1980s in Girdwood.

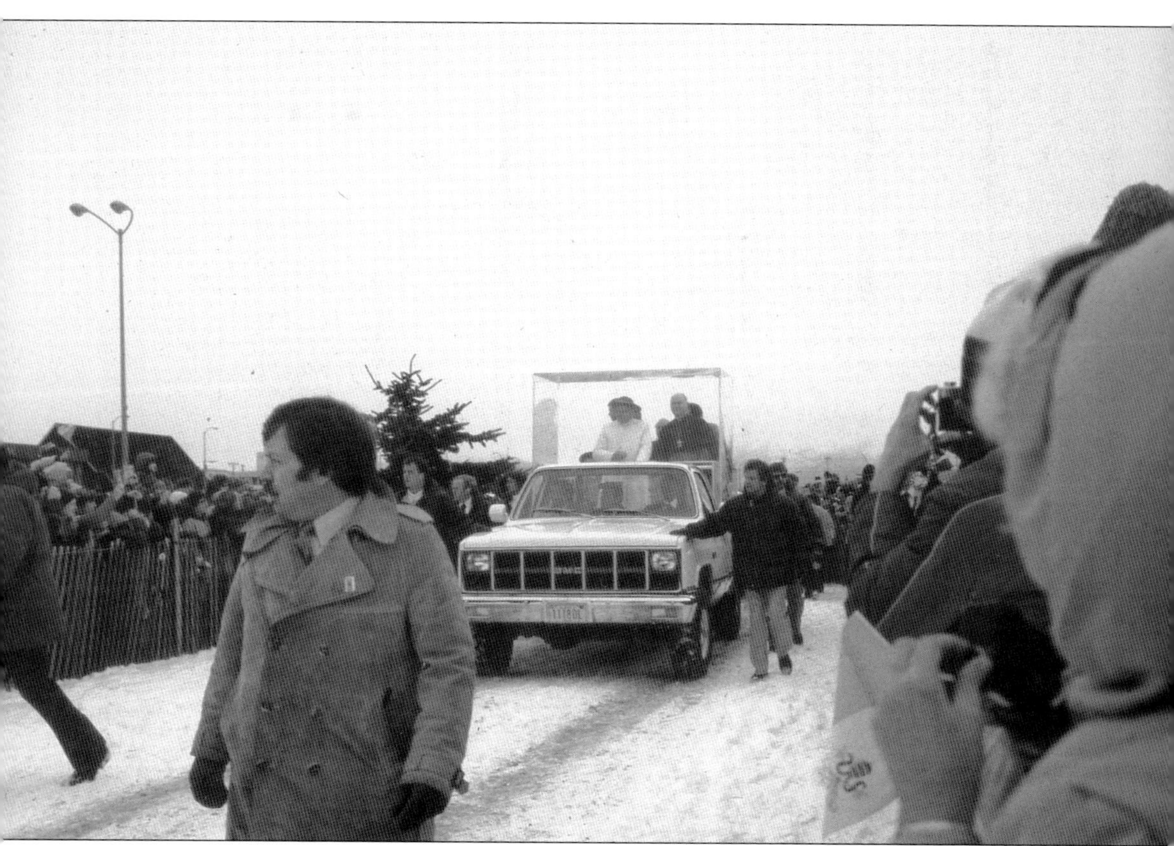

As Anchorage boomed in the late 1970s and early 1980s, national and even international figures expressed greater interest in Alaska, and some even paid its largest community a visit. Pope John Paul II was among the most notable to make the trip. He visited in February 1981 and is seen in this photograph greeting thousands of Alaskans in a modified GMC pickup truck that doubled as a "popemobile" for the day. Nearly 40,000 people attended Mass with Pope John Paul II on the Delaney Park Strip in downtown Anchorage on February 26, 1981. His stop in Alaska was part of a broader Pacific "Peace Pilgrimage" that included stops in Japan, the Philippines, and Guam. He also stopped in Fairbanks. Upon arriving at the airport in Anchorage, Pope John Paul II was greeted by Alaska Native women who gifted him a fur-trimmed parka, which he graciously wore much of the time over his white garments.

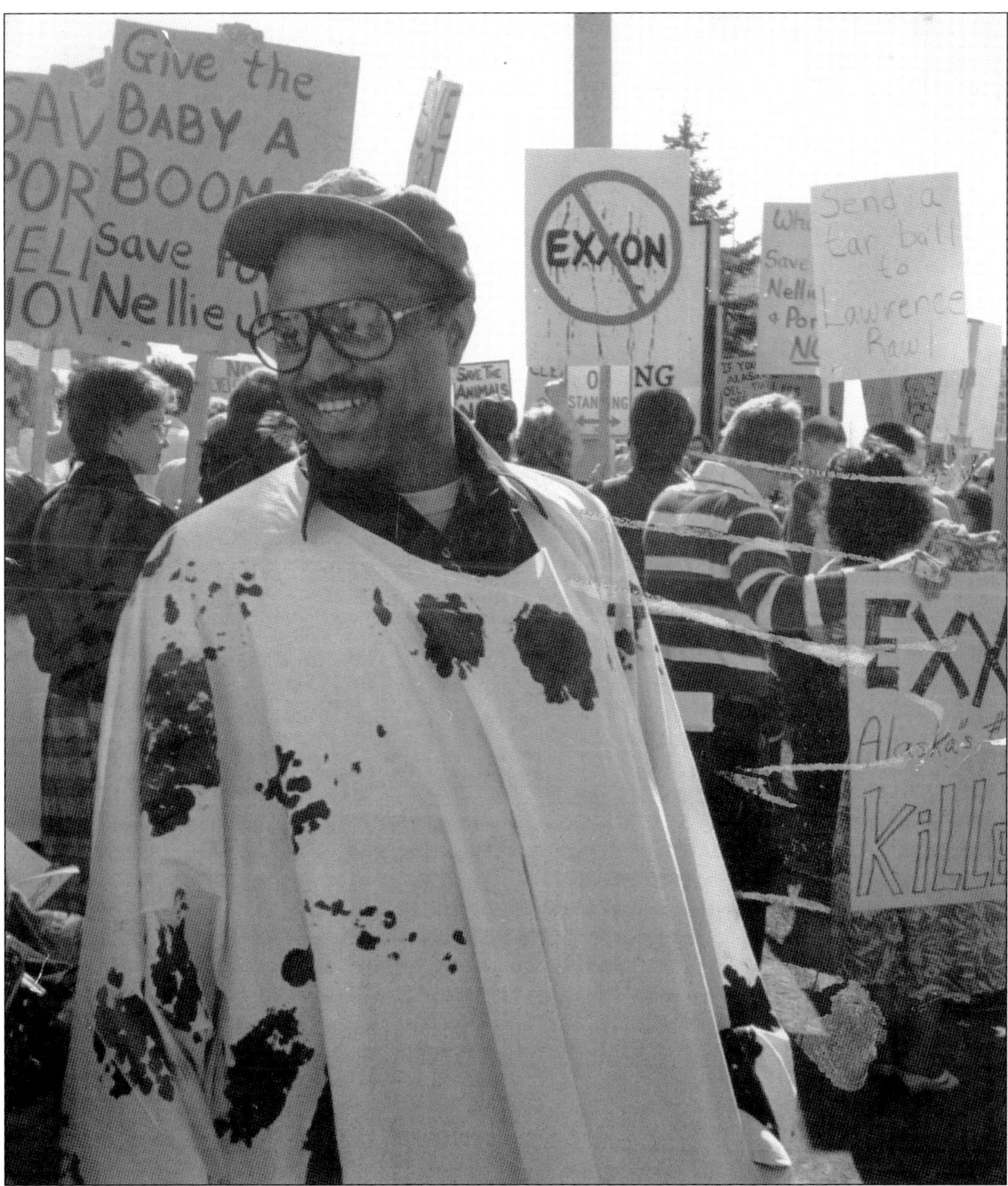

March 24, 1989, is a date that is almost as indelible to Alaskans as March 27, 1964. On that day, the oil tanker *Exxon Valdez* ran aground on Bligh Reef in Prince William Sound. The tanker spilled roughly 11 million gallons of oil into the sound, making it the largest environmental disaster of its kind in American history to that point. Alaskans faced difficult questions about their relationship with the oil industry and the impact that such a disaster had on the state's arguably most precious resources: its natural beauty and wildlife. Many resented the power that the oil industry had accumulated over the years and began to push back. Community activist Cal Williams attended a protest wearing a white sheet covered in black "oil" stains. He was not alone. The reputation of the industry declined as Alaskans grappled with the staggering environmental and financial costs of the cleanup effort. This photograph was taken shortly after the oil spill in 1989 at a rally protesting the Exxon Mobil Corporation, one of the large oil developers in Alaska.

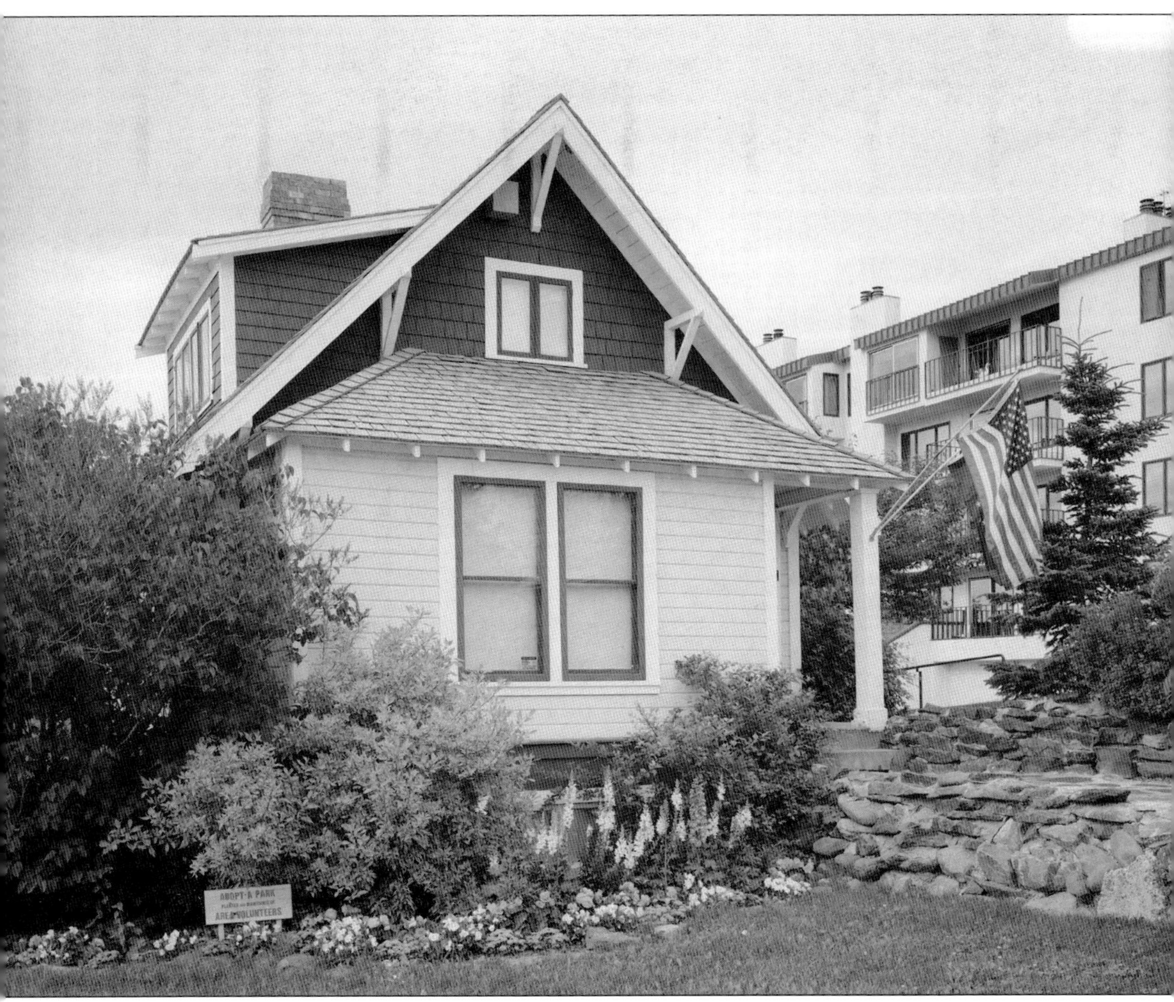

This is a photograph of the Oscar Anderson House at 420 M Street in the late 1980s. The Oscar Anderson House is the first framed wood house in Anchorage. Its construction dates to 1915, and it is found adjacent to Elderberry Park in downtown Anchorage, near the Bootlegger's Cove neighborhood. Oscar Anderson was a Swedish-born immigrant who arrived in the United States in 1901 and then in Anchorage in 1915. He was among the first European settlers to call the area home. Anderson worked several jobs over the course of his life in Alaska, including with the Alaska Engineering Commission, as a small business owner, airline operator, newspaper manager, and even as an oil driller and sawmill operator. He passed away in 1974. The municipality purchased the home and worked with the National Register of Historic Places to list the home in 1978. Just behind the house, which is now a modest museum open to the public, modern condos and apartments are visible. Anchorage is a city that blends the old and new.

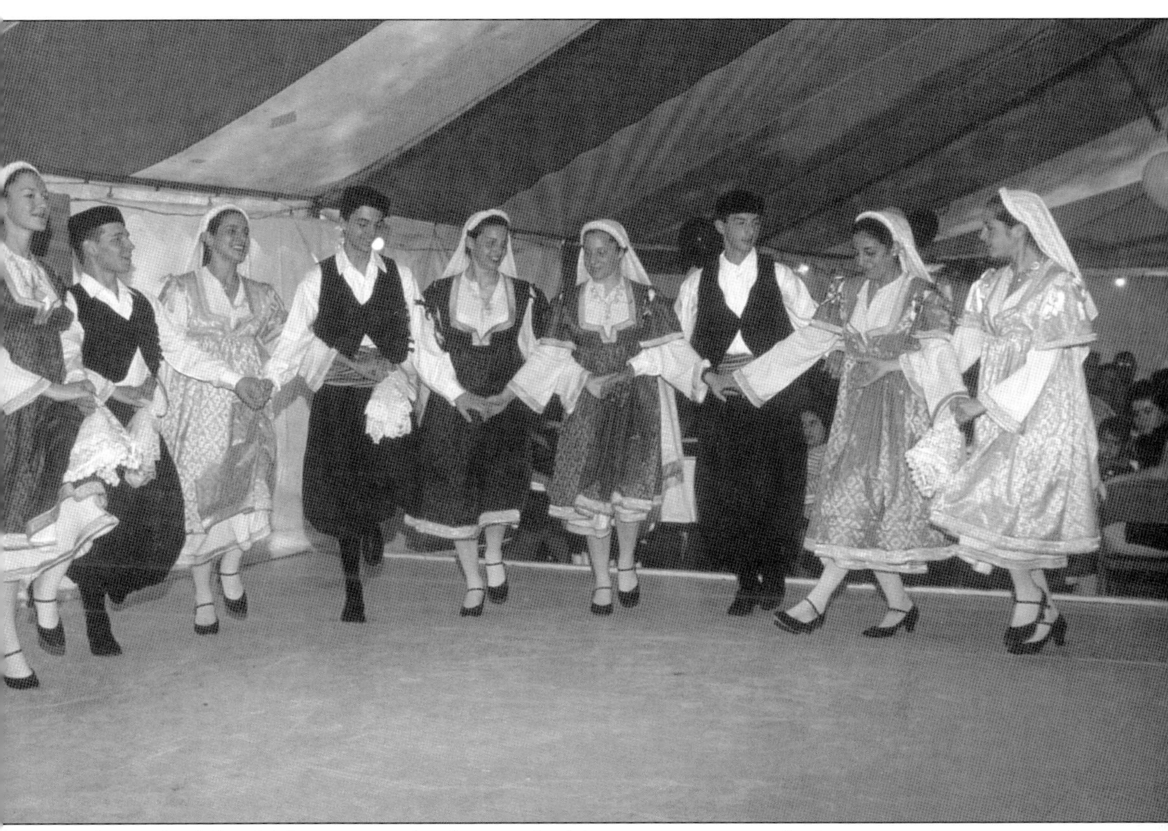

By the end of the 20th century, Anchorage had become increasingly diverse, with an array of languages spoken in the schools. Numerous celebrations around town have emerged to express the global character of the community. Here, a Greek dance troupe enlivens a festival in 2000.

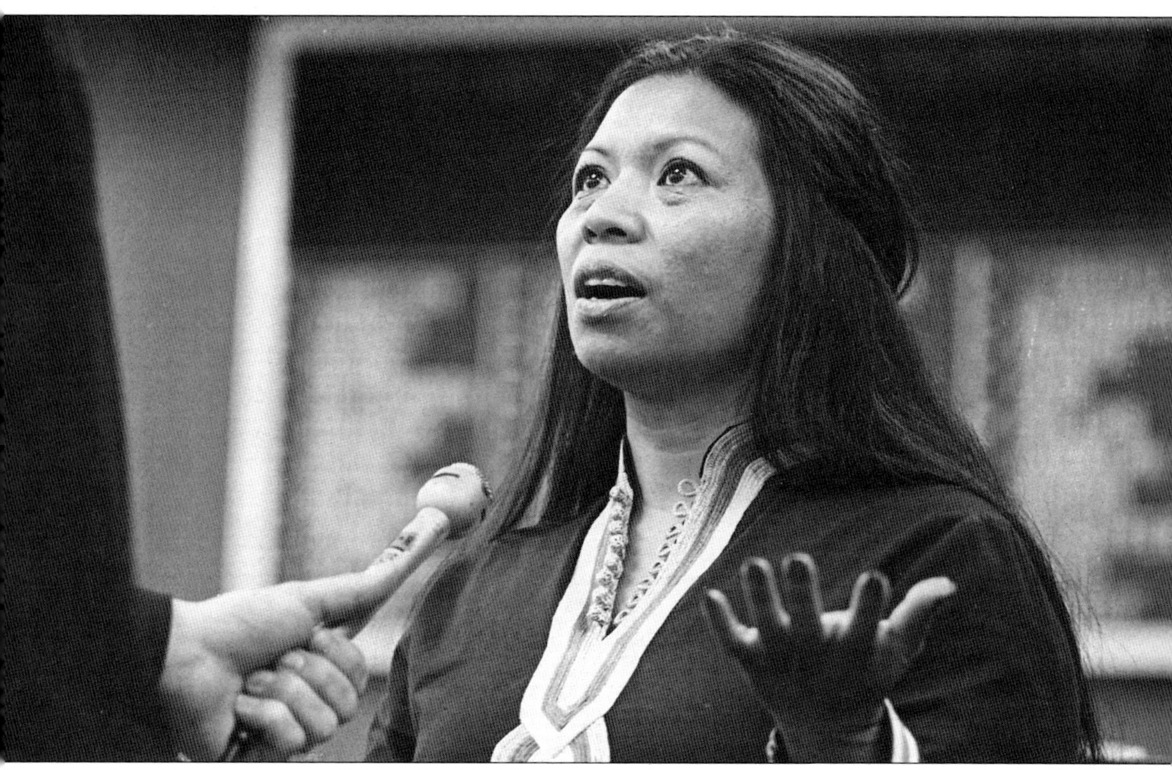

State Representative Thelma Buchholdt responds to an interview in the early 1980s. Buchholdt became the first Filipina American legislator in the United States after her election to the Alaska House of Representatives in 1974; she served her Anchorage district through 1982. Buchholdt was elected to state government in the aftermath of the Watergate scandal and was among a cohort of Democrats at the state and national level who promised more transparent and effective governance. She was also known to work across the aisle to deliver for her district. She even supported the popular Republican Jay Hammond for governor. Buchholdt's rise in politics mapped onto Anchorage's demographic transformation as the municipality grew more diverse and oil reshaped the economy during the 1970s and 1980s. After her political career, Buchholdt completed a law degree and published *Filipinos in Alaska: 1788–1958*, the first and still only publication to provide a detailed exploration of Filipino history in the 49th state.

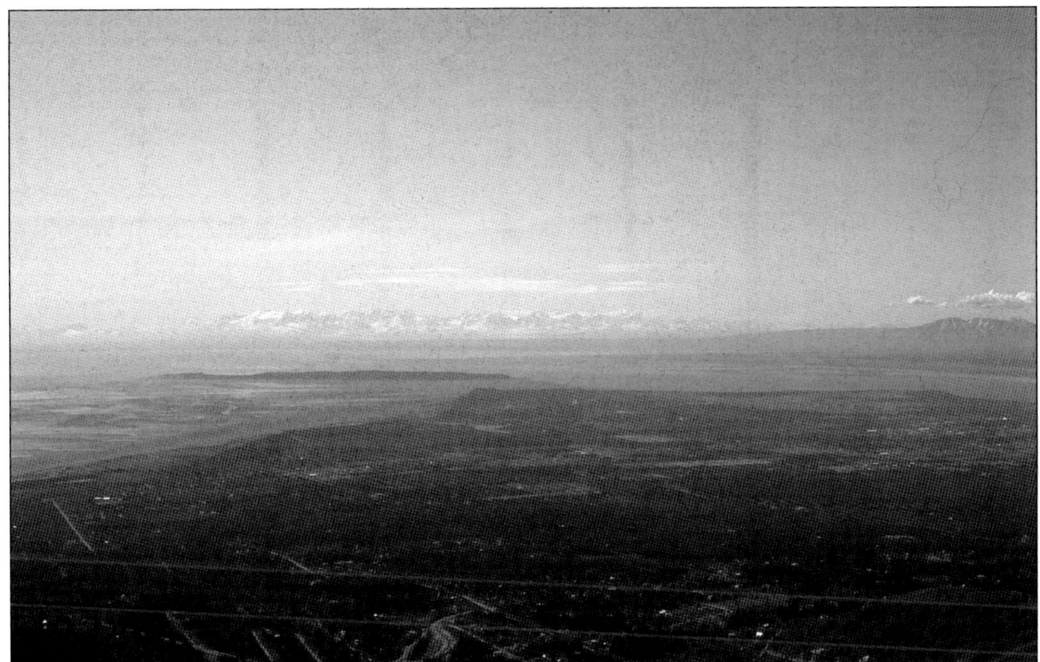

The view from Flattop, the most popular hike in Alaska, entails a scramble up to the 3,500-foot summit. Hikers are rewarded with impressive views of Anchorage, the Cook Inlet, and Mount Susitna (more commonly known as Sleeping Lady), which is seen in the top left of the photograph. Fire Island and the Alaska Range are visible in the center of the photograph.

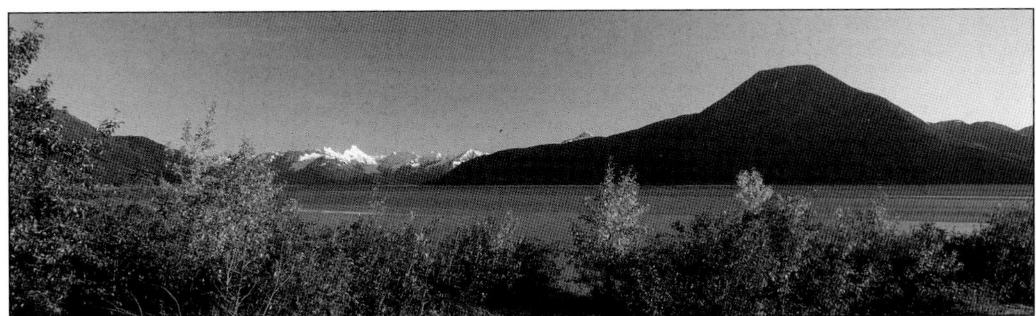

Turnagain Arm is viewed from Anchorage along the Seward Highway in the fall of 2000. The Seward Highway affords stunning views and provides travelers opportunities to pull off to take photographs, hike, camp, fish, or rest for the night at a roadside lodge.

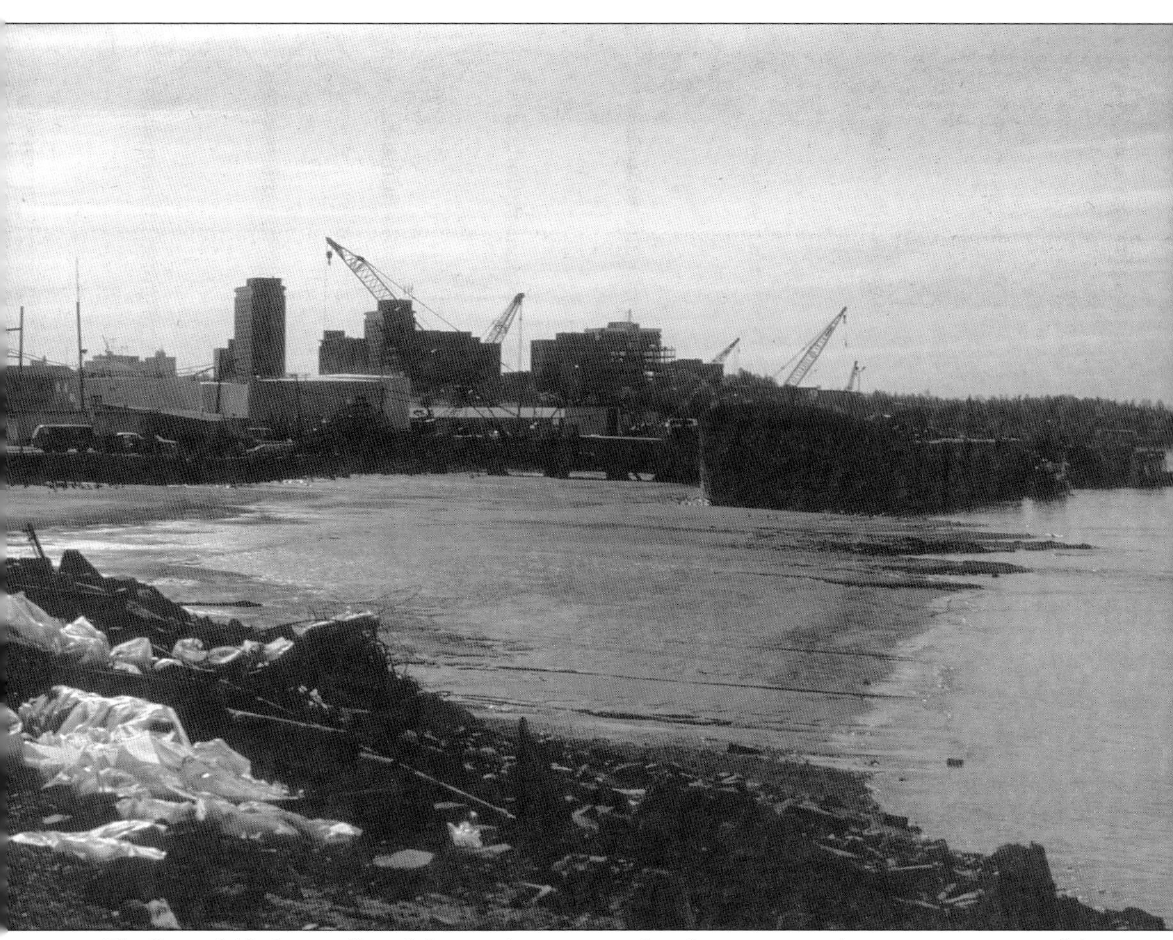

The Port of Alaska, a pillar of the state's commercial and economic infrastructure, is viewed from the mudflats during the summer of 1981. Most visitors come to see Alaska's wild and natural landscapes, but Anchorage and its waterfront have long been sights of industry and commerce. The Port of Alaska has been a consistent source of political hand-wringing and controversy over the years. Its location, adjacent to the mudflats along the Knik Arm just up from the Cook Inlet, is subject to some of the largest tidal ranges in the world, along with periodic freeze-ups during the winter (the port is never fully frozen, but neither is it ice-free through much of the cold season). This has taken a toll on the port and created the necessity for costly repairs and upgrades. But with the state reliant on the port to receive essential goods, Alaskans have been forced to contend with the costly maintenance.

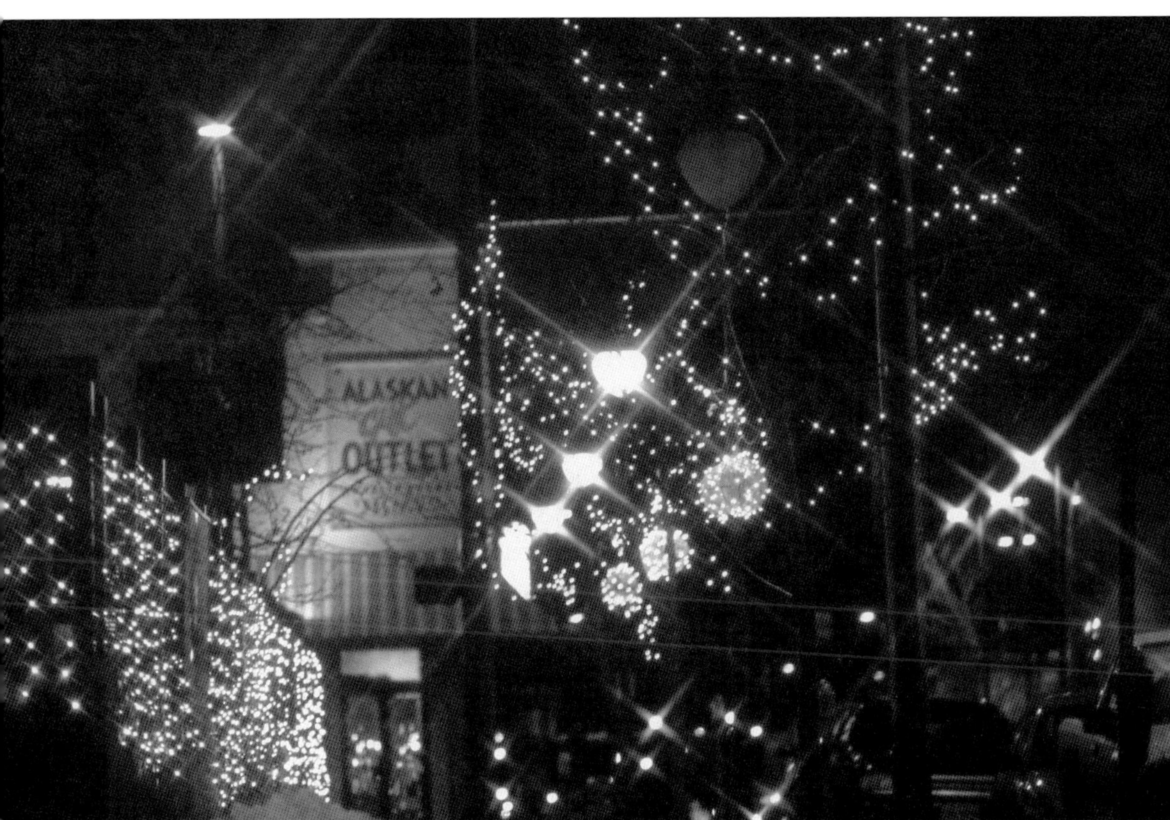

Between the glow of freshly fallen snow reflecting from the moonlight and the twinkle of festive lights, Anchorage's long winter nights are brighter than many may assume. This photograph, taken in the late 1980s around the holidays, depicts a dark but celebratory Anchorage. During the winter solstice, the sun rises in Anchorage after 10:00 a.m. and sets before 4:00 p.m., giving the residents a brief five and a half hours to enjoy the sun as it moves across the horizon at a low angle.

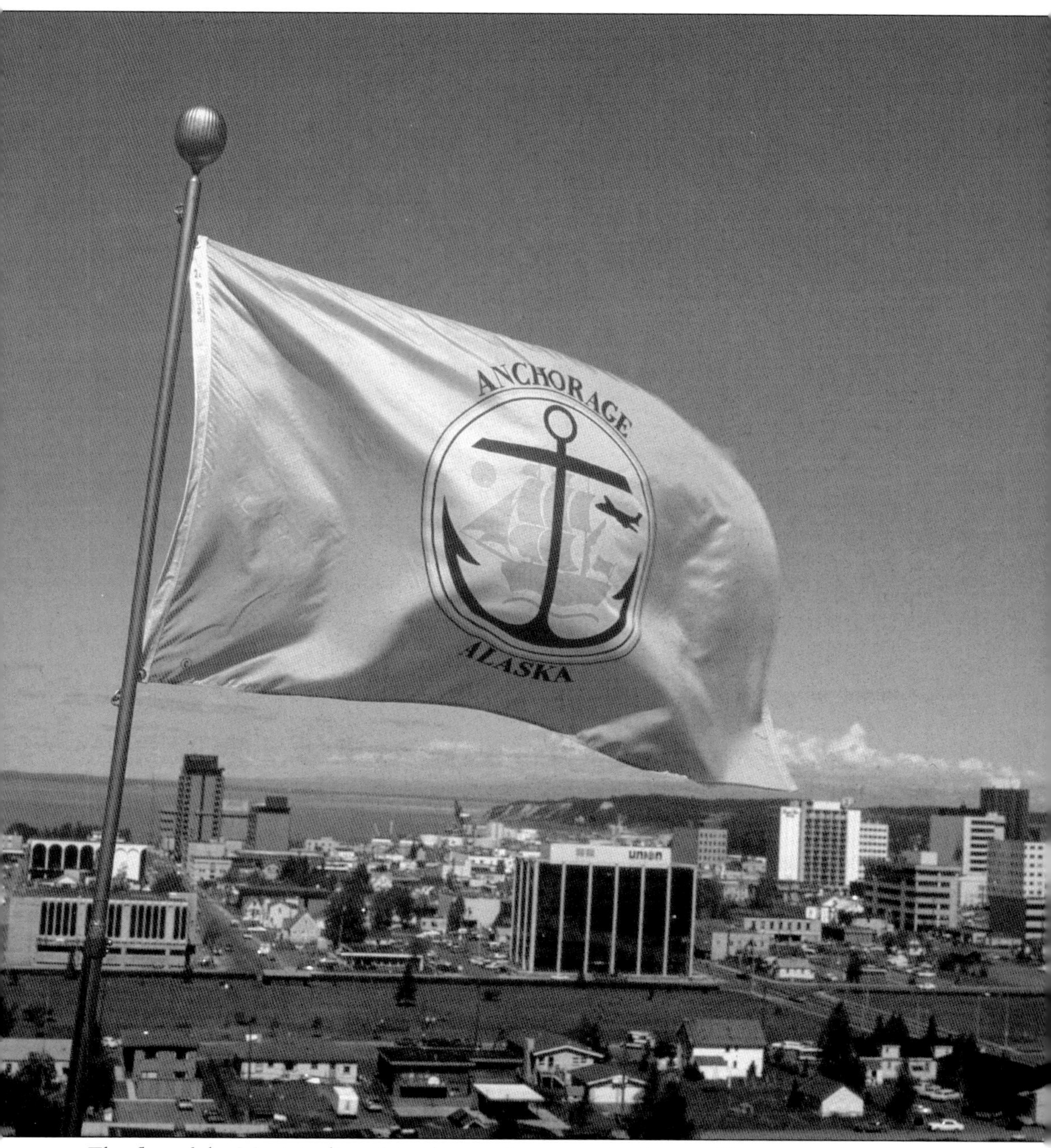

The flag of the Municipality of Anchorage flies over the Pioneer Home, a facility that provides assisted living for longtime Alaskans. The west end of downtown looms in the background. The yellow flag has at its center a blue anchor and a tall ship set as the backdrop. To the right is an airplane. Together, the symbolism demonstrates how Anchorage connects to the world by sea and air travel. Yet there is no allusion to trains or railroads, which was the reason for the town's founding in the first place.

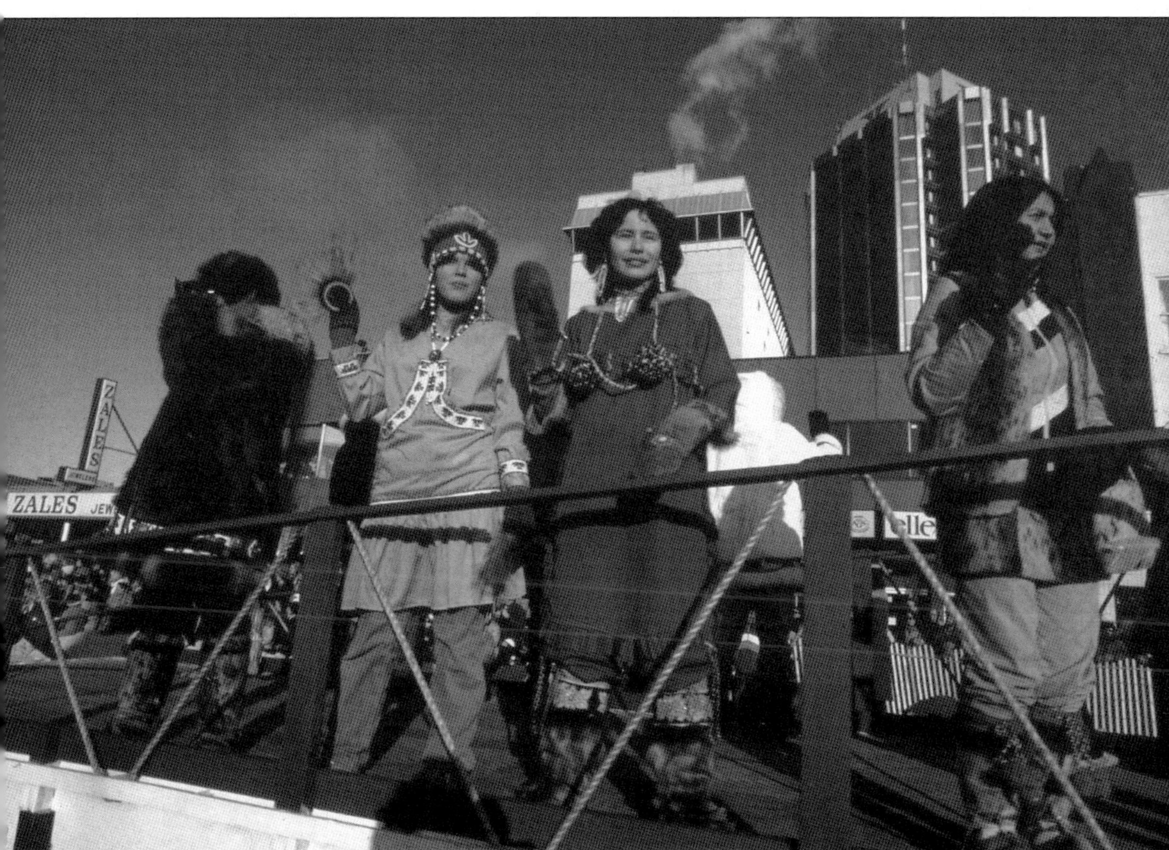

Alaska Native women participate in a Fur Rendezvous parade in 1983. Hotels, emblematic of the rise of the emerging tourism and hospitality sector in Alaska, are viewed overhead. In the background, a Zales jeweler is visible. The photograph nicely encapsulates Anchorage in the final decades of the 20th century. It had become a modern community and commercial center, at once striving to become an international destination with a skyline dominated by hotels and retail outlets yet also a place that remained proudly home to thousands of Alaska Native people and embracing its history.

Bibliography

Atwood, Evangeline, and Phillip Radcliffe. *Anchorage, Star of the North.* Tulsa: Continental Heritage Press, 1982.

Barnett, James K., and Ian Hartman, eds. *Imagining Anchorage: The Making of America's Northernmost Metropolis.* Fairbanks: University of Alaska Press, 2019.

Cloe, John Haile, with Michael F. Monaghan. *Top Cover for America: The Air Force in Alaska, 1920–1983.* Anchorage: Anchorage Chapter of the Air Force Association and Pictorial Histories Publishing Co., 1984.

Cole, Dermot. *Amazing Pipeline Stories: How Building the Trans-Alaska Pipeline Transformed Life in America's Last Frontier.* Kenmore, WA: Epicenter Press, 1997.

Fountain, Henry. *The Great Quake: How the Biggest Earthquake in North America Changed Our Understanding of the Planet.* New York: Crown, 2018.

Haycox, Stephen. *Alaska: An American Colony.* Seattle: University of Washington Press, 2020.

Jones, Suzi, James A. Fall, and Aaron Leggett. *Dena'inaq' Huch'ulyeshi: The Dena'ina Way of Living.* Fairbanks: University of Alaska Press, 2013.

Kari, James, and James A. Fall. *Shem Pete's Alaska: The Territory of the Upper Cook Inlet Dena'ina.* Fairbanks: University of Alaska Press, 2003.

Naske, Claus-M., and Ludwig J. Rowinski. *Anchorage: A Pictorial History.* Virginia Beach: Donning Company, 1981.

Naske, Claus-M., and Herman E. Slotnick. *Alaska: A History.* Norman: University of Oklahoma Press, 2014.

Prince, Bernadine LeMay. *The Alaska Railroad, In Pictures, 1914–1964.* Anchorage: K. Wray's Print Shop, 1964.

Senkowsky, Sonya, and Amanda Coyne. *Alaska Then and Now: Anchorage, Fairbanks, and Juneau.* San Diego: Thunder Bay Press, 2008.

Wohlforth, Charles. *From the Shores of Ship Creek: Stories of Anchorage's First Hundred Years.* Anchorage: Todd Communications, 2015.

About the Cook Inlet Historical Society

Established in 1955, the Cook Inlet Historical Society (CIHS) is a private nonprofit historical society focused on the Anchorage area. Since its founding, the CIHS has worked to foster discussion, research, and publication of the history and ethnography of Anchorage and the Cook Inlet region, as well as of our state and its place in the Circumpolar North. The artifacts and archives collected by CIHS were the start of collections for the Anchorage Museum in 1968. The society actively promotes the public understanding of local history through its annual lecture series at the Anchorage Museum and by coordinating with the museum on historical exhibits. The Cook Inlet Historical Society also supports local and statewide history initiatives, such as the publication of this book. For more information, please visit the CIHS website at www.cookinlethistoricalsociety.org or find us on social media.

Discover Thousands of Local History Books Featuring Millions of Vintage Images

Arcadia Publishing, the leading local history publisher in the United States, is committed to making history accessible and meaningful through publishing books that celebrate and preserve the heritage of America's people and places.

Find more books like this at
www.arcadiapublishing.com

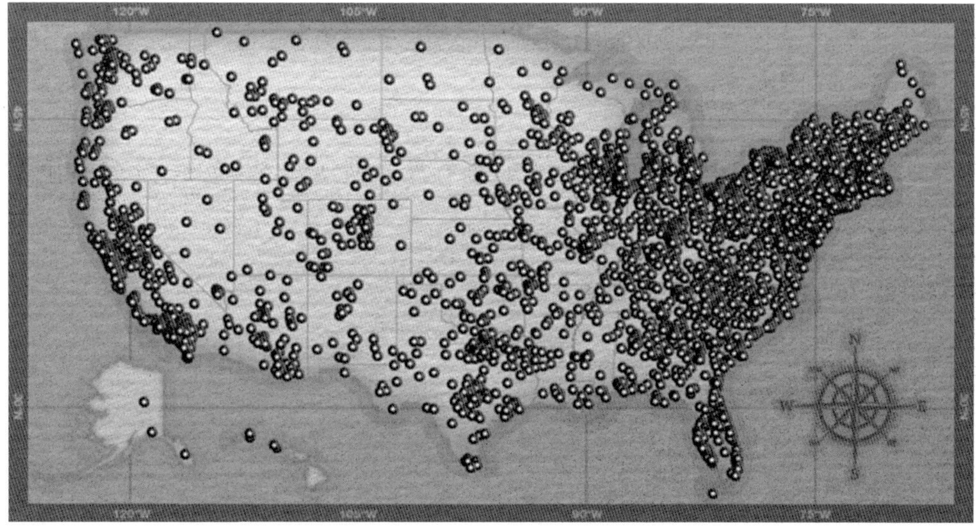

Search for your hometown history, your old stomping grounds, and even your favorite sports team.

Consistent with our mission to preserve history on a local level, this book was printed in South Carolina on American-made paper and manufactured entirely in the United States. Products carrying the accredited Forest Stewardship Council (FSC) label are printed on 100 percent FSC-certified paper.

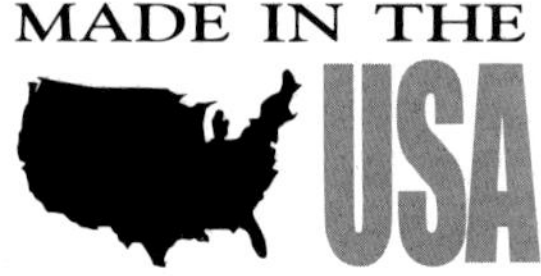